THE EUROPEAN UNION AFTER LISBON

The International Political Economy of New Regionalisms Series

The International Political Economy of New Regionalisms series presents innovative analyses of a range of novel regional relations and institutions. Going beyond established, formal, interstate economic organizations, this essential series provides informed interdisciplinary and international research and debate about myriad heterogeneous intermediate level interactions.

Reflective of its cosmopolitan and creative orientation, this series is developed by an international editorial team of established and emerging scholars in both the South and North. It reinforces ongoing networks of analysts in both academia and think-tanks as well as international agencies concerned with micro-, meso- and macro-level regionalisms.

Recent titles in the series (continued at the back of the book)

Roads to Regionalism
Genesis, Design, and Effects of Regional Organizations
Edited by Tanja A. Börzel, Lukas Goltermann, Mathis Lohaus and Kai Striebinger

New Regionalism or No Regionalism?
Emerging Regionalism in the Black Sea Area
Edited by Ruxandra Ivan

Our North America
Social and Political Issues beyond NAFTA
Edited by Julián Castro-Rea

The European Union after Lisbon

Polity, Politics, Policy

Edited by

SØREN DOSENRODE
Aalborg University, Denmark

Routledge
Taylor & Francis Group
LONDON AND NEW YORK

First published 2012 by Ashgate Publishing

Published 2016 by Routledge
2 Park Square, Milton Park, Abingdon, Oxfordshire OX14 4RN
711 Third Avenue, New York, NY 10017, USA

First issued in paperback 2016

Routledge is an imprint of the Taylor & Francis Group, an informa business

British Library Cataloguing in Publication Data
The European Union after Lisbon : polity, politics, policy. – (The international political economy of new regionalisms series)
1. European Union – Constitution. 2. Constitutional law – European Union countries. 3. Law reform – European Union countries. 4. European Union countries – Politics and government – 21st century. 5. Treaty on European Union, (1992). Protocols, etc., 2007 Dec. 13.
I. Series II. Dosenrode-Lynge, Søren Zibrandt von.
341.2'422–dc23

Library of Congress Cataloging-in-Publication Data
The European Union after Lisbon : polity, politics, policy / [edited by] by Søren Dosenrode.
p. cm. – (The international political economy of new regionalisms series)
Includes bibliographical references and index.
ISBN978-1-4094-3821-2(hardback)
1. European Union. 2. European Union countries –Politics and government – 21st century. 3. Treaty on European Union (1992). Protocols, etc., 2007 Dec. 13. I. Dosenrode-Lynge, Søren Zibrandt von.
JN30.E94118 2012
341.242'2–dc23

2011048735

ISBN 13: 978-1-138-25695-8 (pbk)
ISBN 13: 978-1-4094-3821-2 (hbk)

Contents

List of Figures and Tables

Figures

Tables

Notes on Contributors

Cristina Blasi Casagran holds a Master's degree in European Integration of the Universitat Autònoma de Barcelona and a LL.M in European Law of the Europa Institut of the Universität des Saarlandes. She is currently a PhD candidate in Law at the European University Institute in Florence, Italy.

Blanca Vilà Costa is Director of the University Institute of European Studies at the (IUEE) Autonomous University of Barcelona and Professor of Private International Law, and holds the Jean Monnet Chair in European Community Law. She holds a PhD from the Autonomous University of Barcelona, and an MA in Hautes Etudes Européennes from College of Europe, Bruges.

Søren Dosenrode is Jean Monnet Professor of European Politics and Administration at Aalborg University and director of the Center for Comparative Integration Studies (CCIS) at the same place. He holds an M.Phil. from the University of Copenhagen and a Dr. Phil. from the University of Zürich.

Nico Groenendijk is Jean Monnet Professor of European Economic Governance, and Co-Director of the Centre for European Studies at the University of Twente (NL). He holds a M.Sc. in public administration and public finance and a doctor's degree in public administration, both from the University of Twente.

Per Jansson holds a PhD in Political Science from the University of Lund, and is Senior Lecturer of Political Science at Linköping University. He is director of the master's programme on International and European Relations, and of the MEIA programme.

Lars Niklasson is PhD and Associate Professor in Political Science, Linköping University, where he teaches European and Comparative Politics as well as Political Economy and Public Administration. He was previously a policy analyst and held positions with ministries, agencies and consultancies in Sweden. He has taught at the University of Pittsburgh and Uppsala University, Sweden, where he earned his PhD and is honorary Associate Professor (docent). He is currently chair of the section for Political Science at Linköping University.

Andreas Warntjen is Assistant Professor for European and International Politics at the University of Twente (NL). He studied political science, sociology and law at the University of Konstanz and holds a PhD from the London School of Economics and Political Science.

Wolfgang Zank is Associate Professor of European Studies at Aalborg University and chairman of the board of studies for International Affairs. He holds a Dr. Phil. from Ruhr-Universität Bochum.

List of Abbreviations

ACP	Africa-Caribbean-Pacific
ASEAN	Association of Southeast Asian Nations
BENELUX	Belgium, Netherlands and Luxemburg; customs union and synonymous with the region
Bond	Bond for international development
CARIFORUM	Caribbean Forum
CFSP	Common Foreign and Security Policy
ComPat	Community Patent
CSDP	Common Security and Defence Policy
CT	Constitutional Treaty
EAC	East African Community
EC	European Community
ECB	European Central Bank
ECDPM	European Centre for Development Policy Management
ECHR	European Convention on Human Rights
ECI	European Citizen's Initiative
ECJ	European Court of Justice
ECSC	European Coal and Steel Community
ECtHR	European Court of Human Rights
EDC	European Defence Community
EDPS	European Data Protection Supervisor
EEAS	European External Action Service
EEC	European Economic Community
EFTA	European Free Trade Association
EMU	Economic and Monetary Union
ENP	European Neighbourhood Policy
EP	European Parliament
EPA	Economic Partnership Agreement
EPC	European Political Community (failed proposal 1952–54)
EPC	European Political Cooperation (existing cooperation 1970–92)
EPLA	European Patent Litigation Agreement
EPO	European Patent Office
ESDP	European Security and Defence Policy
EU	European Union
EUES	European Union External Service
Euratom	European Atomic Energy Community
GDP	Gross Domestic Product
IFLA	International Federation of Library Associations and Institutions

IGC(s)	Intergovernmental Conference(s)
IMF	International Monetary Fund
LT	Lisbon Treaty
MC	Median (overall)
MEP	Member of the European Parliament
Mercosur	*El Mercado Común del Sur*, Common Southern Market
ML	Median (majority coalition)
NATO	North Atlantic Treaty Organization
OECD	Organization for Economic Co-operation and Development
OPEC	Organization of Petroleum Exporting Countries
P1… P7	Player 1 through 7
PNR	Passenger Name Records
QMV	Qualified majority vote
R&D	Research and Development
RELEX	External Relations
SEM	Single European Market
SME	Small and Medium-sized enterprises
SQ	Status Quo
SWIFT	Society for Worldwide Interbank Financial Telecommunication
SWOT	Strengths, Weaknesses, Opportunities and Threats
TEC	Treaty establishing the European Community
TEU	Treaty on European Union
TFEU	Treaty on the Functioning of the European Union
UK	United Kingdom
UN	United Nations
UNASUR	*Unión de Naciones Suramericanas*, Union of South American Nations
US	United States
WEU	Western European Union
WTO	World Trade Organization

Introduction

One could almost hear the sigh of relief from the political elite of Europe, when the Lisbon Treaty was finally ratified by Poland in 2009 and could enter into force on 1 December 2009 (after the Czech instrument of ratification was the last to be deposited in Rome on 13 November 2009, much to the dislike of the Czech president, Václav Klaus).

After an extremely long process beginning with the Laeken Declaration of 2001, and ending in 2009, the EU had changed from a Union of 15 members to a union of 27 members, and more 'would like to be members' were waiting. Many hopes and fears were voiced during this long process.

Now, a few years after the entering into force of the Lisbon Treaty, the question remains: what did the Lisbon Treaty actually bring about? Was it just '[...] relatively insignificant in terms of institutional or policy reform', as Hix and Høyland claimed (2011: 11)? Or did they perhaps underestimate it? This question was asked in the Research Group for European Policy Studies (RGEPS) which brings scholars from the European Studies and International Relations departments at the universities of Aalborg, Barcelona Autonoma, Linkoping and Twente together. The result of our deliberations, discussions and presentations is this book, which is also the first tangible result from the Research Group.

I would like to thank Ms Cirkeline Cappel, BA, and Mr Elijag Munyi, MA, for their kind, flexible and competent help with the manuscript, bringing the bits and pieces together under a very tight deadline. I am also indebted to Jean Monnet Professor emeritus Staffan Zetterholm for commenting on three of the chapters in this book.

Søren Dosenrode
Hjermitslevgaard Manor
May 2012

Chapter 1
Exploring the Lisbon Treaty

Søren Dosenrode

The European Union (EU) is the world's greatest trading power. It provides the majority of the day-to-day legislation of its more than 500 million citizens, and is by some described as the world's second superpower (Andrew Moravcsik, 2010).[1] This power is developing, although not smoothly and systematically, but rather in a mix of staccato leaps forward and 'quiet incrementalism'. The latest major development is the Lisbon Treaty. It was ratified after a bumpy journey in December 2009, under the names 'Treaty on European Union' and 'The Treaty on the Functioning of the European Union' (in short: the Lisbon Treaty). The treaty revision process had lasted longer than any previous revision process. It began in Laeken in December 2001 and its aim was a Constitutional Treaty. However, the Constitutional Treaty was turned down by the citizens of France and the Netherlands in 2005, and later the treaty revision was delayed by the 'close to veto' of first the Polish and later the Czech president (in 2007 and 2009 respectively), just to mention a few obstacles. But in the meantime the EU continued growing due to the Eastern enlargements.

The Lisbon Treaty's preamble states:

> DESIRING to complete the process started by the Treaty of Amsterdam and by the Treaty of Nice with a view to enhancing the efficiency and democratic legitimacy of the Union and to improving the coherence of its action, [...].

This statement raises a number of questions; among others: Is the process begun in Amsterdam really completed with the Lisbon Treaty? Was efficiency enhanced by the new treaty? And how about democracy, was it really upgraded?

This book tries to answer these questions. To do so, we analyse the treaty from the classical three angles of political science, namely that of

a. polity, i.e. in a broad sense a political system and the institutions (cf. Windhoff-Héritier 1987: 17), and in a narrow sense a state or a state-like entity. The latter, narrow understanding is primarily used in this volume.
b. politics, i.e. the 'art of government' or the processes and rules used to govern a political entity like a state, and lastly

1 Toje (2011) on the contrary considers the EU a small power.

c. policy, i.e. '[…] an attempt to define and structure a rational basis for action or inaction', as Wayne Parsons (1995: 14) defines it, or simply the policy 'contents' as Windhoff-Héritier phrases it (1987: 17).

By choosing these three angles we will try to identify what is new and analyse it. By doing so we are aware that no 100 per cent agreement on the definitions just mentioned exists, and that the concepts often overlap. It is, for example, hard to make an analysis of the Common Agricultural Policy without looking at the rules (politics) within the area, and if one looks at 'the art of government' (politics), it is hard to leave out the political system itself, the state (the polity). But the three perspectives should provide us with a systematic approach when looking at the Lisbon Treaty.

Before going into polity, politics and policy questions, Søren Dosenrode, in Chapter 2, sets up the frame of the book, mapping the Road to Lisbon. This chapter analyses the development of the European Union from the beginnings in the 1950s until today. As such, it provides the background for the rest of the chapters in this book. The analysis is divided into two main parts: the developments from the Schuman Declaration to the Single European Act and the years after (1950–1991), and the developments from Maastricht to post-Lisbon (1992–2012). The chapter is rounded off by a few considerations on how regional integration happens, and argues for taking a closer look at the insights of the classical theories of regional integration.

In Chapters 3 to 5, the main analysis of the treaty's polity aspects is undertaken. To operationalize the concepts of polity we emphasize the nature of the whole system, when analysing the development of the EU.

In Chapter 3 Søren Dosenrode, assesses the European Union's statehood after the Lisbon Treaty. His starting-point is that until now academia has not yet produced a satisfactory label for the EU. The least satisfactory expression is *sui generis*, implying that the EU is completely unique and has to be treated as such, thus excluding or ignoring other regional integration projects like the federations. This prevents generalizations and eventual theory building. The second popular and only marginally better name used for the Union is 'a political system'. This name was coined by Simon Hix. In this chapter, Dosenrode sets up a model of what a state is (based on mainstream political science), and applies it to the EU. The conclusion is that the EU in fact is a (weak) state.

Wolfgang Zank turns to the central questions of geographical spill-overs, structural power and growing 'agency' post Lisbon in Chapter 4. Zank uses the concepts of 'structural power' and 'agency' for analysis of the external impact of the EU in a historical perspective. According to Zank, a single theory can't explain the development because at different points in time different theories are strong. As it turned out, already in the 1950s the European Coal and Steel Community (ECSC), and later the European Economic Communities (EEC) had a power of attraction and strong impact on the United Kingdom and other neighbours, a process termed 'geographical spill-over' by Ernst B. Haas. In the 1970s and 1980s the EEC could use its power of attraction in order to stabilize democracy in Greece, Spain and Portugal. And in the 1990s the EU gained an unprecedented power for shaping other societies in the process of the eastern enlargement, through the application of strict conditionality prior to membership. The EU used enlargement as a conscious policy in order to export democratic stability and prosperity to the eastern countries. The EU can again be seen as a rational self-interested actor. Also in the European Neighbourhood Policy, the EU can exercise influence, though to a lesser degree than during enlargement.

During the last decades the EU has also increasingly built up agency, and the Lisbon Treaty has added to this. 'Structural power' and 'agency' can go together, in particular if an actor follows 'milieu goals', as the EU does. This is a characteristic of the EU polity in the world.

In the following Chapter 5, Per Jansson analyses the security of the European polity in the Lisbon order. In this conceptually oriented chapter Jansson addresses the prospects and meanings of European security, using the Lisbon Treaty as a point of departure. Jansson is using the security perspective to approach essential questions about European identity, and in particular the coherence and authority of Europe as a political community. For European security to make sense there must be a European polity that not only has the resources and institutional clout to provide effective external actions, but commands legitimacy, a capital of trust. Even though questions pertaining to security are prominent in the reform process, dramatic consequences in terms of how policy is conducted in this field are not to be expected. In the long run, however, the symbolic effects may be considerable.

The next chapters (6 to 8) analyse the politics aspects of the Lisbon Treaty. The Lisbon Treaty could i.a. be considered a 'politics treaty' adding, and changing, procedures, institutions and actors.

Chapter 6, by Cristina Blasi Casagran, is a good example of concrete overlapping of the concepts, as the reinforcement of human rights in the form of the Charter of Fundamental Rights also has strong polity-building aspects. Thus, the chapter could arguably be placed under the headline 'polity', too.

Since the Lisbon Treaty quite a number of amendments concerning human rights have been incorporated into the *aquis*. The new nature of the Charter of Fundamental Rights, which gets the same legal value as the Treaties, as well as the accession of the EU to the European Convention of Human Rights, seem to be the main amendments. But also other larger changes regarding the better protection of human rights are analysed. In particular, changes in the legal basis regarding data protection, external action or the non-discrimination policy will be studied, as well as the new provisions with regard to the guarantee and control schemes.

In Chapter 7 Nico Groenendijk analyses 'enhanced cooperation', which is regarded as being a way out of EU decision-making deadlock and as a major possibility of proceeding with European integration in selected areas. Nico Groenendijk starts out by placing enhanced cooperation within the frame of 'flexible integration' in which he discusses two dimensions (does it take place within or outside the EU-decision making framework? and does it lay within or outside the EU policy domain as outlined by the EU treaty?). Groenendijk proceeds to discuss the dangers and the advantages of enhanced cooperation comparing it to two other possibilities: unitary integration and alternative integration.

Although the mechanism has been in place since the Treaty of Amsterdam, enhanced cooperation has only recently become a reality, in two policy fields: divorce law and the single EU patent. Using these two cases, Groenendijk analyses the pros and cons of enhanced cooperation (as compared to unitary integration and alternative integration). The chapter concludes by pointing out some possible weaknesses of the enhanced cooperation, i.e. the danger that unanimous decision-making can be circumvented, that the policy result may not be progressive, and that the majority in the Council and the Commission do not seem overcautious, when it comes to the application of the requirements on non-distortion of the internal market. The chapter also highlights the obvious advantage, namely the possibility for a large number of states to bypass another group of states when unitary integration does not work (for the smaller group this is, of course, a disadvantage).

The last of the politics chapters is Andreas Warntjen's on Designing Democratic Institutions: Accountability, Responsiveness and the Reform of the Council of the European Union after Lisbon (Chapter 8).

According to Warntjen the widely perceived lack of legitimacy of EU decision-making has prompted a major debate about institutional reform. Improving democratic practice in the Council has been one of the key topics in the debates leading up to the Lisbon Treaty. In general, we can distinguish between two models of democracy. The majoritarian model of democracy builds on the open competition of political camps that enjoy wide-ranging powers to implement their policy agenda once in office. In contrast, the consociational model of democracy relies on inclusiveness, compromises and power-sharing. Warntjen discusses the most prominent topics of the recent debate on institutional reform in the Council (voting threshold, Council Presidency, transparency) in light of these two models of democracy. The current practice of decision-making in the Council resembles the consensual model. Andreas Warntjen concludes that the changes in the Lisbon Treaty are unlikely to make any significant difference in this regard

In the following part (Chapters 9 and 10) policy implications of the Lisbon Treaty are looked into.

In Chapter 9 Blanca Vilà analyses and evaluates the policy-outcome of the Spanish Presidency, which was the first 'trio' under the Lisbon Treaty . The Spanish presidency offers a unique opportunity to analyse both (1) some updated institutional features under the new rules of the Treaty, and (2) the dialectics between the new conditions under which EU presidencies will have to function in the future.

After an introduction to the new '*acquis*' and the increasing institutionalization, this chapter discusses, from a critical perspective, the hard conditions for the policy performance of the Spanish presidency priorities, presenting this experience as a European 'living laboratory' on how to implement the Lisbon Treaty.

Lars Niklasson, in Chapter 10, analyses contradictions in the European market-building. The European Union has embarked on a new strategy for economic growth, known as the EU 2020-strategy. It looks like a well-designed machinery for growth, but in fact it reveals fundamental problems with the EU as a growth-enhancing organization. It is at once very complex and yet too simple to capture all relevant activities by the EU to stimulate economic growth. It is generally limited to policies where the EU already has a mandate, while some policies, such as cohesion policy, are missing.

The strategy is analysed in the light of a long debate on contradictions in EU policy, where the EU is seen as supporting conflicting goals and producing unintended side-effects. Under the surface are very different conceptions of markets and market failure as well as of the role of existing firms and the role of entrepreneurship to support new firms. The strategy reveals that the Commission lacks a mandate for change and that a case is building up for an elected Commission of the EU.

In Chapter 11 Søren Dosenrode sums up the findings in the previous chapters, structured around the elements of polity, politics, policy. One of his conclusions is that the Lisbon Treaty was more of a 'polity and politics treaty' than a 'policy treaty' aiming at deepening more than widening the EU.

References

Moravcsik, A. 2010. Europe, the Second Super Power. *Current History*, 109(725), 91–8.

Parsons, W. 1995. *Public Policy – An introduction to the Theory and Practice of Policy Analysis*. Aldershot: Edward Elgar.

Toje, A. 2010. The European Union as a Small Power. *Journal of Common Market Studies*, 49(1), 43–60.

Windhoff-Heritier, A. 1987. *Policy-Analyse – Eine Einführung*. Frankfurt and New York: Campus Verlag.

Chapter 2
The Road to Lisbon

Søren Dosenrode

Introduction

On 9 May 1950 the French foreign minister Robert Schuman declared:

> Europe will not be made all at once, or according to a single plan. It will be built through concrete achievements which first create a de facto solidarity. The coming together of the nations of Europe requires the elimination of the age-old opposition of France and Germany. Any action taken must in the first place concern these two countries. With this aim in view, the French Government proposes that action be taken immediately on one limited but decisive point. [...] By pooling basic production and by instituting a new High Authority, whose decisions will bind France, Germany and other member countries, this proposal will lead to the realization of the first concrete foundation of a European federation indispensable to the preservation of peace.

Since the Schuman Declaration from 1950 regional integration has moved onwards; sometimes fast and at other times hardly at all, but only once backwards (Luxemburg compromise 1966). The purpose of this chapter, is to give a brief outline of European Union's history from Paris (1950) to Lisbon (2007), as background for the following chapters. The chapter will also show an ongoing regional integration process driven by internal and external pressures, sometimes in the form of crisis. The chapter falls into three parts. The first tells the story of the early history until the beginning of the 1990s. The second part begins with the 'quantum leap' of the Maastricht Treaty and takes us up to the period after the Lisbon Treaty.[1] The chapter ends with a few considerations on what made regional integration happen in Europe and what made it develop.

---

1 Others, like Hix and Høyland (2011: 7–10), argue that *the* great change came about with the European Single Act (ESA). I agree, that the ESA was very important inter alia reintroducing qualified majority voting in the Council of Ministers. But 'Maastricht', building on the ESA both added the qualitative changes e.g. it created the European Union, introduced the European citizenship and subsidiarity and it introduced the co-decision procedure giving the European Parliament a veto-right in the legislative process. Quantitatively a variety of new policy areas were introduced. Thus I find it natural to make a dividing line between the ESA and the Maastricht Treaty.

From the Schuman Declaration to the Single European Act and the years after (1950–1992)

The situation in Europe at the end of the 1940s was not one of idle joy; yes, Nazi-Germany had been defeated, but the costs had been terrifying in the number of lives killed or ruined, in the sheer devastation of material goods (housing and industries damaged), and in the creation of Stalinist dictatorships in Eastern Europe. Moreover, Europe's role as the central continent in world politics had been changed from being the dominant part to being the domineered part. The prediction, ascribed to Aristide Briand, from the interwar years that if Europe did not unite, it would lie helplessly between the hammer of the USA and the anvil of the Soviet Union, had come true.

The Soviet Union did not live up to agreements on free elections in Eastern Europe, and the Cold War had begun, with 'incidents' in Europe like the Prague coup d'etat 1948 and the Berlin Blockade 1948-49. Additionally, the European economy was on the brink of collapse, and was only saved by the Marshall Plan. This was the background for Robert Schuman's and Jean Monnet's plan for European unification: a situation of instability and threat. The negotiations on what was to become the European Coal and Steel Community (ECSC) were conducted right after Mao Tse-tung's winning the Chinese civil war, and under the echoes of the cannons in Korea (1950–53), indicating a situation of international instability and crisis.[2]

Robert Schuman's main aim was to prevent war in Europe, and the main addressee of his invitation was (West) Germany, but all European states were invited. Implicit in this plan, and more explicit in the Pleven-plan (see below) was the question of German rearmament, which the US pressed for; a new, independent German army, five years after the end of World War II was a very emotional question. The prosaic aims of the cooperation were to secure economic expansion, a higher standard of living, higher employment and promotion of international trade. The negotiations soon began and were conducted swiftly. The European Coal and Steel Community started working in 1952 with the six members: Belgium, France, (West) Germany, Italy, Luxemburg and the Netherlands.

2 I will lean on Hermann's conceptualization of 'crisis' (1969: 415): '[…] a situation that (1) threatens high-priority goals of the decision-making unit, (2) restricts the amount of time available for response before the decision is transformed, and (3) surprises the members of the decision-making unit by its occurrence.' He also introduces the 'innovative situation', which is characterized by high threat, surprise, but extended time to reply to the challenge. But the name Hermann chose is unfortunate as it indicates, that if only there is no time-pressure a good outcome is likely. This is not so. A crisis is a turning point and the result may be either good or bad. Thus, I suggest using the term 'constructive crisis' instead. I see the two basically as two kinds of crisis, as each their respective ends of a 'crisis continuum'.

The special thing about the ECSC was the 'High Authority' which should, according to the original plan, have all the supranational[3] power to regulate and rule. But the small states were afraid of the great powers, so they insisted on a 'Special Council' which should only be advisory. This Special Council very soon developed into the powerful Council of Ministers (cf. Monnet 1978: 229). Still, the High Authority did get supranational powers and the treaty included provisions for creating a common market for coal and steel. Additionally, a court was established, to solve eventual disputes, and also an advisory Common Assembly was created.

The European Coal and Steel Community was only meant to be the beginning; the ambition of the French Prime Minister René Pleven was to create a European Defence Community (EDC), a plan he launched in October 1950. Later plans for a European Political Community (EPC) were added. In this, defence, security and foreign policy should be conducted by a supranational organization. The EDC should include a European army led by an institutional setup similar to the ECSC's, that is a Joint Defence Commission, a Council of Ministers, a Court of Justice and a Common Assembly. A far-reaching proposal, but it would solve the question of German rearmament, by placing a new German army under supranational control. After long negotiations, all but one state had signed the treaty. Only France, from where the initiative came, declined. The Korea War and its immediate threat of destabilizing world peace was over and Stalin had died the previous year, so the French Parliament refused to ratify the treaty in 1954, with Charles de Gaulle's *Le Rassemblement du Peuple Français* and the Communists voting it down.

After this fiasco, a certain melancholy and fatigue developed. But the Dutch Minister of Foreign Affairs J.W. Beyen took an initiative leading to a joint proposal from Belgium, Luxemburg and the Netherlands, which was presented at the Messina Conference in 1955. The parties decided to work on plans for economic and energy integration, and the result was the treaties of Rome from 1957 establishing the European Economic Community (EEC) and the European Atomic Energy Community (Euratom) (Dosenrode 1993: 182–200). The treaties entered into force on January 1958. External forces which facilitated the negotiations, by prompting a feeling of instability if not crisis were the Polish unrest in 1956, and the Hungarian uprising the same year, both quelled by Soviet troops. Additionally, the 'end of Empire' became clearer to France, but not necessarily the United Kingdom, with the French defeat at Dien Bien Phu in 1954, and the disastrous joint British- French- Israeli attack on Egypt in 1956. The future French leader, de Gaulle, began to realize that France could not 'go it alone' any more, making him look positively on economic integration in Europe eventually under French leadership, a line he would pursue when he became president a few years later.

3 Nugent (2010: 428) defines supranationalism like this: 'Supranationalism involves states working with one another in a manner that does not allow them to retain complete control over developments. That is, states may be obliged to do things against their preferences and their will because they do not have the power to stop decisions.'

Of the two new communities the EEC turned out to be the most vital and important one. In the Treaty's first article it is decided to establish a European Economic Community. The tasks of the Community are then listed in Article 2 (Rome Treaty, 1957):

> The Community shall have as its task, by establishing a common market and progressively approximating the economic policies of Member States, to promote throughout the Community a harmonious development of economic activities, a continuous and balanced expansion, an increase in stability, an accelerated raising of the standard of living and closer relations between the States belonging to it.

The aim was to create a higher standard of living *and* closer relations between the Member States. The means was a common marked approximation of the Member States' economic policies. So, the aim and means were much more than 'purely' economic, the political aim was there too.

It was stipulated that all internal tariffs and restrictions on internal trade should be removed to create a functioning free trade area. A Common External Tariff should be implemented and also a common external trade policy, the Common Commercial Policy, thus creating the EU's first foreign policy area. Additionally, free movement of capital, persons and services should be introduced (Rome Treaty, 1957, Art. 3).

The institutional pattern both for the EEC and Euratom was the same as that of the ECSC, or rather as what it had developed into, that is a Commission making the policy proposals, a Council of Ministers which acted as legislator, a Court of Justice settling eventual disputes and a Common Assembly advising the Commission and the Council (Rome Treaty, 1957, Art. 4).

Problems came at the beginning of the 1960s, during the détente, when Charles de Gaulle launched the idea of a Union in 1960. De Gaulle suggested a widening of the areas to be included (e.g. military security, culture etc.) but at the same time he wanted to change from the supranational model to a more inter-governmental one, where the heads of state and government should be in the driving seat and meet regularly, assisted by a number of commissions without supranational competencies (Dosenrode 1993: 187). The idea was shelved for about a year when the French foreign minister Fouchet took it forward again, unsuccessfully.[4]

The next problem occurred when the Commission's President, Walter Hallstein, in 1965, launched a number of proposals which inter alia would strengthen the economic autonomy of the Commission and give the European Parliament some influence. De Gaulle not only resisted the basic idea of the plan, but he also tried to press back the supranational elements already working. After months of the 'empty chair policy', when France did not participate in the Community's work, the Luxembourg Compromise was agreed upon in 1966, where one 'agreed to

4 Desmond Dinan has a good chapter on de Gaulle and his plans for Europe (1999).

disagree', and to introduce a de facto veto right, thus rolling back integration (cf. Dosenrode 1993, 203–6). De Gaulle also managed to veto a British (and thus also de facto Danish, Irish and Norwegian) EC membership both in 1963 and 1967. Looking at the 'integration score' of the 1960s it is mixed: de Gaulle did cause setbacks, and rather severe ones, too, but there was much practical progress, too, e.g. abolishing the tariffs, earlier than scheduled, or the construction of the Common Agricultural Policy (CAP), not to forget, extremely important for EU-Law, cases like van Gend en Loos and Costa vs ENEL. De Gaulle's resignation in 1969 lessened tensions, and a number of initiatives were launched, among others the Werner-Plan on Economic and Monetary Union, and the foreign ministers being charged with writing a plan on European Political Cooperation, both offsprings of the Hague meeting of the Heads of State and Government in 1969. Another important decision of that meeting was to open negotiations with Britain, Denmark, Ireland and Norway on accession to the EC (cf. Dosenrode and Stubkjær 2002: 4; Urwein 2003: 23).

The accession of Britain, Denmark and Ireland on 1 January 1973 was a challenge to the EC, as it now included three countries that did not share the idea of a European federation to the same degree as the original six member states. The impulse for speedy integration of the new members was further diluted by the oil-crisis and the following financial crisis of the 1970s. The external pressure, e.g. from the Organization of Oil Producing Countries (OPEC), exhibited the inconsistent attitudes of the Member States towards the Arab-Israeli conflict, with Denmark, Germany and the Netherlands having pronounced pro-Israeli attitudes, compared to Britain's and Belgium's fairly ambiguous stands and France's direct support for the Arab course (Dosenrode and Stubkjær 2002: 81–4). The result was that the Member States opted for individual approaches, and lost out against a united OPEC.

The bad economies of the 1970s and the beginning of the 1980s, as well as the lack of tangible progress within the EC, gave rise to the term 'Eurosclerosis' to characterize a situation with high unemployment and slow job creation and unwillingness to use the EC as the medium to solve problems that were generally shared and too large to be resolved individually (like the EC's low rate of competition and innovation compared to the US and Japan). All this against the background of the Cold War, which was in one of its very cold phases where the US and the Soviet Union to a very large extent decided Europe's fate without asking the Europeans.

The Spinelli Draft Constitution for a European Union, passed by the European Parliament in February 1984, put a certain pressure on the governments of the Member States (cf. Spinelli 1984). Additionally, the Commission presented its plans for a Single European Market, or the Internal Market, in 1985. The basic idea of Commission President Jacques Delors was to 'reinvent' the common market from the original Rome Treaty, centred on the principles of free movement of capital, goods, labour and services. Delors presented 300 measures to be taken to accomplish this aim, including the use of qualified majority vote (QMV) in the Council of Ministers (cf. Nugent 2010: 54).

Altogether, the deplorable economic situation as well as the feeling of being subject to the whims of the superpowers facilitated the passing of what was to be known as the Single European Act. The treaty contained two parts; the programme for the Internal Market and the codification of the European Political Cooperation (EPC), which for the first time was mentioned in a treaty. The success of the Internal Market as well as the introduction of QMV, the institutionalization of the EPC and the introduction of the cooperation procedure, which gave the European Parliament a tiny bit of influence on a limited number of policy fields, paved the way to the Maastricht Treaty, the Treaty on European Union (cf. Dinan 1999: 103–26). Allegedly, Margaret Thatcher has stated that if she had realized the integrative potential of the Single European Act she would have vetoed it – although it is rather doubtful that she actually would have been able to, if it came down to that.

From Maastricht to Lisbon (1992–2011)

Around 1991 the Internal Market was a success, but seemed to have even more unused potential to offer, and the Cold War had come abruptly to an end when the Soviet Union imploded in 1989–91. The end of the Cold War resulted in anxiety and instability especially in Eastern Europe; concretely, the EC had a war going on in its own backyard (Yugoslavia) without the means to intervene. So, pressure for further integration was present, and exploited among others by the President of the Commission, Jacques Delors, German Chancellor Helmut Kohl and French President Francois Mitterrand pressing on (cf. Phinnemore 2003: 48).

Neil Nugent (2010: 55) summarizes the factors leading to the Maastricht Treaty: the Internal Market's functioning had revealed unresolved questions, such as a perceived need for an Economic and Monetary Union and also a need for a 'social dimension' to soften the cold winds of market economy; mechanisms to cope with the unintended effects of the dismantled border controls (crime, drug trafficking etc.); and the longstanding question of democratic legitimacy. Nugent then refers to a number of external factors all relating to the breakdown of the communist bloc.

How would or should Europe develop? It is obvious that the answer to this question created uncertainty after the end of the Cold War, and it was an important factor on the road to Maastricht, too. This anxiety was spelled out in the debates in these years, e.g. in the Danish Parliament (Politiken, 28, 29 and 31 May 1992), where the government and adherents of the Maastricht treaty explicitly referred to the dangers of a reunited Germany outside or only loosely connected to the EC, as well as to the wish of strengthening the EC to be able to integrate the newly freed states if they wanted to.

The Treaty on European Union was agreed upon in December 1991 in the Dutch city of Maastricht, which has given its name to the treaty.

The Maastricht Treaty, entering into force 1 November 1993, was a huge leap forward in terms of regional integration. Institutionally, it brought together the supranational part (European Community) and the inter-governmental part, which it renamed from EPC to Common Foreign and Security Policy (CFSP), and it introduced a whole new group of inter-governmental policy cooperation under the name of Justice and Home Affairs.[5] It set the track for an Economic and Monetary Union (EMU) and it introduced the legislative co-decision procedure, giving the European Parliament a veto right to proposals from the Commission.[6] In spite of its importance, reading through the treaty leaves the impression of a rather messy text.

Former Secretary General of the Council of Ministers, Niels Ersbøll, in conversation with this author, once said that the mistake made when concluding the agreement leading to the Maastricht Treaty was to fix a date for its revision. But it had one (in article N of the treaty), and it stipulated that an inter-governmental conference (IGC) should be convened in 1996, and already in 1994, in Corfu, the European Council appointed a 'Reflection Group' to prepare the next IGC. The Reflection Group did not deliver a significant document, and when the IGC began it moved slowly, mainly due to British obstruction which lasted until Labour won the general election in 1997 (cf. Nugent 2010: 60). The Amsterdam Treaty was signed in October 1997 and entered into force in May 1999.

'Agreement was reached at Amsterdam on a rather modest treaty.' So the words of George and Bache (2001: 136) and Dinan go so far as to call the treaty 'a failure' (1999: 182). Considering the run- up to the agreement as well as the contents of the treaty itself, this seams a rather harsh judgment. Looking at the new treaty, the role of the so-called cooperation procedure was reduced and the use of the co-decision procedure was extended; the European Parliament's role under co-decision was strengthened; the use of QMV in the Council was increased. The principle, that a group of Member States should be allowed to work closer together than the rest was introduced (Enhanced Cooperation was the name given to it later).[7] The Schengen Agreement (until then extra-EU) was included in the treaty; the CFSP was strengthened to include certain security questions (Petersberg tasks) and the post of a High Representative was created (formally also secretary-general of the Council of Ministers), with Javier Solana as the first to have the post. The Amsterdam Treaty managed to clean up a bit of the mess in the Maastricht treaty, as well as to strengthen the Union. But despite the pressure for institutional reforms to cope with the expected Eastern enlargement, it did not manage to prepare the Union significantly for that. Before judging it too negatively one has to remember

5 This construction is often referred to as the pillar system.

6 The contents of the Maastricht Treaty as well as the negotiations leading up to it have been described in numerous books. I refer to Nugent (2010) and to Lauersen and Vanhoonacher (1992).

7 See also Groenendijk, Chapter 7 in this volume, for an analysis of Enhanced Cooperation.

that a treaty reflects the willingness of the Member States' governments and one has to remember the 'luxury' of not having major acute internal or external crisis to put pressure on the governments – the Dayton Agreement had been signed in November 1995 but the embarrassment of having the US solve yet another European war was still felt.

Looking at the EU's close neighbourhood, the Eastern and Central European states (with the notable exception of ex-Yugoslavia) managed their transitions from one-party states under Soviet dominance to 'Western-style' democracies fairly well, and in 1998 it was decided to open membership negotiations with six of them. But, considering that the EU had enlarged from 12 to 15 members in 1995 (the 'EFTA enlargement'), the question of the EU's ability to cope, especially concerning the institutions, was put on the agenda and a new IGC was called for 2000, but this time with the proviso that it should be finished by the end of 2000 (cf. Danish Parliament 2001). The brief of the IGC was to look into institutional matters to prepare for the expected Eastern enlargement (Nugent 2010: 62). It should among other things consider the maximum size of the Commission but it merely stipulated that each state should have one commissioner, thus taking the 'second one' from the large states; it settled the number of members of the EP weights of vote in the Council. Also the use of QMV was extended, but modestly so. But it did add the European Security and Defence Policy (ESDP) to the treaty. The Nice Treaty was signed on 26 February 2001 and came into force on 1 February 2003. Participants have told this author that it was a very chaotic European Council ending the IGC in Nice, also lasting nearly four days instead of the planned two. Did the treaty live up to the expectations? Yes, but only as a stop-gap solution, as the questions of decision-making efficiency had not been solved. With the danger of being unjust, my claim is, that the only genuine additions to the Treaty on European Union resulting from the Nice summit were the Charter of Fundamental Rights and the European Defence and Security Policy, (ESDP).[8]

A charter of fundamental rights 'smells' very much like a constitution and that is where such rights are normally placed. The idea of a charter originated at the European Council in Cologne in 1999, where the conclusions read:

> The European Council takes the view that, at the present stage of development of the European Union, the fundamental rights applicable at Union level should be consolidated in a Charter and thereby made more evident.

And considering that the EU is an evolving legal system,[9] it makes good sense to secure the fundamental rights of the citizens if they should clash with EU-law.[10]

8 See also Blasi, Chapter 6 in this volume.

9 Cf. Blasi, Chapter 6, and Dosenrode, Chapter 3 in this volume.

10 In annex IV it was stated: 'Protection of fundamental rights is a founding principle of the Union and an indispensable prerequisite for her legitimacy. The obligation of the Union to respect fundamental rights has been confirmed and defined by the jurisprudence

But at the Nice European Council a decision to include the Charter of Fundamental Rights in the treaty was stopped by opposition of some states (especially Britain). Instead it was decided to include it as a protocol without juridical binding force.

Already in Nice in 2000, the question of bringing the Union closer to the citizens was mentioned as central and was placed on the agenda. Additionally the terrorist attack on the World Trade Centre and the Pentagon made a heavy impact on the EU and brought security as a topic in its own right to the European agenda. A few days after the attack, the European Council met in Brussels to analyse the implications of the attack and to take precautions. 'Antiterrorism' turned out to be a word which could speed up cooperation (broadly) within 'Pillar 3' Justice and Home Affairs. In October they confirmed their intentions of pressing forward. A Danish senior diplomat told this author in 2003 that 'the attack on Twin Towers brought integration within Justice and Home Affairs 10 years forward in one day'. An assessment which EU Justice Commissioner Vitorino shares, according to Den Boer (2003: 1), as the terrorist attack according to him has led to a 'giant leap forward' for EU Justice and Home Affairs cooperation.[11] [12] The fight against terrorism had entered the EU agenda to stay.

When the Heads of State and Government meet in Laeken in December 2001, they decided to launch a Convention for the Future of Europe. One important motive for the convention was, as indicated, democratic concerns (Laeken Declaration 2001):

> At the same time, the Union faces twin challenges, one within and the other beyond its borders. Within the Union, the European institutions must be brought closer to its citizens. Citizens undoubtedly support the Union's broad aims, but they do not always see a connection between those goals and the Union's everyday action. They want the European institutions to be less unwieldy and rigid and, above all, more efficient and open. Many also feel that the Union should involve itself more with their particular concerns, instead of intervening, in every detail, in matters by their nature better left to Member States' and regions' elected representatives. This is even perceived by some as a threat to their identity. More importantly, however, they feel that deals are all too often cut out of their sight and they want better democratic scrutiny.

Another concern was Europe's security and stability in a globalized world (Laeken Declaration 2001):

---

of the European Court of Justice. There appears to be a need, at the present stage of the Union's development, to establish a Charter of fundamental rights in order to make their overriding importance and relevance more visible to the Union's citizens.'

11 I refer to Monica Den Boer's analysis for details.

12 This 'crisis driven' integration fits the basic idea of neo-functionalism theory, cf. Dosenrode 2011.

> Beyond its borders, in turn, the European Union is confronted with a fast-changing, globalised world. Following the fall of the Berlin Wall, it looked briefly as though we would for a long while be living in a stable world order, free from conflict, founded upon human rights. Just a few years later, however, there is no such certainty. The eleventh of September has brought a rude awakening. The opposing forces have not gone away: religious fanaticism, ethnic nationalism, racism and terrorism are on the increase, and regional conflicts, poverty and underdevelopment still provide a constant seedbed for them.

Using a 'convention method' was due to the positive experiences of the convention which drew up the Charter of Fundamental Rights in 2000, and the method should help give the result a larger legitimacy, and Mario Teló (2011: 14) argues that one succeeded in this respect.

The Convention consisted of 105 members, representing the heads of states and government of the member states as well as of the candidate states, the member states and the candidate parliaments, the European Parliament and the European Commission. Additionally, there was a presidency consisting of Valery Giscard d'Estaing and two vice-presidents, Guliano Amato and Jean-Luc Dehane (cf. Convention 2003).

The Convention on the Future of Europe elaborated a draft for a Constitutional Treaty, which was delivered to the Heads of State and Government in June 2003.[13] The Constitutional Treaty (CT) abolished the three pillar system, and it clearly strengthened the cooperation within Justice and Home Affairs by making it subject to supranational decision-making procedures, removing it from the inter-governmental sphere. It suggested a more permanent presidency of the European Council and a European Minister of Foreign Affairs. It included a 'solidarity clause', and extended power to the European Parliament through the co-decision procedure, and it attempted to make the treaty more uniform by incorporating both the Treaties of Rome and the Nice Treaty in one. It also included the Charter of Fundamental Rights (Convention 2003). According to Nugent (2010: 73), the treaty's importance lay in the specific provisions for EU-structures, institutions and decision-making procedures, as well as the highly symbolical name 'constitution'.

During the end phase of the Convention's work the US led an attack on Iraq in March 2003 which split the EU in what US Defence Secretary, Donald H. Rumsfeld, rather arrogantly called 'New Europe' (his supporters) and 'Old Europe' (those not supporting the invasion). This split did not, of course, support the federalization of the Common Foreign and Security Policy at all.[14]

---

13 The nature of the CT has been discussed; was it a treaty, a constitution or something in-between? Teló (2011: 19) quotes Giuliano Amato, the Convention vice-president for calling it a hybrid or a hermaphrodite, half male, half female.

14 Interestingly, this split did not seem to stop the cooperation between France and the United Kingdom. Begun with the Saint-Malo declaration from 1998 it has developed on a pragmatic basis until the two states in 2010 agreed to share hangar ships for their naval jets.

The Constitutional Treaty was discussed over the next year and signed in October 2004 … and turned down by the French and Dutch populations in the middle of 2005. After this, the European Council decided to establish a 'period of reflection', which lasted until June 2007 when the so-called 'Reform Treaty' was presented (cf. Nedergaard 2010: 34).

The launch of the Reform Treaty was made together with the clear understanding that a) the EU would not be able to work with the new Eastern European states on board unless the decision-making was made more efficient, i.e. supranational, and b) that it would be freed of too many 'federal' symbols. The negotiations were conducted largely under German leadership, but concluded in Lisbon, hence the name 'the Lisbon Treaty'.

Decision-making procedures were made more supranational in two ways: a) by making the co-decision procedure the 'ordinary' way of legislating in the EU, thus strengthening the European Parliament considerably, and b) by creating the position of a permanent president of the European Council, securing continuity and a more general view of EU-matters than a national presidency can be expected to take.

The Union's ability to act externally was strengthened by a number of means: a) merging the external services of the Council and the Commission into a European External Action Service, b) strengthening the role of the High Representative by making her Vice-President of the Commission, permanent Chair of the Foreign Affairs Council and executive of the European External Action Service, as well as the one assisting the commission's president when he attends the European Council.

The 'pillar structure' introduced by the Maastricht Treaty was abolished, and the majority of the policy areas under the heading of 'Justice and Home Affairs' were moved to the supranational decision-making procedure. Also, the Charter of Fundamental Rights got legal status, although only as a protocol.[15] Altogether, one witnessed a federalization of policy areas previously regarded as 'no go areas' for the EU.[16]

The Lisbon Treaty was signed by the heads of state and government in December 2007 and entered into force on 1 December 2009. It may be considered 'Plan B', as the Constitutional Treaty was aborted in 2005. But it is a Plan B which contains approximately 95 per cent of the original CT and it did strengthen the European Union considerably.[17]

All together the development of todays EU came about through a long series of treaty revisions (one might even write: an ongoing process of treaty revisions),

---

15 That the Charter was made legally binding prompted opt-out for British and Polish citizens so that the Charter does not create new rights for their citizens which could be brought to the Court of Justice.

16 Concerning terrorism as policy area, Keukeleier and MacNaughtan (2008: 239) refer to the lack of actual progress in spite of the institutions made.

17 Mario Teló (2011: 14) is slightly more conservative, fixing the figure at 90 per cent.

in a few cases they merely codified praxis, like the Single European Act codifying the European Political Cooperation, but they all introduced closer cooperation furthering regional integration in Europe. The latest of these treaty revisions is the 'Lisbon Treaty', which this book sets out to analyse.

What made regional integration happen in Europe?

This is not the place to begin a thorough discussion of regional integration theory, but I would like to draw attention to a general trend which seems to prevail[18]:

The large integrational leaps took place in times of internal or external crisis and insecurity which could be interpreted as examples of 'federal integration' á la Reiker-McKay (cf. Dosenrode 2011). This goes for the founding of the ECSC (1951) and the EEC (1957) during the Cold War. The background for the next 'leap', the European Single Act (1986), was that Europe was economically lagging way behind the US and Japan, and that the 'New Cold War' had clearly shown the world that Europe's fate was not a matter for the Europeans but for Russia and the US (one example was the Reykjavik summit in 1986 between the presidents of the Soviet Union and the US). The end of the Cold War and the breakdown of the Soviet Empire (1989) created uncertainty in Europe and was a huge incentive for the Maastricht Treaty from 1992 (one important question was how to 'tie up' a reunited Germany). The intergovernmental conference leading to the Amsterdam Treaty, 1997, would probably not have been convened had it not been for the Maastricht Treaty calling for a revision (this also explains why the result of it was important, but not exciting). And Nice in 2000? An important reason for the Nice Treaty was the upcoming Eastern Enlargement, where six states were eager to join, and the institutions had to be adjusted – here the lack of serious pressure (internal or external) may help in explaining the meager result of it.

The EU remained attractive for non-members, there was a certain uncertainty about EU-US relations and the world had changed after 9–11, bringing insecurity (and thus security) back on the agenda. These were forces pressing for the Laeken Declaration and the following European Convention – but the feeling of being threatened disappeared while the Convention was convened and this was one of several reasons why the Constitutional Treaty was not ratified in 2005 (another was purely domestic matters in France and The Netherlands). But the EU was now large in terms of member states and there was a distinct feeling that it could not work without an institutional reform. Thus the pressure for reform came from within, and although it was obvious that the EU needed it, there was no mood among the heads of state and government for an ambitious treaty, the strain was not big enough. In this sense, following the federal approach, the Lisbon Treaty (2007) is surprising as to its contents and importance which is not easily explained by that theory (cf. Chapter 11 in this anthology).

---

18 See also Zank, Chapter 4 in this volume.

But integration is made by man, and is not automatic, and a federal approach does not explain it all. This was clearly shown in the 1970s with the Oil Crises, where the nine EC-Member States were cleverly out-maneuvered by OPEC. And the following economic crisis of the 1970s which – in spite of its gravity – did not promote supranational endeavors; perhaps due to the comparably large inclusion of the three new Member States (1973) with a distinct inter-governmental approach. Their socialization took time and hindered further supranational development. The access of Greece (1981) did not make integration easier, whereas the entry of both Portugal and Spain (1986) did not seem to give the same institutional trouble.[19]

This very (!) sketchy look at the correlation between crisis and regional integration does provoke us to take a look at the insights of the classical theories of regional integration (e.g. federalism in the Rieker-McKayan version and Neo-Functionalism in a Philippe Schmitter version), they might very well have been given up too hastily (cf. Dosenrode 2010, 2011).

References

Convention on the Future of Europe. 2003. http://european-convention.eu.int/, accessed March 2011.

Danish Foreign Office. July 2007. http://www.euo.dk/emner/reformtraktat/reform/um_redegoerelse/, accessed February 2011.

Danish parliament (question on the Eastern enlargement). 2001. http://www.euo.dk/dokumenter/ft/paragraf_20/alle/20003071/

Den Boer, M. 2003. 9/11 and the Europeanization of anti-terrorism policy: A critical assessment. *Notre Europe Policy Papers* No.6.

Dinan, D. 1999. *Ever Closer Union – An Introduction to European Integration.* 2nd edn, London: Macmillan.

Dosenrode, S. 1993. *Westeuropäische Kleinstaaten in der EG und EPZ.* Chur & Zürich: Verlag Rüegger.

Dosenrode, S. 2010. Regional Integration: Bringing the Classics Back in? *The Icfai University Journal of International Relations*, 4(1–2).

Dosenrode, S. 2011. Federalism Theory and Neo-Functionalism: Elements for an analytical framework. *Perspectives on Federalism*, II(3).

Dosenrode, S. and A. Stubkjær. 2002. *The European Union and the Middle East.* Continuum and University of Sheffield Press.

European Council, Presidency Conclusions – Cologne European Council (3 and 4 June 1999). http://www.ena.lu/.

George, S. and I. Bache. 2001. *Politics in the European Union.* Oxford: Oxford University Press.

---

19 Still, one has to remember that all new Member States sign up to the goal of a European Union (cf. Phinnemore 2003: 47).

Hermann, C.F. 1969. International Crisis as a Situational Variable, in *International Politics and Foreign Policy*, edited by J.N. Rosenau. New York: The Free Press.

Laeken Declaration on the Future of the European Unon. 2001. http://european-convention.eu.int/pdf/lknen.pdf , accessed March 2011.

Laursen, F. and S. Vanhoonacker, eds. 1992. *The Intergovernmental Conference on Political Union*. Maastricht: Institute Européen d'Administration Publique.

Monnet, J. 1976. *Mit Liv*. Copenhagen: Forum.

Moravcsik, A. 2006. The European Constitutional Compromise and the neofunctionalist legacy, in *The Disparity of European Integration*, T.A. Börzel (ed.). Oxon: Routledge.

Nedergaard, P. 2010. *Lissabon Traktaten – En Politologisk Analyse*. Copenhagen: Jurist- og Økonomforbundets Forlag.

Nugent, N. 2010. *The Government and Politics of the European Union*. 7th edn. Houndmills: Palgrave.

Parsons, W. 1995. *Public Policy*. Aldershot: Edward Elgar.

Phinnemore, D. 2003. Towards European Union, in *European Union Politics*, M. Cini (ed.). Oxford: Oxford University Press.

Politiken; leading Danish newspaper.

Rome Treaty. 1957. http://www.eurotreaties.com/rometreaty.pdf, accessed February 2011.

Schuman, R. 1950. *Schuman Declaration*, http://europa.eu/abc/symbols/9-may/decl_en.htm , accessed February 2011.

Spinelli. 1984. Draft Treaty Establishing the European Union. *Official Journal of the European Communities*, No C 77/33, Tuesday, 14 February.

Teló, M. 2011. Before and after the Lisbon Treaty: What political integration for Europe? Paper, Regional Integration in Europe and Africa, University of Pretoria, February 2011.

Treaty of Lisbon amending the Treaty on European Union and the Treaty establishing the European Community (2007) 2007/C 306/0. http://eur-lex.europa.eu/JOHtml.do?uri=OJ:C:2007:306:SOM:EN:HTML

Urwein, D.W. 2003. The European Community: From 1945 to 1985, in *European Union Politics*, M. Cini (ed.). Oxford: Oxford University Press.

Chapter 3
Assessing the European Union's Statehood[1,2]

Søren Dosenrode

Introduction

In an important article from 1996 James Caporaso characterizes the 'state of the art' concerning analysing the nature of the European Union (EU), and his conclusion is still correct (1996: 30):

> Today, the study of European integration is moving into a post-ontological stage; scholars are less concerned with how to categorize than how to explain process and outcome, paying less attention to 'the nature of the beast' [...]. Indeed, in some literature, the EU is simply assumed to be a polity, and analysis of policy-making within specific issue areas proceeds much as it would within domestic polities (Hix, 1994).

Academia has not yet produced a satisfactory label for the EU.[3,4] The least satisfactory expression is *sui generis*, implying that the EU is completely unique and has to be treated as such, thus excluding or ignoring other regional integration projects like the federations and thus preventing generalizations and eventual theory building (Dosenrode 2010, 2011). The second popular, and only marginally better name used for the Union, which was coined by Simon Hix (Hix 1994) is that of a political system. It is a fluffy, but popular, approach (e.g. Majone 2009; Hix and Høyland 2011,[5] Teló 2011). When I call the concept 'political system' fluffy,

1 This chapter is a development of my chapter 'The EUropean Federation' from 2007 and is heavily revised and updated.

2 Due to the outline of this chapter as well as to the space available, certain issues like the development of the European Council, the citizen's initiative etc. will be looked into in Chapter 11.

3 Rosamond (2000: ix) draws attention to the importance of doing one's conceptualizations and blame the 'rugged state of health' for theories of European integration on this.

4 Zielonka (2006: 1) claims the opposite when he writes, disapprovingly, that 'The dominant paradigm is state-centric: The EU is on its way to becoming a kind of Westphalian federation with a central government in charge of a given territory.' This statement is later weakened when Zielonka (2006: 2) writes that: 'Although hardly any work explicitly claims that the Union is a state in the making, [...]' Neither of these statements are supported by references. I do not agree with his statement.

5 One section is titled 'What is the EU? A Political System but not a State'.

it is because it is very broad, including everything from a parish in the Danish church[6] to a state like Russia and thus it does not help us much when we try to pin down the nature of the EU.[7]

Caporaso then argued that the European Union was an 'international state' but he rejected the idea that it was a traditional state in the Webian sense (1996: 35–6):

> Wars, religious conflict and taxation were critical for the construction of nation-states, much less so for the EU.[8] And later [...] European integration is polycentric and lacking in a single, centralized, political location. This is not fertile ground in which political responsibility and legitimacy can take root.

Is this really so? The purpose of this chapter is to analyse the statehood of the EU after the Lisbon Treaty was ratified. The reason for doing this exercise is simple; should the EU actually be 'some kind of state', analysing it would be easier insofar as we would get rid of the academically unsatisfactory notion of *sui generis* and we could use the whole armoury of concepts from traditional political science, including comparative government, when dealing with the Union. This chapter will begin by discussing and defining 'statehood' before it applies this concept to the EU in its Lisbon Treaty version. The chapter aims at contributing to the discussion of 'what is the nature of the EU' so my focus is 'the state' or 'statehood', but I will occasionally draw a few parallels to one particular kind of state, namely the federation.[9]

---

6 I use Hix and Høyland's model of a political system (2011: 12–13) to illustrate my point. (1) In a Danish parish, there is a stable and clearly defined set of institutions for collective decision-making (the parish council) and through the order of business the relations between the council and the members, between the council and the priests as well as within the council are regulated. (2) The parish members may seek to realize their desires through parties at the elections for the council or through some of the ecclesiastical interest organizations. (3) The collective decisions in the parish council have significant impact on the distribution of economic resources (the council decides on the annual budget), and (4) through i.e. the annual parish meetings new demands are raised and put into the system.

7 Zielonka's approach, to analyse the EU as a neo-medieval paradigm does unfortunately not create clarity by adding yet another category to put the EU into, especially as the definition of 'empire' is all-embracing, not much more focused than 'a polity'.

8 This argument is surprising as it argues a primacy of the process over the result.

9 Elazer defines a federation as (1987: 1) '[...] a comprehensive system of political relationships which has to do with the combination of self-rule and shared rule within one matrix of constitutionally dispersed powers.' In a federation the governmental system is divided between the federal or supranational level and the member states giving each level at least one policy area to act autonomously within. Sovereignty is divided between the member states and the federation; together they posses the sovereignty of the federation.

State and statehood

The state is in its most basic definition a community, Gemeinschaft, of people as Aristotle told us 2300 years ago (1970: 63). A community which is made by man and which is needed to protect human beings' survival. On this basis, communities have developed from the time of 'hunters and gatherers', via the first agricultural settlers and tribal states, the growing division of labour, to industrialization and now the post-industrial society, at least in the Western world. Parallel to the modes of production the organization of the community has developed, too: anarchy, tribes, feudalism, absolutism, the modern state, and some would claim the post-modern state.[10] Power has as a general rule been accumulated and centralized in increasingly larger units.

This is not the place to make a survey of the classical theories and philosophies of state as we find them in Aristotle, Han Fei, Iben Kaldun, Machiavelli, Hobbes, Bodin, Loch and so forth. Instead, we go right to the so-called 'modern state', which is the result of centuries of centralization of power, legitimated by scholars like Bodin's and Hobbes' idea of sovereignty, power and domination. But are 'state' and 'statehood' adequate concepts today? Yes; states are still the single most important units in the international system. They sign treaties, they construct the framework within which transnational firms are operating, they levy taxes and distribute the majority of welfare, and they conduct wars. This does not imply that other organizations are not important, too, and that such organizations do not have significant international importance. But Unilever, British Petroleum, Credit Suisse or, for that matter, Al Qaeda, do not have the same international policy-shaping ability as a state has: the transnational companies do not sit in the UN Security Council. Statehood is still a very attractive status to achieve, something one is willing to die for and to let other people die for, as we have seen lately in Southern Sudan. Statehood is still a very strong and vivid concept.

Seen from inside, the state is still today fundamentally characterized by the features Max Weber emphasized in his analysis right after World War 1: for a unit to be regarded as a state it has to have a legitimate monopoly of power within its borders. In other words, there exists a hierarchy within the state; someone who has a right to rule over somebody. Using the term 'Westphalian' as a label on a classical understanding of the concept 'state', Caporaso (1996: 34) sums Weber's ideas up like this:

> The Westphalian state is the Weberian ideal in which monopolies of legitimate violence, rational bureaucracies and centralized policy-making authority correspond to territorially exclusive political orders.

10 In this analysis I will stay within the analytical frame of modernity.

Approaching the state from *outside*, classical international public law tells us that a state consists of three basic features: a people, a territory and a government.[11] If one of these elements is missing there is no state. The state is subject to international public law; there is no one above it, and no one may legislate on its behalf. This may sound trivial and outdated, but it is still the basic principle which constructs the fundamental structures of the international society and which is laid down in the Charter of the United Nations (Art. 2.1).

But 'state' and 'statehood' are by no means unproblematic concepts, and in this sense they are perhaps typical political science concepts insofar as there are various definitions of what a state concretely is. One reason for this diversity is that the object of investigation changes over time – although it can be discussed how much the basics actually have changed when one keeps Aristotle in mind. Another, perhaps more important, reason is that the state is perceived through the ideological spectacles of the one trying to come to grips with it.[12]

If one should find a 'mainstream definition' of a state, Dunleavy and O'Leary is a safe bet. They have tried to condense five characteristics of what they describe as a modern state[13], seen from an organizational point of departure (1987: 2):

1. The state is a recognizably separate institution or set of institutions, so differentiated from the rest of its society as to create identifiable public and private spheres.
2. The state is sovereign, or the supreme power, within its territory, and by definition the ultimate authority for all law, i.e. binding rules supported by coercive sanctions. Public law is made by state officials and backed by a formal monopoly of force.

---

11 In other words the Montevideo criteria. Some critics of the hypothesis, that the EU possesses a statehood of its own, have claimed that the question of the 'moving borders' of the EU, of a clearly defined physical base, is a grave problem, cf. Jansson Chapter 5 in this volume. This author disagrees, recalling that the frontiers of, e.g., the United States of America or Russia in the 18th and 19th centuries were equally 'blurred' without calling their statehood into question. The problem of moving borders is also mentioned by Zielonka (2006: 1) in his thought-provoking argument for the EU resembling a neo-medieval. But, it should be remembered, that the borders of the EU are always clearly defined, there is no doubt as to the borders of the Union today.

12 A number of schools of thought or traditions exist when analysing 'the state': 1) pluralists (e.g. Laumann and Knoke 1987; Richardson and Jordan 1979), 2) new right (e.g. Mitchell 1980; Shand 1984), 3) Marxists (e.g. Habermas 1976; Jesop 1990; Poulantzas 1978), 4) elitists (e.g. Aberbach et al. 1981; Vogel 1987), and 5) neo-pluralists (Dahl 1985; Galbraith 1974; Lindblom 1982; Luhmann 1979), although there are clear overlaps among some of them.

13 The European Union adheres to democratic norms and values (see below), and Dunleavy and O'Leary focus on the modern, democratic states, too. The following discussion of state and statehood does the same, but it is recognised that certain characteristics will also be found in totalitarian regimes.

3. The state's sovereignty extends to all the individuals within a given territory, and applies equally, even to those in formal positions of government or rule-making. Thus sovereignty is distinct from the personnel who at any given time occupy a particular role within the state.
4. The modern state's personnel are mostly recruited and trained for management in a bureaucratic manner.
5. The state has the capacity to extract monetary revenues (taxation) to finance its activities from its subject population.

But these organizational characteristic are basically of a domestic nature, and overlook the state as foreign political actor in the international system. Thus I add a 6th characteristic:

6. The state has, or rather tries to uphold, the official monopoly to conduct foreign relations.

Also the Dunleavy and O'Leary model does not pay much attention to the factors which make states 'stick together'. One could add several, including economic coherence etc. but I limit myself to the following two factors:

7. To secure endurance and stability a modern state must build upon a core-culture common to a vast majority of, if not all, citizens. This core culture is the fundament of the values, rules and laws governing the civil society.[14]
8. The state is the focal point of the population's loyalty (is a political community).

A last important addition has to be made to the model of Dunleavy and O'Leary. It is a fairly static model, with a certain 'either-or' connotation. But as state formation as well as the development of a state can be looked at as a process, some would even look at a state as an organism, it is important to add the dynamic element. Thus one should consider the characteristics as *continua*, where a certain polity can score from 'high' to 'low'.[15] From the analyst's point of view, this is

---

14 When discussing the concept of 'culture' it is important to distinguish between the underlying or core-culture, and the present manifest culture. To the former belongs the fundamental world-view and understanding of human nature; the common highest values etc. The manifest culture includes guiding morals and rules and societal structures (for a thorough discussion, see Gullestrup 1992: 38–49). It is important to remember, that albeit there is a common core-culture it does not imply that the manifest culture is or has to be identical in all entities (an example is the diversity of the Christian churches in Europe; they share a common core culture, but the manifest culture or form includes such different branches as the Roman Catholic, the Orthodox, the Reformed, and the Protestant churches).

15 The processual element is always present, but it is less important as soon as the polity in question has been recognized as 'a state'. When this has happened, the mere

not making things easier as it unfortunately implies that it is getting less clear-cut when a polity is 'a state'. But it creates the possibility to draw a more correct picture of a certain polity at a certain time in history.

To get a rudimentary overview of forms of states one could construct a simple matrix with four rooms: the first axis would contain two basic forms of organizing states: the unitary state and the federal state, the second axis would describe the degree of centralization i.e. strong/tight and weak/loose. In the category 'strongly centralized unitary state' one would find Denmark and France; in the group of weakly centralized or decentralized unitary states one would find, e.g., Italy or Spain, the latter being a de facto asymmetrical federation. The category of strongly centralized federations would, e.g., contain Austria, whereas Belgium would be an example of a weakly centralized or decentralized federation.

These examples in the matrix (Table 3.1) are mentioned simply to remind us that forms of states are highly different, being products of geography, culture and history, and that we should keep our minds open to new 'untraditional' forms of state.[16]

Table 3.1 Forms of states

	Unitary State	*Federal State*
Strong/tight	Denmark, France	Austria
Weak/loose	Italy Spain	Belgium

Analysing the statehood of the EU

As mentioned in the introduction a lot has been written about the 'unique' nature of the EC/EU. For years, especially lawyers could claim that the EU was *sui generis*, and political scientists discussed the EU as 'a lot of governance' etc.[17] After Maastricht, Amsterdam, Nice and Lisbon these positions are getting harder to uphold, as the EU has changed qualitatively and, quantitatively and it is worth remembering that the political aim of the EU always was a federation (cf. Robert Schuman's Paris Declaration).

To structure the discussion of the statehood of the EU, the extended Dunleavy and O'Leary model set-up in the previous part will be applied here. To stress the processual element, one should, as mentioned above, consider the following criteria

recognition bares a conserving element in itself towards the preservation of the obtained status, towards the outside world, although the state may be degenerating inside.

16 Lijphart (1999) shows this diversity of states and governments in his analysis of 36 countries.

17 For a survey, see, e.g., Rosamond (2000: Ch. 7).

as continua on which a certain polity can 'score' from 'high' to 'low', indicating that a state is in an ongoing 'process' of development.[18] This unfortunately implies that it is getting less clear cut when a political system is 'a state'.

Dunleavy and O'Leary's first point was that the state should be a recognizable separate institution, which should create identifiable public and private spheres. The Union does have these institutions (Art. 13 TEU, see also Part six, TFEU). Had the Constitutional Treaty been passed, the federal character of the EU would have been obvious. But giving the European Council the official status of an institution, as well as the creation of a permanent President of the European Council, stresses its role as a collective presidency (like the one in Yugoslavia in the years after Tito's death until the state was dissolved) (Arts 13 and 15 TEU).[19] The President of the European Council represents the Union both internally and externally.[20] The role of the European Council is to give impetus to the Union and to lay down the broad policy lines. The European Commission has several tasks similar to those of a 'normal' government. Its main functions are to initiate legislation and to supervise its implementation, to be a broker of interests and a guardian of the treaties.[21] Over the last decades – since Jacques Delors retired – the Commission has gradually lost legitimacy and its role has become more difficult. The Joint Study (2010: 60) points to several reasons:

> The main causes would appear to be: the extension of the areas of EU intervention, the successive enlargements, the successive Treaty reforms – including increasing powers for the European Parliament and demands for more democracy in the system.

---

18 The question of 'score' indicates a quantitative approach. In this article it is not so, in that sense I follow the same approach as Hix and Høyland (2011: 10) when they write of 'approximate measures'. Thus the 'score' indicated in this article must be taken as tentative and is of a qualitative nature.

19 See Chapter 11, Dosenrode, in this volume for an analysis of the permanent presidency.

20 Nedergaard rightly suggests, that in due course the presidency of the Commission and the presidency of the European Council are likely to be merged into one (2010: 59), thus creating a presidency like the French or American one.

21 The wording of Art. 17.1 (TEU) is 'The Commission shall promote the general interest of the Union and take appropriate initiatives to that end. It shall ensure the application of the Treaties, and of measures adopted by the institutions pursuant to them. It shall oversee the application of Union law under the control of the Court of Justice of the European Union. It shall execute the budget and manage programmes. It shall exercise coordinating, executive and management functions, as laid down in the Treaties. With the exception of the common foreign and security policy, and other cases provided for in the Treaties, it shall ensure the Union's external representation. It shall initiate the Union's annual and multi-annual programming with a view to achieving inter-institutional agreements'.

One way of restoring the lost legitimacy was to involve the European Parliament directly in the election of the President and the Commission's members. But 'Lisbon' did not change the role of the Commission fundamentally. The same cannot be said of the European Parliament. The Lisbon Treaty enhanced the powers of the European Parliament, the directly elected representatives of the European peoples (Art. 14 TEU). By renaming the 'co-decision method' the 'Ordinary Legislative Procedure' and extending its application in such a way that approximately 75 per cent of all EU legislation needs the consent of the Parliament, the first chamber gained substantial powers (Nedergaard 2010: 63; Joint Study 2010: 31). Also, the Parliament is now fully part of the budgetary process, with all the powers this implies (Art. 314 TFEU), but it still lacks the opportunity to propose new legislation in a way which is binding for the Commission (the EU government). In relation to the Commission, the Treaty (Art. 17.8 TEU) stipulated that: 'The Commission, as a body, shall be responsible to the European Parliament', thus on the one hand giving the Commission democratic legitimacy like any Western government, but also, on the other hand, taking some of the Commission's independence.

How is it that the European Parliament could extend its power, again? The Joint Study gives two explanations (2010: 31): first:

> [...] not only was there a significant level of representation [...] of MEPs in the Convention [...] but the Parliament moreover had to give its formal consent, as with any treaty change, and therefore had to be taken seriously. Secondly, at the time, many Member States' delegations overly focused on other institutional innovations [...], whilst others sought precisely to ensure that the Parliament's powers were enhanced in order to strengthen democratic accountability. [...] The result was that there was very little serious assessment of many of the new provisions.

The Council of Ministers very much resembles a second chamber in a federation, a senate, which brings the territorial dimension to the legislative process (Art. 6 TEU). The Council is still a very strong institution representing the governments of the Union, and compared to the EP it still has a number of privileges stressing the Union's intergovernmental elements,[22] although one should not forget that the number of policy areas where the Council decides with Qualified Majority Voting was extended to approximately 75 per cent, leaving only approximately 25 per cent intergovernmental.

Altogether, the Lisbon Treaty made the federal character of the Union more visible (cf. Figure 3.1).

Adding to this, the EU has a strong, independent court (Court of Justice of the European Union, e.g. Art. 19 TEU) as well as an independent central bank (European Central Bank (ECB), Art.127 TFEU) issuing the only legal tender in 17 of the 27 member states. The Lisbon Treaty also conferred juridical personality on the whole of the Union so that it now can enter treaties like, e.g., the European Convention on Human Rights (Art. 47 TEU).

---

22 Intergovernmental understood as 'consensus' or veto-power.

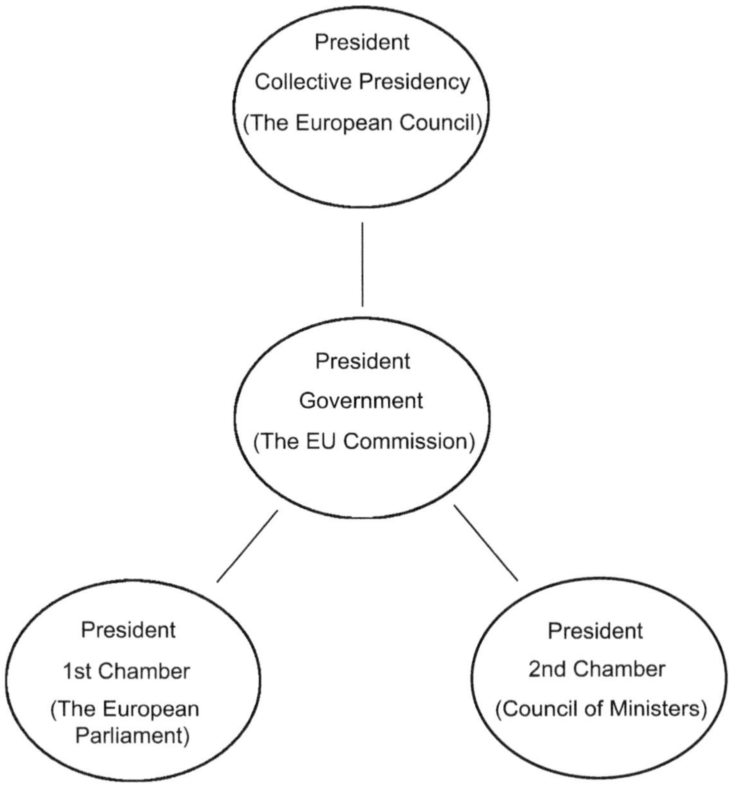

Figure 3.1 The governmental system of the EU

With the Lisbon Treaty, the Union also adopted the Charter of Human Rights as a legally binding protocol (Arts 6 and 51 TEU). Such charters are normally only placed in constitutions. Adopting it and giving it legal character stresses the constitutional nature of the Union's treaties.[23] This is also the case with the Union's citizenship, conferred additionally to the member states' citizens and giving additional rights, e.g. concerning consular help (Art. 20 TFEU).[24] This dual citizenship has lately (March 2011) been used as a basis for giving parents of EU citizens the right to stay

23 I refer to Michael Longo (2006), Joseph Weile's extensive works, e.g. 1999, 2002, and Malene Wind (2003). See also Blasi, Chapter 6 in this volume.

24 Art. 20.2 TFEU reads: 'Citizens of the Union shall enjoy the rights and be subject to the duties provided for in the Treaties. They shall have, inter alia:

(a) the right to move and reside freely within the territory of the Member States;

(b) the right to vote and to stand as candidates in elections to the European Parliament and in municipal elections in their Member State of residence, under the same conditions as nationals of that State;

and work within the Union (cf. Zambrano). Thus, citizenship is much more than merely a symbol conferring a number of rights upon its holders. This was made clear when the word 'complementary' as used in the previous treaties was changed to 'additional' in the Lisbon Treaty (Art. 20.1 TFEU).

On the symbolic level, the Union has a flag and an anthem, although they are not mentioned in the treaties.

Lastly, it is worth mentioning that the Lisbon Treaty included Art. 222 (TFEU), the 'solidarity clause' stipulating that:

> The Union and its Member States shall act jointly in a spirit of solidarity if a Member State is the object of a terrorist attack or the victim of a natural or man-made disaster. The Union shall mobilize all the instruments at its disposal, including the military resources made available by the Member States, [...].

Thus, it is evident that the EU constitutes a distinct public sphere, contrary to the private sphere, and that the EU tentatively 'scores' high on this continuum.

The second of Dunleavy and O'Leary's characteristics stipulates that the state is the supreme power within its territory and by definition the ultimate authority for all laws. It is a central notion that we as citizens accept that the state issues binding decisions. Equally important is that no other state interferes with the internal affairs of another state and legislates on its behalf. If the state enters into international treaties, including obligations for its citizens, they will have to be 'transported' into national law first.

The EU issues legislation, which is directly applicable to the citizens in the member states (the doctrine of direct effect). The legislation is passed by the Council of Ministers, the Second Chamber, in which representatives of the 27 member states sit. The legislation is often passed by qualified majority vote, which implies that, e.g., a Danish minister may very well vote against a proposal, but if there is the needed majority, the act of legislation will be applicable in Denmark anyway. Should a member state choose not to follow EU legislation it can be brought before the Court of Justice of the European Union and be forced to follow the law. Thus, the member states do not possess the ultimate authority any longer. Also important in this context is the fact that an EU citizen may sue 'its' state at the European Court of Justice if the person feels his/her rights are neglected, and with

---

> (c) the right to enjoy, in the territory of a third country in which the Member State of which they are nationals is not represented, the protection of the diplomatic and consular authorities of any Member State on the same conditions as the nationals of that State;
>
> (d) the right to petition the European Parliament, to apply to the European Ombudsman, and to address the institutions and advisory bodies of the Union in any of the Treaty languages and to obtain a reply in the same language.

These rights shall be exercised in accordance with the conditions and limits defined by the Treaties and by the measures adopted thereunder.'

the Lisbon Treaty 'rights' include human rights too.[25] Approximately 75 per cent of all new 'national' legislation originates in Brussels.[26] For countries that have joined the third phase of the EMU and thus transferred their entire monetary policy competencies to the ECB, the amount of European laws applicable is higher.[27] Thus it does not seem an exaggeration to recognize that the EU, to a very large extent, has the right to issue legislation binding for the individual member states, and to enforce the law, should a member state decline to comply with it. But there is room for the member states to legislate within certain policy areas.[28] Does this pose a problem in regard to the second criterion? On the contrary, and especially if we look at federalism theory.[29] The federal government has certain autonomous competencies, and the states have others.[30] Together, these two levels constitute the federation, which is, as a whole, sovereign to the outside world. It is exactly here that the discussion of a catalogue of competencies is extremely relevant: which competencies are best placed at the member state level, and which are best placed at the Union level? According to the federal approach it is important to have such a catalogue of competencies, with clear dividing lines, so as to protect the states from creeping centralization at the federal level. With 'Lisbon' these lines of demarcation were laid down in Arts 3 and 4 of the Treaty on the Functioning of the European Union. Additionally, one should mention the subsidiarity principle (e.g. TEU Arts 5 and 12, protocol no. 2), which states that a decision should only be made at the European level, if it is not better made at the national one. This principle is there to prevent the eroding of the member-states and ensure that decisions affecting the citizens are made as close as possible to them. Also, to prevent excessive EU legislation, the national parliaments have received rights of petition if they feel that the Union is exaggerating its powers and not adhering to the subsidiarity principle (TFEU Art. 69).

Thus, this second characteristic has been fulfilled, too, and tentatively the EU 'scores' high.

---

25 See also Blasi in Chapter 6 in this volume.

26 Apart from the directly applied legislation, one has to add the 'socialized' laws, which are national, but made in an 'EU-fashion', which had otherwise not been used. One may talk of 'socialization' (Dosenrode in Dosenrode 2002) or 'osmosis' (Rasmussen in Dosenrode 2002).

27 The role of the Court of Justice, as a proactive interpreter of the treaties especially when it acts on references for preliminary ruling, should not be underestimated. Often the findings of the Court of Justice have later been put into the treaty, as in the example of art. 2 TEU 'equality' which stems from the judgments of the Court of Justice.

28 Another important novelty is the so-called 'citizens initiative' art. 11, paragraph 4 TEU, giving citizens of the Union the right to propose new legislation, see also Chapter 11, Dosenrode, in this volume.

29 Cf. Holzinger and Knill (2000: 6), and Börzel and Rise (2000); but Lepsius (2000) is critical of this approach.

30 See Klöti (1997: 6–8).

The next two characteristics are fairly quickly dealt with. The third stipulated that legislation should be applicable to all without exceptions due to rank or position. This also applies to EU law (cf. Art. 288 TFEU). The laws are applicable to everybody it addresses. Over the years, the Court of Justice has interpreted EU legislation and its applicability. One central case was the Van Gend en Loos from 1963. In its ruling the court decided that the treaties gave directly applicable rights to the citizens of the then European Economic Community. On the basis of this ruling as well as other 'classical' cases a sophisticated interpretation of states' and citizens' rights and duties under EU law has been constructed (cf. Hartley 2010 or Fairhurst 2007). Equally, the observation that the state's personnel are mostly recruited and trained for management in a bureaucratic manner is applicable to the EU, e.g. the civil servants are mostly recruited through competitions, 'concours', and they are trained in a traditional bureaucratic manner. Thus, both characteristics tentatively 'score' high on the continua.

The question whether the EU has the capacity to extract monetary revenues (taxation) to finance its activities is an important one. To be able to finance one's activities is just as central for a state as for a citizen: 'No resources, no activities'. The Union does have the ability to levy taxes, but it is very limited. This implies that EU institutions, to a very large extent, depend on financial contributions from the member states, thus restricting their freedom of action. The Lisbon Treaty did include the possibility of introducing an EU tax and the President of the Commission, Barroso, as well as the European Parliament have been pushing, but so far in vain (e.g. Europolitics 2010): the member states are not willing to relinquish one of their two ultimate sources of power, the other being the right to introduce treaty changes. Therefore, this criterion is only marginally fulfilled. Turning to federations one recognizes that the situation where the federal government has no, or very limited, resources of its own is not unknown, e.g. the German Empire was constructed in this way, and Otto v Bismarck's memoirs (1928) clearly show his frustration when he had to go to the German states to secure resources for his projects. But the tentative 'score' of this characteristic is low.

The sixth characteristic concerned the state as foreign political actor. As discussed in detail elsewhere (Dosenrode and Stubkjaer 2002: 1–34), the Union for some time possessed an international actor capability of its own.[31] An actor capability which by far exceeds that of some of the individual member, states, e.g. that of Belgium, Denmark, Finland, Ireland, the Netherlands and Sweden.[32]

31 Allen and Smith (1990) coined the concept of 'presence' in 1990. Summarized very crudely 'presence' is about impact in the international system. Whether a state or not, the EU has an impact on the surrounding world. If the EU had not been there things would have looked differently.

32 Space prevents a thorough discussion of actorness, but let me briefly refer to Gunnar Sjöstedt. Sjöstedt wrote *the* seminal work on EC (EU) actorness in 1977. To be an international actor the entity in question must possess two essential qualities (15f): autonomy and actor capability. Autonomy implies that the unit is discernible from its environment,

But the actor capability is mixed. Until the Lisbon Treaty was implemented, one part (the supranational one) was conducted by the Commission, another (the intergovernmental) was conducted by the Council of Ministers, which since the Amsterdam Treaty has appointed a High Representative of the EU, and the third part was kept by the member states.[33]

The Lisbon Treaty created the European External Action Service, which amalgamated the units of the Commission and of the Council that had been in charge of external relations. In spite of the trouble relating to the creation of this new service, it has clearly made the EU more visible on the global stage, and the fusion has enhanced the foreign political capacity of the Union.

Although there is a part of foreign policy left to the member states, this part, too, has been restricted insofar as the member states may not take actions running contrary to the Union's foreign policy. In other words, the foreign-political freedom of action of the member states, one of the prime prerogatives of national sovereignty, has been reduced, at least on paper. Thus, the EU possesses the foreign political actor capability but it is shared with the member states. The Lisbon Treaty enforced this tendency in several ways: the High Representative's position has been strengthened considerably. She is now both a Vice-President of the Commission and President of the Foreign Affairs Council and she assists the Presidency of the European Council when it meets.[34,35] The High Representative now heads the foreign services of the Commission and the Council secretariat thus – potentially – being able to stop rivalry between the civil servants in the Council and in the Commission, and use resources better, avoiding duplication (these advantages have not materialized at the time of writing, cf. Chapter 11 in this anthology). The European External Action Service represents the Union in third states, and the heads of mission have been given the title 'ambassador'

---

and that it has a minimal degree of cohesion. Actor capability implies the 'unit's capacity to behave actively and deliberately in relations to other actors in the international system' (1977/16). To operationalize his definition, Sjöstedt defines a set of variables. An important insight of Sjöstedt's is that being an international actor is not the same as being, e.g., a superpower. Actorness is a quality, which can vary in strength, as one sees when looking at the international system today, with the USA at one end of the continuum and Fiji at the other. Using his criteria, it is possible to argue that the EU is an international actor in its own right, although it is not (yet?) a superpower. Sjöstedt has been criticized, but I find his approach basically sound. Since then a number of works have been written, e.g. Allen and Smith (1990), Hill's contributions (e.g. 1993), Bretherton and Vogler (1999), Jørgensen's contributions (e.g. 2007), Keukeleier and MacNaughtan (2008), Moravcsik (2009) and Zank, Chapter 4 in this volume.

33 Looking at federations, this is not a unique case; e.g. the Swiss cantons have some limited foreign political powers.

34 Cf. Allen and Smith (2011: 210–15).

35 In the Constitutional Treaty a similar post was created and labelled 'Foreign Minister', but it sounded 'federal' and the name – but not the competencies – were removed from the Lisbon Treaty.

(which is an important symbolic change). Additionally, the High Representative, as permanent head of the Foreign Affairs Council, adds continuity and potentially strengthens the coordination between the work of the Commission and the Council.[36]

Already before the Lisbon Treaty was ratified Andrew Moravcsik (2009) wrote of the Union's foreign policy capacity:

> The world today is bipolar. We have seen that there are, and will remain for the foreseeable future, two global superpowers: the United States and Europe. Only these two actors are consistently able to project a full spectrum of 'hard' to 'soft' power internationally. European countries possess, moreover, an unmatched range of civilian instruments for international influence. Because the post-Cold War world continuously becoming a more hospitable place for the exercise of distinctively European forms of power, and because Europe favours the substantive outcomes of such trends, it has facilitated the rise of European influence over the past two decades. There is every reason to believe Europe's rise in power will continue.

Whereas I might find the prose slightly exaggerated, I agree with Moravcsik's analysis of the EU's potential, especially after Lisbon, but considering the trouble launching the European External Action Service and the Union's recent problems finding a common platform on Belarus, the tentative 'score' on this element would be 'medium'.

An important factor (characteristic 7) in 'state-building' in a democracy is to ensure stability and endurance. As mentioned, this presupposes a core culture common to a vast majority of, if not all, citizens. From a sociological point of departure, one cannot amalgamate two units with different core cultures and expect them to last. It is not enough to declare one's belief in 'human rights' and 'democracy', as such declarations might just serve as political rhetoric to obtain a political aim. A common understanding of the central concepts like 'democracy', 'human rights' and 'rule of law' is essential. To build a sustainable state, one has to share the core culture. According to Uffe Østergaard (1993: 406) the European core consists of four elements:[37]

---

36 See Part Five of the TFEU, The Union's External Actions, for details. For additional analysis, see the Joint Study, pp. 139–62.

37 Samuel P. Huntington (1993: 5) also stresses the basic importance of culture. He divides the world into 'civilizations' of which the Western is one and the Orthodox another. He writes on Western values and their uniqueness: 'At a more basic level, however, Western concepts differ fundamentally from those prevalent in other civilizations. Western ideas of individualism, liberalism, constitutionalism, human rights, equality, liberty, the rule of law, democracy, free markets, the separation of church and state, often have little resonance in Islamic, Confucian, Japanese, Hindu, Buddhist or Orthodox cultures. Western efforts to propagate such ideas produce instead a reaction against "human rights imperialism" and a

adherence to the French republican, political ideal,
participation in the modernization following the (British) industrial revolution,
incorporation of the German romantic idea of collective and individual identity,
all of the previous based on the fundament of Catholic and Reformed – but not Orthodox – Christianity

Culture is not static; it develops over time, among other reasons, due to socialization. Common beliefs as to how 'things are done' are built over the years.

In the Treaty itself the European values are listed in article 2 (TEU) as:

> The Union is founded on the values of respect for human dignity, freedom, democracy, equality, the rule of law and respect for human rights, including the rights of persons belonging to minorities. These values are common to the Member States in a society in which pluralism, non-discrimination, tolerance, justice, solidarity and equality between women and men prevail.

But values which cannot be protected might turn out to be useless. Thus, in Art. 7 of the TEU, the Union institutions are given means to protect these values and – after a complicated process – eventually suspend some of the rights of a member state not respecting them. The case of the Hungarian media law, passed in December 2010, was a first test case which ended with the Hungarian government amending the law satisfying the European Commission (Reuters).[38] At the time of

---

reaffirmation of indigenous values, as can be seen in the support for religious fundamentalism by the younger generation in non-Western cultures. The very notion that there could be a "universal civilization" is a Western idea, directly at odds with the particularism of most Asian societies and their emphasis on what distinguishes one people from another. Indeed, the author of a review of comparative studies of values in different societies concluded that "the values that are most important in the West are least important worldwide"'.

38 The International Federation of Library Associations and Institutions (IFLA) has summarized the case as follows: [...] 'The EU Commission has required Hungary to prove that the Act does not violate the EU regulations. There is fear that with the Act Hungary aims at suffocating criticism of its policy. In particular the following aspects should be reviewed:

- The opposition newspapers protested the draft Act in Hungary by issuing in December blank first pages, without any text. The requirement of balanced information in electronic media has been formulated so that it may trespass the freedom of expression and people's right to free information;
- The question about the restriction of foreign programmes and the high penalties: are the penalties so high that they may lead to the closing of a media? Can the restrictions be used unduly for cases that the Authority doesn't like?
- The registration duty which concerns even private persons maintaining blogs; in the opinion of the EU Commission the registration duty restricts too much the organization and offering of services.'

writing 'the jury is still out' concerning the new Hungarian constitution which has caused the Commission launch accelerated infringement proceedings against the Hungarian government, as it may infringe the EU-treaties.[39]

The EU will tentatively 'score' medium to low at the continuum. A number of the Eastern and Southern European states do not live up to the definition suggested by Østergaard e.g. Bulgaria, Romania and Greece, and these countries do give the European Union reason to contemplate whether these states were allowed into the Union prematurely.[40] Huntington (1993) would merely note that it was unwise to try to amalgamate entities from different civilizations such as the Western and the Orthodox ones.

I have included the last point – that the state is a community – with some hesitation, and perhaps it would be more adequate not to consider it a characteristic, but as a condition for endurance and stability (as mentioned in the beginning of this chapter, Aristotle looked at states as a community). Historically, a feeling of community or loyalty to the state has not been a condition either to found a state or to be able to talk of a state at all. Still, loyalty towards the state, a certain feeling of community, is the glue which ensures stability of the modern state.[41] And how then is the feeling of community within the European Union? Vaclav Havel searched in vain for the heart of the EU in a speech at the European Parliament in spring 1994, and later the late president of the Commission, Delors, launched a project aiming at giving Europe a soul. Both incidents indicate that the feeling of community is fairly low.[42]

---

39 'Under new Hungarian legislation, 274 judges (including judges at the Supreme Court) are being compulsorily retired in contradiction to EU rules. The government also receives powers over the data protection authority that contradict the EU Treaties, which require the independence of national data protection authorities (Article 16 of the Treaty on the Functioning of the European Union/TFEU, Article 8(3) of the Charter of Fundamental Rights) and the independence of the national central bank (Articles 130 and 127 TFEU, Article 14 of the Statute of the European System of Central Banks and of the European Central Bank). Hungary's central bank is part of the European System of Central Banks (ESCB) and the Hungarian Central Bank Governor has a seat in the General Council of the European Central Bank, which is the ECB's third decision-making body.' European Comission 2012.

40 Examples are Romania nominating a minister with alleged contacts to organized crime as EU-Commissioner; Bulgaria and Romania not fighting corruption in government and administration; and Greece faking her accounts to give the impression that the state deficits were not as large as they were in reality, when applying for membership of the EMU, with disastrous results for the whole Euro Area.

41 The dissolution of Yugoslavia and Czechoslovakia are illustrative examples of states where the feeling of community and loyalty did not exist to a high degree.

42 The question of transfer of loyalty has been discussed in several of the integration theories, e.g. Federalism (e.g. Etzioni (1965)) and neo-functionalism (e.g. Rosamond 2000: 52).

But in an old Eurobarometer survey (April 2002: 14),[43] one reads the following comment:

> Fifty-three per cent of EU citizens feel to some extent European, compared with 44% who only identify with their own nationality. In 9 of the 15 Member States, the European sentiment outweighs the exclusive identification with one's nationality.

And if one consults a Eurobarometer survey from spring 2011 (p. 51) 62 per cent of those citizens asked stated that they felt a citizen of the EU, whereas 36 per cent did not and 2 per cent were neutral.[44]

The creation of a common European currency, the adoption of a flag and a national hymn, the exchange programs for students and scholars, the same design of driver's licences and passports, all have to be seen as attempts to create a common identity,[45] a community. Seen with federal eyes, the above-mentioned score is fairly good. Experience from various federations (e.g. Switzerland) clearly shows that a citizen can feel loyal both to his state and the federal state as was actually argued in the Federalist Papers more than 200 years ago. As a matter of fact, a feeling of loyalty towards the Member State is essential if a federation is to remain. Without this loyalty a federal state will very soon turn into a unitary state. Still, the empirical evidence at my disposal is too weak to draw strong conclusions, but very tentatively this characteristic would 'score' medium to low.[46]

The European Union – a state, but not a super power

The previous analysis has indicated that the EU fulfills the stipulated characteristics for being a state, apart from being able to levy taxes – these characteristics are only fulfilled marginally, although the treaty opens the possibility of their being developed without having to change the present treaty. Thus, it seems reasonable to conclude that the Union does possess its own statehood (this especially holds true, if one looks at the EU with a federalism approach, as I have argued previously,

43 It has not been possible to obtain newer data from Eurostat. One could imagine that the situation had changed after the eastern enlargements.

44 In four Member States less than 50 per cent felt like EU citizens: Bulgaria, Greece, Latvia and the United Kingdom.

45 A number of books have been written on the European identity. I refer to Demossier (2007) for a qualitative approach, and to Green (2007) for an empirical approach. See also Jansson, Chapter 5 in this volume.

46 See also Chapter 11, Dosenrode, in this anthology.

Dosenrode 2007[47]).[48,49] But the European Union's statehood is not strong, as is the case with some states.

As mentioned, it is important to see the development of a state as a never-ending process, in this sense any state is an open-ended model. The situation described above is basically a 'snapshot' of the present situation concerning the statehood of the EU. Had one made the same exercise for the EC in 1960, 1970, 1980 and 1990 one would see a clear development towards 'more stateness'. It is, of course, impossible to say definitely whether the statehood of the Union will develop further or not,[50] but it is likely that it will continue, as the majority of states decided to hand over their monetary autonomy to the EU, thus cementing the EU as a unit, a state.[51]

One consequence of this conclusion, if it is accepted, is that the days of *sui generis* or political system, are over. It implies that we can use the toolbox developed in (comparative) politics and government, to mention a few, when we analyse the EU. But it is important not to make the faulty equation: the EU is a state = the EU is a superpower. This 'either – or' is wrong. The Union possesses statehood, but it is not a strong state and it is far from being a superpower in a classical meaning of the word, in spite of Moravcsik's statement quoted above. This wrong equation prompted Tony Blair to denounce the EU as a federal superstate in 2003 (Blair 2003). But equally, not being a superpower does not necessarily imply that the EU is a small state, as Toje (2011) claims. The EU is able to influence the international system when economic matters are in play, and plays a very active role outside Europe, too (cf. above). So I agree with Giegereich and Wallace writing 'the EU punches below its weight in international diplomacy [...]' (2010: 452).[52]

---

47 A number of features in the Lisbon Treaty makes this clearer: the addition of a catalogue of competencies and the upgrading of the EU-Citizenship, see Chapter 11 in this volume.

48 This is not the place to begin a discussion of which kind of state the EU is. I refer inter alia to Buzan (1983), who distinguishes between super-states and weak states; Caporaso (1996) discussing the international state; McKay (2001) calling the EU a federation; Vivien Schmidt (2006) using the word 'regional state'; Dosenrode (2007) arguing that the EU is a (messy) federation; Ian Manners (2010) discussing the EU's normative power; and Teló (2011) claiming that it is a mixed constitution.

49 If the EU fulfils the criteria of a state the question of its legitimacy is urgent. There is a host of literature on the topic; I refer to Vivien Schmidt (2006) and Mario Teló (2011) for interesting discussions. See also Niklasson, Chapter 10, and Dosenrode, Chapter 11, in this volume.

50 Majone (2009: 20-21) argues for diversified integration, where some groups of states will advance further than others.

51 At the time of writing the economic crisis (first a liquidity crisis, then a debt crisis) has prompted a number of economic decisions to tighten and coordinate the economic policies within the Euro Area member states. These decisions will in the words of French president Nicolas Sarkozy '[...] lead to greater economic integration' (the *Telegraph* 21 July 2011).

52 I find it puzzling that scholars accepting Malta, Monaco, Somalia or Vatican City as 'states' have great difficulties when it comes to the EU.

On the theoretical level, the assumption of the EU as a state challenges intergovernmentalism (e.g. Moravcsik 1998) as well as the multilevel governance approach (e.g. Börzel 2010); to the former, it denies the absolute and unrivalled supremacy of the member-states and to the latter because it now places a government, albeit a weak one, firmly in the Union; no more governance *without* government. Relating to Zielonka's neo-medievalism thesis, it looks like the EU is developing in the direction of a federal version of his 'neo-Westphalian state' model, although 'Neo-Westphalia' in his 2006 book seems less elaborated and more like a caricature than the neo-medievalism model does.

Accepting the EU's statehood also gives rise to more speculative thoughts within international relations. On the one hand, we have seen the accumulation and centralization of power over the centuries from tribes to cities, to feudal states, to nation states and shortly to two super-powers, of which now only the USA is left as hegemon. On the other hand, we witness more or less successful attempts of regional cooperation and integration taking place in the world, e.g. the African Union, ASEAN, European Union, Mercosur, UNASUR etc.: perhaps the beginning of a multi-polar system, with all its weaknesses and dangers (cf. Waltz 1979)?

Closing remarks

The Lisbon Treaty was basically 'Plan B' after the abortive Constitutional Treaty.[53] But Lisbon has strengthened the Union considerably, although the treaty itself is still a frightful mess, quite a bit like the old Swiss pre-1999 constitution or the present Austrian one. This is partly due to the fear of the 'f-word' (f for federalism) in some, especially northern, European states and due to the way the Union has developed; a long series of struggles between those who would like to see a federation ('United States of Europe') and those who yearn for a solid inter-governmental cooperation. But each time the treaties have been amended or changed, the result has been wider and/or deeper integration.[54] Peter Nedergaard is right, when concluding that the Lisbon Treaty is yet another typical example of compromising between visions of the future Europe.

The Lisbon Treaty tightened the governmental web of the union considerably by strengthening the European Parliament, the European Council and in the way that it ties the national parliaments much closer in the legislative procedure than

53 I subscribe to the statement of the Joint Study (2010: 189): 'Treaties have a way of surprising their drafters. This will most likely also happen with the Lisbon Treaty'.

54 Majone (2009: 1), himself a subscriber to EU as a polity, claims that one of the operating principles behind the integration of the EU is to make a fait accompli, not telling the public what really goes on, to make opposition and debate useless. But by not telling the people of Europe what the end goal is, it can never be achieved.

hitherto, and it gives the European citizens the right to bring proposals to the Commission, which the Commission will have to consider.[55]

In 2001 David McKay wrote the words below, which I have previously quoted approvingly; they are even truer today than then (2001: 3):

> Claims that the EU – [...] – is *sui generis* and can be explained only in terms of its unique structure and evolution look inappropriate given the increasingly state like status of the Union.

References

Aberbach, J.D. et al. 1981. *Bureaucrats and Politicians in Western Democracies*. Cambridge, MA: Harvard University Press.

Abromeit, H. 2000. Contours of a European Federation. Paper presented to ARENA, Oslo.

Allen, D. and M. Smith. 1990. Western Europe's Presence in the Contemporary International Arena. *Review of International Studies*, 16(1).

Allen, D. and M. Smith. 2011. Relations with the Rest of the World. *Journal of Common Market Studies*, 49, Annual Review.

Aristotle. 1970. *Politik*. Zürich: Ex Libris.

Blair, T. 2003. EU Superstate Ruled Out. Sky News http://news.sky.com/skynews/Home/Sky-News-Archive/Article/200806412355577, accessed March 2011.

Blondel, J. 1996. *An Introduction to Comparative Government*. New York: Praeger Publishers.

v. Bismarck, O. 1928. *Gedanken und Erinnerungen*. Stuttgart und Berlin: I.H. Gotta'sche Buchhandlung Nachfolger.

Börzel, T. 2010. European Governance. *Journal of Common Market Studies*, 48(2).

Börzel, T. and T. Risse. 2000. Who is Afraid of a European Federation. Paper, Symposium: Responses to Joschka Fischer. http://www.jeanmonetprogram.org/papers/00/00f0101.html, accessed January 2011.

Bretherton, C. and J. Vogler. 1999. *The European Union as a Global Actor*. London: Routledge.

Buzan, B. 1983. *People, States & Fear – The national security problem in international relations*. Brighton: Wheatsheaf Books.

Caporaso, J.A. 1996. The European Union and Forms of State: Westphalian, Regulatory or Post-Modern? *Journal of Common Market Studies*, 34(1).

Dahl, R. 1985. *A Preface to an Economic Theory of Democracy*. London: Polity Press.

Demossier, M. (ed.). 2007. *The European Puzzle – The Political Structuring of Cultural Identities at a Time of Transition*. New York: Berghahn Publishers.

Dosenrode, S. (ed.). 2002. *EU-rettens påvirkning af dansk ret*. Aarhus: Systime.

55 This citizen's right is also known in Switzerland and California.

Dosenrode, S. (ed.). 2007. *Approaching the EUropean Federation?* Aldershot: Ashgate.
Dosenrode, S. 2010. Regional Integration: Bringing the Classical Theories Back In? *The Icfai University Journal of International Relations*, IIII(1–2).
Dosenrode, S. 2011. Federalism Theory and Neo-Functionalism: Elements for an analytical framework. *Perspectives on Federalism*, II(3).
Dosenrode, S. and A. Stubkjær. 2002. *The European Union and the Middle East.* Continuum and University of Sheffield Press.
Dunleavy, P. and B. O'Leary. 1987. *Theories of the State.* London: Macmillan Press.
EP. 2010. State of the (E)Union: The Europe of today and tomorrow debated in the EP http://www.europarl.europa.eu/news/public/focus_page/008-80686-195-07-29-901-20100714FCS78876-14-07-2010-2010/default_p001c006_en.htm, accessed February 2011.
Europa-Barometer. April 2002, No. 56. http://ec.europa.eu/public_opinion/archives/eb/eb56/eb56_en.pdf , accessed January 2011.
Eurobarometer, Spring 2011. http://ec.europa.eu/public_opinion/archives/eb/eb75/eb75_publ_en.pdf , accessed September 2011.
European Commission. 2012. European Commission launches accelerated infringement proceedings against Hungary. http://ec.europa.eu/economy_finance/articles/governance/2012-01-18-hungary_en.htm, accessed January 2012.
Europolitics. 2011. EP pushes for new own resources. http://www.europolitics.info/institutions/ep-pushes-for-new-own-resources-artb284865-33.html, accessed February 2011.
Ezioni, A. 1965. *Political Unification – a Comparative Study of Leaders and Forces*. New York: Holt, Reinhart & Winston.
Fairhurst, J. 2007. *Law of the European Union.* 6th edn. Harlow: Pearson & Longman.
Galbraith, J.K. 1974. *Economics and the Public Purpose.* Harmondsworth: Penguin Press.
Giegereich, B. and W. Wallace. 2010. Foreign and Security Policy – Civilian Power Europe and American Leadership, in *Policy-Making in the European Union*, 6th edn, Helen Wallace et al. (eds). Oxford: Oxford University Press.
Green, D.M. 2007. *The Europeans – Political Identity in an Emerging Polity.* Boulder: Lynne Rienner.
Gullestrup, H. 1992. *Kultur, kulturanalyse og kulturetik.* Akademisk Forlag.
Habermas, J. 1976. *Legitimation Crisis.* London: Heinemann Publ.
Hartley, T.C. 2010. *The Foundations of European Union Law – An introduction to the constitutional and administrative law of the European Union.* 7th edn. Oxford: Oxford University Press.
Hill, C. 1993. The Capability-Expectation Gap, or conceptualizing Europe's International Role. *Journal of Common Market Studies*, 3(3).
Hix, S. 1994. The Study of the EC: The Challenge to Comparative Politics. *West European Politics*, 17, 1–30.

Hix, S. 1999. *The Political System of the European Union*. Houndmills: Palgrave.
Hix, S. and B. Høyland. 2011. *The Political System of the European Union*. 3rd edn. Houndmills: Palgrave.
Holzinger, K. and C. Knill. 2000. Eine Verfassung für die Europäische Föderation – Kontinuierliche Weiterentwicklung des Erreichten. Paper, Symposium: Responses to Joschka Fischer. http://www.jeanmonetprogram.org/papers/00/00f1401.html, accessed January 2011.
Huntington, S.P. 1993. The Clash of Civilizations? *Foreign Affairs*, 72(3).
International Federation of Library Associations and Institutions. 2011. The New Press and Media Act in Hungary, http://www.ifla.org/en/publications/the-new-press-and-media-act-in-hungary, accessed 20 August 2011.
Jackson, R. and G. Sørensen. 1999. *Introduction to International Relations*. Oxford: Oxford University Press.
Jessop, B. 1990. *Putting the Capitalist State in Its Place*. Cambridge: Polity Press.
Joint Study. 2010. The Treaty of Lisbon – A Second Look at the Institutional Innovations, Joint CEPS, EGMONT and ECP Study. http://www.epc.eu/pub_details.php?cat_id=1&pub_id=1150, accessed August 2011.
Jørgensen, K.E. 2007. The State of EU Foreign Policy – Constituting a Global Player, in *Approaching the European Federation?*, S. Dosenrode (ed.). Aldershot: Ashgate.
Keukeleier, S. and J. MacNaughtan. 2008. *The Foreign Policy of the European Union*. Houndmills: Palgrave.
Klöti, U. 1997. *Federalism in Europe*. Distinguished Guest Lectures Series, no 1, Aalborg University, Board of Studies for Social Science & Public Administration.
Klöti, U. et al. 1999. *Handbuch der Schweizer Politik*. Zürich: NZZ Verlag.
Laumann, E.O. and D. Knoke 1987. *The Organizational State*. Madison: University of Wisconsin Press.
Lepsius, M.R. 2000. Die Europäische Union als Herrschaftsverband eigener Prägung. Paper, Symposium: Responses to Joschka Fischer. http://www.jeanmonetprogram.org/papers/00/00f1201.html, accessed January 2011.
Lijphart, A. 1999. *Patterns of Democracy*. New Haven and London: Yale University Press.
Lindblom, C. 1982. Still muddling, not yet through. *Public Administration Review*, 39, 517–36.
Longo, M. 2006. *Constitutionalising Europe – Processes and Practices*. Aldershot: Ashgate.
Luhmann, N. 1979. *Trust and Power*. New York: Wiley Ltd.
Madison, J., A. Hamilton and J. Jay. 1987. *The Federalist Papers*. London: Penguin Books.
Majone, G. 2009. *Europe as the Would-Be World Power*. Cambridge: Cambridge University Press.
Manners, I. 2010. As You Like It: European Union Normative Power in the European Neighbourhood Policy, in *The European Neighbourhood Policy in*

Perspective – Context, Implementation and Impact. R. Whitman and S. Wolff (eds). Basingstoke: Palgrave Macmillan.
McKay, D. 1999. *Federalism and European Union – A Political Economy Perspective*. Oxford: Oxford University Press.
McKay, D. 2001. *Designing Europe – Comparative Lessons from the Federal Experience*. Oxford: Oxford University Press.
Mitchell, W. 1980. An anatomy of state failure, in *Making Bureaucracies Work*, edited by C. Weiss and C. Barton. Beverly Hills: SAGE Publishers.
Moravcsik, Andrew. 1998. *The Choice for Europe – Social Purpose and State Power from Messina to Maastricht*. London: UCL Press.
Moravcsik, A. 2009. Europe: Quietly Rising Superpower in a Bipolar World. Paper.
Nedergaard, P. 2010. *Lissabon Traktaten – En Politologisk Analyse*. Copenhagen: Jurist- og Økonomforbundets Forlag.
Poulantzas, N. 1978. *State Power and Socialism*. London: Verso.
Rasmussen, H. 1994. *EU-ret og EU-institutioner i kontext*. Copenhagen: Karnov.
Rasmussen, H. 2002. Eksemplets magt – Om Dansk Rets frivillige reception af EU-ret, in *EU-rettens påvirkning af dansk ret*, S. Dosenrode (ed.). Aarhus: Forlaget Systime.
Reuters (7 March, 2011): Hungary amends media law http://www.reuters.com/article/2011/03/07/us-hungary-media-vote-idUSTRE7265RN20110307, accessed January 2012.
Richardson, J.J. and A.G. Jordan 1979. *Governing Under Pressure*. Oxford: Martin Robertson Press.
Rosamond, B. 2000. *Theories of European Integration*. London: Palgrave.
Schmidt, V.A. 2006. *Democracy in Europe*. Oxford: Oxford University Press.
Shand, A. 1984. *The Capitalist Alternative – An Introduction to Neo-Austrian Economics*. Boston: Harvester.
Sjöstedt, G. 1977. *The External Role of the European Community*. Farnborough: Gower.
Sørensen, G. 2001. *Changes in Statehood – The transformation of international relations*. Houndmills: Palgrave.
Teló, M. 2011. Before and after the Lisbon Treaty: What political integration for Europe? Paper, 'Regional Integration in Europe and Africa' at the University of Pretoria, February.
Treaty of the European Union: http://eur-lex.europa.eu/JOHtml.do?uri–OJ:C:2007:306:SOM:EN:HTML, accessed January 2011.
Toje, A. 2010. The European Union as a Small Power. *Journal of Common Market Studies*, 49(1), 43–60.
Treaty on the Functioning of the European Union (consolidated version): http://eur-lex.europa.eu/JOHtml.do?uri=OJ:C:2010:083:SOM:EN:HTML, accessed January 2011.
United Nations, Charter of: http://www.un.org/en/documents/charter/index.shtml, accessed January 2011.

Vogel, D. 1987. Political Science and the Study of Corporate Power. *British Journal of Political Science*, 17, 385–408.

Waltz, K.N. 1979. *Theory of International Politics*. Addison-Wesley.

Weiler, J. 1999. *The Constitution of Europe – 'Does the New Clothes have an Emperor?' and other Essays on European Integration*. Cambridge: Cambridge University Press.

Weiler, J. 2002. A Constitution for Europe? Some Hard Choices. *Journal of Common Market Studies*, 40(4).

Wind, M. and J. Weiler. 2003. *European Constitutionalism beyond the State*. Cambridge: Cambridge University Press.

Zambrano. 2011. Case C-34/09 Court of Justice of the European Union.

Zielonka, Jan. 2006. *Europe as Empire: The Nature of the Enlarged European Union*. Oxford: Oxford University Press. (University Press Scholarship Online).

Østergaard, U. 1993. *Europas Ansigter – Nationale stater og politiske kulturer i en ny og gammel verden*. Copenhagen: Rosinante.

Chapter 4
Geographical Spillovers, Structural Power and Growing 'Agency' Post Lisbon

Wolfgang Zank

Introduction: EU's external 'structural power' and 'agency'

On various occasions EU declarations have expressed ambitious aims of shaping world affairs by exporting the union's own model, at least partly. The Lisbon Treaty is one example among many. In Article 21 it states:

> The Union's action on the international scene shall be guided by the principles which have inspired its own creation, development and enlargement, and which it seeks to advance in the wider world: democracy, the rule of law, the universality and indivisibility of human rights and fundamental freedoms, respect for human dignity, the principles of equality and solidarity, and respect for the principles of the United Nations Charter and international law .... It shall promote multilateral solutions to common problems, in particular in the framework of the United Nations.

As the text goes on, the EU shall 'safeguard its values' and 'fundamental interests'. In academia there have been many debates about whether policies are driven by interests or based on values. Apparently, for the authors of the Lisbon Treaty there does not seem to be a contradiction between the EU's interests and values. I think this is basically correct: by promoting its values, as e.g. specified in the treaty, the EU serves also its own (long-term) interests. I shall give substance to this postulate further below in this paper.

Besides promoting democracy and the rule of law and preserving peace, Article 21 mentions explicitly fostering 'the sustainable economic, social and environmental development of developing countries, with the primary aim of eradicating poverty'. It is not specified what this means in practice. At least it does not mean that EU aid should primarily go to the poorest countries. Instead, most aid flows to the EU's relatively wealthier neighbourhood. But the following point is rather specific, namely to 'encourage the integration of all countries into the world economy, including through the progressive abolition of restrictions on international trade'. The EU also wants to 'help develop international measures to improve the quality of the environment', give humanitarian aid in the case of natural or man-made disasters and promote 'multilateral cooperation and good global governance'.

All in all, the treaty formulates a programmme of influencing matters globally. However, it is, of course, a question whether the European Union actually can shape affairs outside its own borders. In the academic literature a variety of views are to be found. Often quoted until today has been Christopher Hill's diagnosis in 1993 of a 'Capability-Expectation Gap'. More recently, but before the ratification of the Lisbon Treaty, Bastian Giegerich and William Wallace also came to a rather sobering assessment (Giegerich and Wallace 2010: 452–4):

> The EU punches below its weight in international diplomacy – including in the international institutions through which civilian power might best be exercised. Dependence on the US for hard security and for managing extra-European security threats betrays idealist claims to distinctively civilian power .... European cooperation in foreign policy has gone beyond the framework of sovereign state diplomacy, but still remains far short of an integrated single policy, with integrated diplomatic, financial and, and military instruments.

But in some newer publications the tone is quite different. One example is an article by Andrew Moravcsik. In his view the EU is the 'second superpower', the only one besides the US effectively influencing matters on a global scale. As he explains (Moravcsik 2010: 93):

> In fact, Europe today is more effective at projecting civilian power globally than any other state or non-state actor. And Europeans have demonstrated, contra realist claims, that such instruments of power can be extremely influential. Some of these tools are wielded by a unified Europe, some by European governments acting in loose coordination, and some by European governments acting unilaterally.

In his view Europe is not only projecting civilian power. Also its military power is 'far more formidable ... than most observers acknowledge'. Europe's defence expenditure has a share of 21 per cent of world spending. This is considerably less than the US's 43 per cent, but much more than China's 5 or Russia's 3 per cent. In the past decade EU member states deployed between 50,000 and 100,000 soldiers in combat roles outside their home countries. Numerous interventions and peace-keeping missions have been led by Europeans. But notwithstanding its considerable military power, 'Europe is, in contrast to the United States, a "quiet" superpower', applying economic influence, international law, 'soft' power (bringing others to your way of thinking) and 'smart' power, which combines military and civilians means (Moravcsik 2010: 93).

I basically share Moravcsik's view. And as I will argue in more detail below, it is highly likely that the EU's role will increase further. This is, on the one hand, due to institutional changes such as the ones the Lisbon Treaty brought. But perhaps much more important, there are powerful global trends which bring most countries closer to the EU model and make them partners for the EU. The Lisbon Treaty's basic principles of EU's external action, as quoted above, are increasingly becoming global principles.

I find it very useful to distinguish between the EU's influence as an actor and EU's 'structural power'. The 'capability-expectation gap', which many authors rightly have assessed, pertains mainly to Europe's role as a unified actor. But it should be underlined that things have changed considerably in this respect. The Lisbon Treaty brings a further strengthening of Europe's 'actorness', e.g. by establishing the European External Action Service. But another matter is 'structural power'. In abstract terms Susan Strange defined it as the 'power to shape and determine the structures of the global political economy within which other states, their political institutions, their economic enterprises and (last, not least) their scientists and other people have to operate' (Strange 1994: 24f, as quoted in Holden 2009: 12). This power can be *purely* structural. As Patrick Holden explains: a state 'may be deemed to have structural power in that its sheer economic size relative to others (and their dependency on its markets) means that its internal rules and systems will spill over to others whether it wants it or not' (Holden 2009: 12f). Holden mentions the US as an example of a state with such structural power, but it is certainly also the case with the European Union.

The concept of structural power has been debated in various forms. Social constructivists have spoken of 'normative power'. The neo-Gramscian school has claimed that certain dominant discourses have systematically empowered some groups, to the disadvantage of others, the most important example being mainstream economic theory. While not denying that norms or types of discourses are important, I want to put much more emphasis on material facts, first and foremost economic structures.

Structural power and agency can go together, in particular if actors pursue 'milieu goals' (Holden 2009: 12). The US did this successfully after 1945 when shaping important characteristics of the global economic system. And the EU has been successfully doing this the last decades, first mainly in its near surroundings, but increasingly with a broader reach.

In order to understand how and why the EU has acquired formidable structural power and important agency, we should go back in time. As it will become apparent, there is not one theory which can explain everything. Instead, different theories have explanatory value at different points in time.

The emergence of a new union

On 9 May 1950 French Foreign Minister Robert Schuman presented a novel proposal: France, West Germany and other interested countries should create a common market for coal and steel, with common institutions and regulations. But the project was not mainly about economics. The first words of Schuman's declaration were *la paix mondiale* – world peace. Europe should unite in order to protect world peace. But the unification of Europe could not be achieved in one stroke. Rather, in the first place *réalisations concrètes* should first create de facto solidarity (*une solidarité de fait*) (Schuman Declaration). One point was not negotiable for Paris: The High Authority and other institutions of this coal and steel union should have supranational competences, with the right to generate decisions which were binding for the member states. This should not just be a scheme for intergovernmental cooperation, but a first step to proper political unification. Belgium, West Germany, Italy, Luxemburg, and the Netherlands accepted. But for the British government any infringement of national sovereignty was unacceptable at that time. Consequently, the United Kingdom stayed outside the European Coal and Steel Community (ECSC), founded by the Treaty of Paris, 18 April 1951.

Presumably, federalism theory, as pioneered by William Riker, delivers the best theoretical explanation: states accept some loss of sovereignty to a new supranational body when being confronted with a threat that seemed to be too great to be addressed by one nation state alone. And the threats were multiple. On the one hand a divided Europe had to face Stalin's mighty Soviet Union, and the promise of US protection did not remove all anxieties. Furthermore, West Germany's recovery was seen – not least by the United States – as necessary for the economic reconstruction of Western Europe and for its defence, and with this basic decision the other European countries had to live. But this opened also the possibility of the revival of old power rivalries. The solution was to firmly anchor West Germany in Western Europe (Knipping 2004: 63).

Riker, coming from the 'Realist' school in international relations, argued on a basis of rational choice. But we must supplement it with some constructivist considerations. Threats are in the eye of the beholder. Why did some countries accept the French proposal and others not? Presumably the experience of occupation just a few years before had left a sense of vulnerability in some countries, but not, e.g., in Switzerland or the United Kingdom. Geography was perhaps also important in this context, because the Channel and the Alps had prevented occupation during the Second World War. Geographical factors could perhaps be integrated into a strict rational-choice argumentation, but for instance the case of Denmark saying no would still remain a puzzle: Flat, certainly a prime target of any Soviet attack, and also having experienced German occupation. Here we have to revert to peculiarities of the Danish political discourse.

The project of a European Defence Community (EDC) failed in August 1954 in the French National Assembly. After Stalin's death (March 1953) the international situation looked much less threatening than in 1950, and the Gaullists deemed the EDC as an intolerable infringement of national sovereignty. But European integration made progress nevertheless. Rather silently. For instance, the European Coal and Steel Community gained a piece of competence in foreign policy when it opened missions in the US and elsewhere. The institutions of the ECSC, in particular the High Authority, became new actors who worked systematically for intensifying integration. Because the ECSC had real supranational powers, interest groups and political parties began to organize themselves on a community-wide level, formulated demands to the new centre and provided it with input, thus reinforcing the integrationist drive. Ernst Haas, the pioneer of neo-functionalism, analysed these processes meticulously. The concept of spill-over was central in his analysis: If certain conditions are fulfilled, then integration in one field will create systematic pressures for extending integration to other fields. Haas highlighted the importance of elites. Their actions towards more integration were often motivated by rather narrow interests, not by grand ideological designs. Also, those politicians who had high ambitions about Europe often strongly diverged in what they meant by, e.g., the unification of Europe. But in Haas's scheme rational self-interested actors brought much progress to integration. These processes will finally create a new political community (Haas 2004: 16):

> *Political integration is the process whereby political actors in several distinct national settings are persuaded to shift their loyalties, expectations and political activities towards a new centre, whose institutions possess or demand jurisdiction over the pre-existing national states. The end result of a process of political integration is a new political community, superimposed over the pre-existing ones* (emphasis in the original).

Given the point that the nation states and national sovereignty were strongly planted in peoples' minds, such a process of superimposing a new community above them could not be expected to progress smoothly. Consequently, the history of European integration has been littered with crises. But the crises have mainly delayed further integration steps for some time. Admittedly, in the case of defence the delay lasted some 45 years before a new, more modest start was done. But there has never been an unravelling of the treaties, or members leaving.

Throughout the history of the EU spill-over effects have been rather silent, but powerful, motors of integration. And they prepared the ground for new bolder political initiatives. The way towards the Treaty of Rome (25 March 1957) and the foundation of the European Economic Communities shows this. On the one hand there were strong functional arguments for extending the common market from just coal and steel to all products. But there was again strong political will behind it.

At a conference in Messina the foreign ministers of the six ECSC countries agreed on the principles of a common market. But as their final declaration (again) emphasized, this was not only about economics, but deemed necessary in order that Europe could retain its place in the world, and, slightly contradictory, 'to give Europe its influence ... back'; raising standards of living was also continually mentioned. Echoing the Schuman Declaration the foreign ministers stated that 'Europe should be constructed in the first place in the economic field' (Herbst 1996: 227f).

The West German cabinet minister Ludwig Erhard voiced objections, advocating more integration in the world market instead. Chancellor Konrad Adenauer underlined the primacy of political considerations (Herbst 1996: 231):

> The current international situation contains extraordinary dangers. In order to avert them ... decisive actions are needed. To these belong first and foremost a clear positive German position as regards European integration .... In case of successful integration we will be able to put ... the weight of a united Europe on the scales in negotiations about both security and [*German*] re-unification. On the other hand can serious concessions from the Soviet Union not be expected, as long as Europe's division gives it the hope to drag one state or the other to its side, thereby to destroy the cohesion of the West and to initiate the stepwise incorporation of Europe into the system of satellites.

Again federalism theory – integration in order to avert a threat – can explain matters to a large extent. And after the Rome Treaty came into force, spill-over effects made themselves felt even stronger than before. When, for instance, it comes to the new institutions as new agents for more integration, we can quote Walter Hallstein, the first president of the Commission. According to him, the Commission provided 'a constant reminder of a Community interest transcending the interests of each of the participants'; being independent it could 'play the role of honest broker between the governments and bring political weight to bear to ensure that formulas for agreement ... [were] found' (Kassim 2007: 171). And early on, e.g., the project of a monetary union came on the agenda, when in 1961 tensions in the Bretton-Woods System led to a revaluation of the deutschmark and the Dutch guilder by 5 per cent. This was seen by many as being in contradiction to the aim of a common market, in particular to the rules of rules of the (future) Common Agricultural Policy. In October 1962 the European Parliament passed a resolution advocating the stepwise transition to monetary union (Tietmeyer 2005: 23f).

Geographical spill-over and the power of attraction

Of particular importance in our context, Haas observed a process by which 'countries not initially members of the regional grouping ... [found] it desirable to deepen their ties with the integrating *bloc* ...' (Haas 2004: 316). About the United Kingdom Haas wrote in 1958 (Haas 2004: 317):

> A geographical spill-over is clearly taking place. In its unique British form it rigorously rejects any federal trimmings and continues to rely on intergovernmental 'association'. But it grants not only the need for more and more intimate economic contacts in areas of activity until recently considered the sacrosanct preserve of national governments, but even the necessity for decision by majority vote among ministerial delegates. All other things being equal, it is

> as inconceivable that this form of cooperation should not result in new patterns of profound interdependence as it is unlikely that the General Common Market [*a proposed Free Trade agreement between the EEC and the UK*] can avoid a species of political federalism in order to function as an economic organ.

The market of the six gained an increasing importance for the UK, but as to its concrete regulations the UK had no say. Her exporters could expect systematic disadvantages when the EEC made progress at constructing a common external tariff. American investors preferred the EEC and by-passed the UK (Knipping 2004: 145). As again Haas observed: 'Fear of isolation thus became a potent catalyst to the spill-over process as the feeling gained ground that supranational integration was here to stay' (Haas 2004: 315). British Prime Minister Harold Macmillan even spoke of a 'continental blockade' (Holden 2009: 16). But whereas Britain heroically resisted the Napoleonic one, this time she gave in.

In 1961 the UK filed a first application for membership, vetoed by French President Charles de Gaulle. He saw the United Kingdom as a kind of Trojan horse of the United States. He vetoed also a second application in 1967. But finally in 1973 the UK gained membership, together with Denmark and Ireland. Norway's accession was blocked by the voters in a referendum.

With Denmark and the UK two countries joined whose elites showed very little enthusiasm at the idea of creating a new political community 'with jurisdiction over the pre-existing nation states'. But when calculating their interests they came to the conclusion that the emergence of the EEC had changed the landscape to such an extent that they were better off as members, in spite of many misgivings. The interests at stake were, on the one hand, economic ones; Britain was disadvantaged as an exporter and as a location for investment. And political ones: Without membership others could make decisions which substantially impacted on Britain. Consequently, it was not so much that the original six could export their ideas to the UK. UK politicians were as adverse to giving up sovereignty as before. But European integration had created facts which British politicians had to factor into their calculations. And this made British membership look like the lesser evil.

Haas' 'geographical spill-overs' can be seen as an impact of the EU's 'structural power'. Thus, already in the 1950s, when there was little external 'actorness' of the EEC, it had already acquired substantial structural power over neighbours, However, only over neighbours with a pluralistic democratic political system and an open market economy. In these days there were no spill-overs to, e.g., Czechoslovakia.

So strong was the attraction of the EEC on Denmark and the UK that not even important judicial developments which were abhorrent to the supporters of national sovereignty could make them withdraw membership applications. The European Court of Justice, in so-called 'landmark decisions' in the beginning of the 1960s, had made it explicit that the legal acts of the EEC were indeed superior to national law. In case of norm conflict every community norm trumps every national norm, even constitutional norm. Community law had also direct effect on the citizens; they could use it to directly go to court. In general, decisions by the European Court have had a strong impact on the EEC/EU, driving integration further. Many scholars have portrayed the ECJ as a political actor. But in my view the expansion of EU law can best be explained in terms of neo-functionalism. Legal systems have to be consistent, so many norms conflicting with the Rome Treaty (or subsequent treaties) had to be altered. In many cases the politicians making and ratifying the treaties were not aware of their often far-reaching consequences.

Leading politicians in Denmark and the UK were truly unsympathetic to the idea that the new centre could gradually acquire more competences. They could entertain the hope that they could prevent such a development because any treaty revision required unanimity. The 'Luxemburg Compromise' of January 1966 established unanimity also as the main principle for passing legal acts in the council of ministers. But as it turned out, in spite of many veto points the development towards a new community could not be stopped. It took a longer time than Haas had expected, but it took the direction Haas saw.

Enlargement as democracy support and stability export

When the military and authoritarian regimes in Greece, Portugal and Spain fell, the EEC's power of attraction made itself felt immediately. This gave a new kind of 'structural power': explicit membership conditions. The European Council declared in April 1978 that 'respect for and maintenance of representative democracy and human rights in each Member State are essential elements of membership in the European Communities' (Smith 2003: 110). The heads of states and government thereby sent a clear signal that the three Mediterranean countries could become members, provided that they consolidated democracy. This was also meant as support and encouragement for the democratic forces in these countries who could point to the enormous material benefits which the countries could expect in case of membership: Free access to the EEC market, free mobility for workers, money from the European Social Fund and the European Regional Development Fund, and not the least the high prices for agricultural products.

On the side of the existing members there was also some scepticism, e.g. with a view to the prospect of massive immigration from the Iberian Peninsula. But concerns such as these could not prevent the new enlargements. Anchoring democratic stability in these countries remained the overarching issue.

Supporting democratic stability came again on the agenda when the Soviet Union collapsed. Countries such as Poland and Hungary asked for membership early on, but did not get a promise during the first years. The union – after the Maastricht Treaty the European Union – offered association treaties with favourable trade conditions and assistance, but carefully avoided any mention of membership. Leading politicians such as François Mitterrand and Helmuth Kohl did not regard an eastern enlargement as realistic in the near future. However, in

1991 it became apparent that the association policy was insufficient for anchoring stability in the region. In August 1991 the coup against Gorbachev created a widespread sense of alarm, Yugoslavia was tormented by civil war, but also in many other places the eruption of violence looked possible, for instance in the Baltic states with their Russian minorities, or in Romania. Even the democratic front-runner, Poland, looked unstable after the breaking-up of the Solidarity.

The EU commission drafted several documents which showed the way an eastern enlargement could be done without diluting the union. Essential were the principles that new members had to fulfil specified criteria, and that they had to implement the whole *acquis communautaire* before accession. Finally, in June 1993, after the ratification of the Maastricht Treaty was secured, the EU summit in Copenhagen declared a membership offer to a first group of eastern neighbours, which was extended successively to in all ten of these countries, plus Cyprus and Malta. The conditions were democracy, rule of law and protection of minorities, administrative capacities to be able to shoulder membership obligations, and a market economy which could stand the competitive pressure of the Internal Market.

The commission was set to monitor closely the progress towards fulfilling the criteria and implementing the *acquis*. The EU also financed a string of assistance programmes in order to facilitate the transition. This process gave the EU an unprecedented power for transforming these societies. Membership was very attractive, but it could be gained only by reforming the institutional settings, following the often very detailed demands from the EU side.

We can see this as a case of overwhelming structural power, combined with targeted actorness. The EU leadership acted as a rational self-interest actor in uncertain and potentially dangerous surroundings. There are numerous statements, such as the one by British Prime Minister John Major in 1993: 'through community membership we can consolidate democracy and prosperity across our continent. Without it, we risk turmoil among neighbours in Eastern and Central Europe and endanger our own long-term prosperity and stability' (Zank 2005: 39).

There was no such thing as 'rhetorical entrapment', as postulated by some in academia, simply because EU leaders had been very careful to avoid lofty promises (Zank 2005: 38–52). When the offer for membership came at the Copenhagen summit in 1993, it was given after long and detailed deliberations. Also, countries such as Spain which had been singled out as not having an interest in eastern enlargement, but which allegedly were pushed into acceptance by 'rhetorical action', shared the same concern for stabilizing Eastern Europe. Furthermore, Spain had a strong interest that the EU increase its efforts at stabilizing the Mediterranean, together with France and Italy. Successfully they pushed for a big initiative, materialized in November 1995 with the Barcelona Conference. The 'real watershed', in Ricardo Gomez' words, on the way to Barcelona 'was the Essen summit in December 1994 .... Behind the scenes, the agreement to hold the conference formed part of an inter-governmental deal in which the Mediterranean member states accepted that eastern enlargement had to be the EU's number one priority in exchange for a significant political gesture towards the south' (Gomez 2003: 70). Rational actors in short. The operation can basically be seen as a success.

Currently, a similar process is under way in Croatia. Ukraine, Moldova and Georgia have declared their intention to join, the power of attraction has reached the Caucasus. In principle, the EU could use its transformative power also towards Turkey. But the accession process is currently (2011) stagnant, not least due to the negative positions of Nicolas Sarkozy and Angela Merkel towards Turkish membership.

Structural power through offering a stake in the internal market

With the launch of the Global Mediterranean Policy in 1972, arguably the first example of a coherent foreign policy, the EEC tried an exercise in exporting stability southwards. New association agreements and financial and technical assistance should bring more economic cooperation and dynamism and thus stability to the region. A Mediterranean Free Trade Area was the long-term goal (Zank 2009b: 130f). However, success was very limited for many years. On the one hand, all Arab Mediterranean countries followed inward-oriented models of 'Import-Substitution Industrialization' or outright socialist planned economy. And the regimes were authoritarian and not much interested in cooperation with Europe, except Morocco and Tunisia. Under these conditions, few cross-border transactions could take place, there was little 'geographical spill-over', if any. Europe had, thus, neither much structural power nor agency influence because the policies of the major member countries had many divergent characteristics. In the 1970s a slow process of intergovernmental coordination of foreign policy began, but there were not yet common institutions.

But matters were gradually changing. Beginning with Egypt's *Infitah* ('Opening') for more foreign investment, a process of slow and often inconsistent transition towards open market economies began. Often it needed a severe currency or debt crisis and a Structural Adjustment Programme, monitored by the International Monetary Fund (IMF) to start the process in earnest. The regimes practised for many years a 'Chinese solution': maintaining authoritarian rule, but trying to modernize in technical and administrative terms and to gain efficiency through open market economies. The EU became interesting as an export market, as a source for imports and investment, and as a provider of funding and technical assistance. By 1995 the economic climate had changed to such an extent that the Mediterranean Arab countries (except Libya) signed the Barcelona Declaration, which mentioned a Mediterranean Free Trade Area as a long-term goal. They also accepted political and cultural dialogue on many levels.

With the launch of the European Neighbourhood Policy in 2004, the EU formulated the goal of giving the neighbouring countries a 'Stake in the Internal Market'. EU legal norms to regulate markets have become very complex, and often exports to the EU become blocked because the products do not comply with

EU standards, for instance in the field of food safety. But the EU can assist in building the capacities to comply.

In the context of the ENP many of the neighbour countries have build-up a dense network of institutionalized cooperation and dialogue on all levels. For instance Morocco and Tunisia, but increasingly also, e.g., Egypt, have begun to implement sections of the EU's *acquis I* into their own legislation. This means that a process of 'deep integration' has begun with the EU: Not only reforms at the border such as tariff reductions ('shallow integration'), but also reforms behind the borders, in fields such as technical norms, competition legislation or subsidies. The Arab League and its programme of a Greater Arab Free Trade Area (GAFTA) has so far only produced 'shallow integration' (Zank 2010). In addition, institutions such as the court system or the administration of public spending became subject to a process of EU-aided modernization.

We can interpret these developments again as geographic spill-over. One condition has been the above-mentioned transition to open market economies, but another is also the deepening of European integration. After the launch of the Internal Market Programme in 1985 the EU generated a huge set of legislation in order to remove non-tariff barriers among its member states and to create common rules for the market. One condition for it was the introduction of qualified majority voting in the council of ministers. This substantial progress at political integration can be seen as a spill-over of economic integration. But the *internal* Market increased also the EU's *external* reach because it made the EU much more attractive for foreign exporters and investors. Previously, the market was de facto fragmented, successfully exporting to one member country did not mean that it was easy to export also to the neighbouring EU member. But with the Internal Market it has become much easier to make money in the whole union, although the Internal Market is not yet completed.

Structural power and the ACP countries

Since the signing of the Yaoundé Convention in 1963 and then the Lomé Convention in 1975 the EEC/EU has entertained institutionalized cooperation with the former European colonies. In particular, these ACP-countries (Africa, Caribbean, Pacific) had preferential access to the EU market, also in agriculture. In addition, they received EU development aid. The EU became actually the biggest aid donor in the world. In addition, member countries have had their own aid policies. However, preferential access or aid does not seem to have given the EU much leverage.

But matters seem to have changed in the last decade. In 2001 the EU granted tariff- and quota-free access to the Least Developed Countries under the 'Everything-but-Arms' Programme. But this was made conditional on the country in question signing international conventions, for instance against child labour.

This way the EU got some leverage for its policy of strengthening international rule by law.

Another form of leverage resulted from a ruling within the World Trade Organization (WTO), which declared preferential agreements of the type Yaoundé/ Lomé as being incompatible with the WTO rules. Consequently, the Cotonou Agreement between the EU and the ACP-countries provided for the drafting of so-called Economic Partnership Agreements (EPA). According to the agreements groups of ACP-countries should liberalize market access among themselves and for the EU within 25 years. The EU would also provide more aid. These EPA agreements were supposed to be signed by 2008, but the process was slow and protracted. By 2010 only the Caribbean countries (CARIFORUM) had signed a comprehensive agreement, including services and investment, and the East African Community (EAC) had initialled an interim goods agreement. In sub-Saharan Africa 19 out of 46 have initialled an interim agreement, and ten have signed one (Bond and ECDPM 2010: 15). Other countries, e.g. Nigeria, opted for market access to the EU under the *General System of Preferences*. The process has created much animosity, with African leaders accusing the EU of bullying its positions down on poor people in Africa. Consequently, the necessity for altering the old system of preferential access for the ACP-countries has indeed given the EU some structural power, understood in the way that the EU more effectively could push for economic opening in some countries But using this structural power has incurred a loss in reputation.

In general, Europe's structural power has been limited. On the one hand, many African states are still rather closed in economic terms. This impedes not least the cooperation among them and hinders economic development. But it also reduces possibilities for geographical spill-over from the EU. Many of the regimes are authoritarian and thus not very interested in cooperation with outside actors if this implies the risk of de facto interference. And contacts with the EU imply exactly this. For those regimes China is therefore a much more sympathetic partner. For many of these countries there is the additional problem that the strength of their institutions is still rather limited. This makes any kind of institutionalized cooperation with them – usually a strong side of the EU – weak in its effects.

Economic development and democracy

The transition to open market economies has been a worldwide process. Mainstream economists have recommended it for decades, if not centuries, and the dismal results of socialist systems and closed 'Import-Substitution Industrialization' have vindicated their positions.

Open market economies want to export to the big EU market. This has increased the cooperation possibilities and the potential for geographical spill-overs on a worldwide scale. One example is the increasing cooperation of the EU with Mercosur. Also, a process of taking over parts of the EU's *acquis* has begun. Another example is China. The network of institutionalized cooperation has become so dense that, e.g., David Shambaugh, of George Washington University, spoke of an 'emerging axis': one 'of the most important, yet least appreciated developments ... has been the dramatic growth in ties between China and Europe' (Shambaugh 2004: 243). He pointed to a high and increasing level of economic ties, but also to numerous projects of technical cooperation and at the many institutionalized political dialogues, including an annual summit. Many of these meetings generated new treaties and brought about a convergence of views on many fields. The development of these close ties is understandable because both sides have an interest in increasing cooperation, which is deemed to be mutually beneficial. Being open economic systems, China and the EU are interdependent with the world at large and have a common interest in contributing to its stabilization.

There are also points of irritation, e.g. when EU leaders meet the Dalai Lama. And also as to China the EU has an interference agenda, understood in the way that it wants to support a transition to democracy and respect for human rights, until now without much success. But there is a certain long-term optimism on the side of the EU. For instance, the Commission formulated in its strategy paper on China from 1995: 'EU policy is based on the well-founded belief that human rights tend to be better understood and better protected in societies open to the free flow of trade, investment, people, and ideas' (Mattlin 2009: 103). The human rights situation has indeed improved in relative terms. Very dramatically so if compared with the Great Famine 1958–61 and the Cultural Revolution.

The EU policies seem also to be based on a belief in modernization theories. They postulate a connection between a process of modernization and economic development, as measured, e.g., by (non-oil) GDP per head, and democracy. As Ronald Inglehart put it (Inglehart 2000: 92):

> It tends to transform a society's social structure, bringing urbanization, mass education, occupational specialization growing organizational networks, greater income equality, and a variety of associational developments that mobilize mass participation in politics. Rising occupational specialization and rising education lead to a workforce that is independent minded and has specialized skills that enhance its bargaining power against elites ....
>
> Economic development is also conducive to cultural changes that help stabilize democracy. It tends to develop interpersonal trust and tolerance, and it leads to the spread of post-materialist values that place high priority on self-expression and participating in decision making.

General developments in the world during the last decades seem to vindicate such a position. Many East Asian countries experienced strong economic growth and then indeed introduced democracy. The same was the case in most of Latin America, where military regimes were in power still in the 1970s in most countries.

Furthermore, if modernization theory is basically correct, then an EU-type of policy which supports modernization and economic development is also by implication very supportive for democratization.

Policies such as the European Neighbourhood Policy (ENP) can strengthen these pro-democracy effects by building up close patterns of cross-border cooperation and transactions on all levels. Many experts, but also ordinary people, come into stable working relations with Europeans, the EU-system or member countries. And these member countries and the EU are built on democracy and rule by law. The many transactions imply therefore a tacit demonstration of how democracies work.

Recent developments in Tunisia and Egypt are in concordance with this view. A policy such as the ENP presupposes, of course, that the EU works with the regimes in place. After the revolutions in Tunisia and Egypt many observers were highly critical of the close connections which some European leaders had with the autocrats and their entourages. Some media argued that the Europeans had 'supported' or 'buttressed' these regimes. Here we have to distinguish carefully: Some European top politicians indeed performed poorly. That was bad agency. But cooperating with the regimes – in principle, not necessary in all concrete forms – was a condition for Europe's structural power with its pro-democracy implications becoming effective.

Concluding remarks

The ECSC and EEC/EU were explicitly constructed with a view to enhancing Europe's standing in the world. Federalism theory can explain much of the coming about of the treaties, whereas neo-functionalism can contribute with powerful insights on the day-to-day developments. But although the international situation occupied a central place in the minds of the EU's founding fathers, it took a long time before the EU actually acquired 'actorness'. Foreign policy was mentioned for the first time in the Single European Act of 1987 and institutionalized as an EU matter in the Maastricht Treaty. But only in strictly intergovernmental terms, and this meant in an inefficient way. It needed the tragedies of the Yugoslav civil wars and then the Kosovo crisis to make the EU build up its own military capabilities for peace-keeping operations. But the EU cannot project strong military power. It can therefore not give protection to countries under potential military threats. In this respect the US is the only superpower.

The Treaty of Lisbon has strengthened the EU's 'actorness' by creating an External Action Service and a High Representative, anchored in the commission and chairing the meetings of the council of ministers in this field. This will presumably strengthen the cohesion of EU policies. The External Action Service will presumably also intensify processes of socialization of diplomats to common European positions. But the Lisbon Treaty retained the principle of unanimity in foreign policy. This will restrict the number of concrete positions and actions. But it has been possible to agree to some broad strategic principles which laid the basis for common long-term policies such as the ENP and its many programmes. These can have quite an impact and give substantial contributions to processes such as the transition to market economy.

Much earlier than 'actorness', the ECSC/EEC acquired 'structural power' and generated geographic spill-overs. They came about by the construction of a common market under supranational regulation. The progress to 'deep integration' under the Internal Market programme strengthened this aspect because it increased the attractiveness of the EU's market. The EU could use its power of attraction in order to stabilize its surroundings through the perspective of giving membership, based on conditions. In particular, under the eastern enlargement the EU acquired an unprecedented power for shaping the societies in neighbouring countries. Without a membership perspective a neighbourhood policy is much weaker. But the attractiveness of the EU market, in combination with assistance, has given the EU influence.

Two global processes have increased the possibilities of the EU. On the one hand there has been the worldwide trend of transition to open market economies. This has profoundly transformed the international system by dramatically increasing interdependence. Factors highlighted by the so-called Realist School, such as military power, have not become completely irrelevant. But in relative terms they have decreased substantially. And this makes the lack of strong military capabilities on the side of the EU less important, whereas the strong sides of the EU become more important. These are the big market and a policy which aims actively at including others as far as possible in this market. In this respect the US is much weaker because 'trade paralysis' has blocked the US congress once again.

In some very critical studies the transition to a market economy is depicted as the result of Western structural power. Mainstream economics, which advocated such a transition, becomes depicted as an ideology which systematically favours capitalistic interests, and the conditionality, which for instance the IMF has practised in its Structural Adjustment Programmes, bulldozed markets open, under heavy social costs. I have a different view: socialism and other forms of closed economies have been practised worldwide. By 1960 only about 20 per cent of the world population lived in open economic systems (Sachs and Warner 1995: 12). But the closed systems failed everywhere, dismally. Economic mainstream theory has simply been correct, at least as to this point. And the IMF could mainly become powerful towards countries if these countries previously had opted for non-performing closed systems and ended in severe debt crises. There have also been cases where countries 'innocently' ended in a crisis, e.g. after the oil-price shocks in the 1970s, or recently Ukraine during the financial crisis. But in these cases no tough Structural Adjustment Programme was imposed, because this was not necessary. One can, of course, view economic mainstream theory as a form of ideological structural power because it indeed favours some solution to others. But is has become so powerful because the very critical theories, when put into practice, failed so dismally.

Also, a transition to democracy has been a worldwide process, and this means that the EU gets better partners. Authoritarian regimes have accepted economic cooperation, but have tried to avoid any spill-overs into political spheres. Democracies are much more willing to cooperate in many more fields with the EU, often not least with a view to stabilizing democracy and rule by law: central aims of the EU.

If these considerations are correct, we can expect a further increase in both the EU's actorness and in its 'structural power'.

References

Bond and ECDPM. 2010. *The EU and Africa. The policy context for development.* http://www.ecdpm.org/Web_ECDPM/Web/Content/Download.nsf/0/3355884C1EE2D093C12577E700482338/$FILE/EU%20and%20Africa%20policy%20context%20for%20development_BOND&ECDPM.pdf.

Gaens, B. et al. (eds). 2009. *The Role of the European Union in Asia. China and India as Strategic Partners*. Farnham and Burlington: Ashgate.

Giegerich, B. and W. Wallace. 2010. Foreign and Security Policy. Civilian Power Europe and American Leadership, in *Policy-Making in the European Union*, 6th edn, H. Wallace et al. (eds). Oxford: Oxford University Press.

Gomez, R. 2003. *Negotiating the Euro-Mediterranean Partnership. Strategic Action in EU Foreign Policy?* Aldershot and Burlington: Ashgate.

Haas, E. 2004 (1958]. *The Uniting of Europe: Political, Social and Economic Forces 1950–1957*. Notre Dame, IN: University of Notre Dame Press.

Hay, C. and A. Menoon. 2007. *European Politics*. Oxford: Oxford University Press.

Herbst, L. 1996. Option für den Westen. Vom Marshallplan bis zum deutsch-französischen Vertrag, 2nd edn. München: dtv.

Hill, C. 1993. The Capability-Expectations Gap, or Conceptualizing Europe's International Role. *Journal of Common Market Studies*, 31(3), 305–28.

Holden, P. 2009. *In Search of Structural Power. EU Aid Policy as a Global Political Instrument*. Farnham and Burlington: Ashgate.

Kassim, H. 2007. The Institutions of the European Union, in *European Politics*, edited by C. Hay and A. Menon, Oxford: Oxford University Press, 168-99.

Knipping, F. 2004. *Rom, 25. März 1957. Die Einigung Europas*. München: dtv.

Mattlin, M. 2009. Thinking Clearly on Political Strategy: The Formulation of a Common EU Policy toward China, in *The Role of the European Union in Asia. China and India as Strategic Partners*, B. Gaens et al. (eds). Farnham and Burlington: Ashgate, 95–120.

Moravcsik, A. 2010. Europe, the Second Superpower. *Current History*, March, 91–8.

Sachs, J. and A. Warner. 1995. Economic Reform and the Process of Global Integration. *Brookings Papers on Economic Activity*, 1, 1–118.

Schuman Declaration, http://europa.eu/abc/symbols/9-may/decl_fr.htm.
Shambaugh, D. 2004. China and Europe: The Emerging Axis. *Current History*, September, 243–8.
Smith, K.E. 2003. The Evolution and Application of EU Membership Conditionality', in *The Enlargement of the European Union*, M. Cremona (ed.). Oxford: Oxford University Press, 105–40.
Strange, S. 1994. *States and Markets*. London: Pinter.
Tietmeyer, H. 2005. *Herausforderung Euro. Wie es zum Euro kam und was er für Deutschlands Zukunft bedeutet*. München/Wien: Hanser.
Zank, W. 2005. The Politics of Eastern Enlargement: Historical Reconstruction and Theoretical Conclusions. *European Research Unit, Series of Occasional Papers*, 38, Aalborg University, 56 pages.
Zank, W. (ed.). 2009a. *Clash or Cooperation of Civilizations: Overlapping Integration and Identities*. Farnham: Ashgate.
Zank, W. 2009b. The Gradual Europeanization of North Africa: From 'Arab Socialism' to a 'Stake in EU's Internal Market', in *Clash or Cooperation of Civilizations: Overlapping Integration and Identities*, edited by W. Zank. Farnham: Ashgate, 109–46.
Zank, W. 2010. The Dynamics of Overlapping 'Shallow' and 'Deep' Economic Integration: Greater Arab Free Trade Area and European Neighbourhood Policy in the Mediterranean. *The IUP Journal of International Relations*, 4(1 & 2), 101–30.

Chapter 5
European Security in the Lisbon Order

Per Jansson

> The state is invisible; it must be personified before it can be seen, symbolized before it can be loved, imagined before it can be conceived.
>
> Michael Walzer (1992: 66)

Introduction

It seems necessary to constantly remind ourselves that the EU is and always was primarily a project of peace and security. And in broad terms this project has, of course, been a successful one. What makes the post-World War II European experience unique is the development of a successively expanding security community (Deutsch 1957; Adler and Barnett 1998; Checkel and Katzenstein 2009: 12). This makes it particularly important to evaluate the meaning and prospects for European security at turning points of institutional development of the union. The focal point of this volume is Europe after the Lisbon Treaty (LT), and this chapter will accordingly discuss the prospect of European security in this context. My take on this subject will not be a close analysis of the LT as far as this concerns institutions and policies of security, however. Rather, the LT will serve as the starting point for a more wideranging discussion on the meaning and prospects of European security. Thus, this essay attempts to outline a set of arguments and interpretations on the state of European security post-Lisbon, but in this it is also a reflection on the state of the European institutions and the European polity itself.

Focusing on the LT as such risks a top-down perspective assuming that constitutional and institutional reform is the self-evident motive force of political developments. The choice of perspective is also connected to another danger associated with a discourse on security: that of framing our understandings of security, threats, and means of policy-making in terms of the nationstate. Certainly, the state remains for a foreseeable future a main focus of political identification as well as organization, even in Europe, but to underline the obvious: European security (or insecurity) is formed in a world where spatial and cultural borders are becoming increasingly fluid, and where the nature of threats and even the meaning of security are becoming more complex. My starting point will therefore be that the context is a wider one, that it may be helpful to view the Lisbon reforms and the overall development of the European polity in a perspective of a continuing process of political development with a global reach. In Robert Cooper's famous essay of

2003, the European Union is depicted not as a security community of states, but as the most advanced example of a political system in which traditional notions of sovereignty and the model of the bureaucratic nation-state is being replaced by a transparent system of governance. As such, Europe emerges as a postmodern society, located in a still modern, and part pre-modern, world (Cooper 2003).

Broadly speaking, the topic can be approached at different levels of analysis. The level of policy is one. For example, we have reasons to ask what concrete programmes and actions are intended or implied by the LT? Another level is that of institutions: what institutional arrangement are created or affected by the treaty and its implementation? A third level may be referred to as the symbolic one. Here we take the treaty into view as an essentially communicative phenomenon, implicated in and in turn affecting a network of understandings about Europe, the European polity, the meaning of European identity, and European security; the meaning of this and any other international treaty will not be found in the rights and obligations that it defines, i.e. the treaty terms as such, but in the nature of the relationships that it establishes, in the ethical characters thus inscribed on the parties involved (and those left outside). Obviously these levels are interconnected to some extent. Policies, for example, may have a significant element of symbolism, intended or not. But in the following discussion attention will primarily be paid to the symbolic implications of the LT.

Community and security

Understanding of European security runs up against several difficulties, which at least need to be pointed out and recognized. The topic is problematic for the simple reason that there can be no incontestable meaning attached to European security (cf. Burgess 2009). What constitutes Europe and thus the meaning of European can possibly be provisionally settled, although this seems a slim chance. As for security, this has been referred to as an *essentially* contestable concept, i.e., the meaning of security is not only difficult to discern; we are bound to disagree about this meaning since the ideological content of the concept rules out any objective standards of determination.[1] The point is not that security is a complicated notion, but that the very nature of security, like that of other essentially contested concepts, inevitably precludes agreement (Buzan 1991: 7; cf. Smith 2005). This does not, however, imply that security is a meaningless or useless notion. This is clearly not the case, since so much political as well as academic concern seems to be connected to various conceptions of security: national, international, collective, common, human, and so on. As suggested by these distinctions, the concept of security attains substance in relation to specific referent objects, such as the state,

1 The classic exposition of the idea of essential contestable concepts is W.B. Gallie's article 'Essentially Contested Concepts', in *The Importance of Language*, M. Black (ed.). Englewood Cliffs, NJ: Prentice Hall, 1962, 121–46.

the international system, individual human beings or mankind as a whole. The problem is, of course, that this move towards the referent objects of security merely pushes the conceptual quandary in another direction, towards other concepts which themselves are contested. Nevertheless, security is an important value in many different contexts, and we have every reason to try to unveil how conceptions of security and insecurity are construed.

As long as the state is taken to be the referent object, security may be defined in relation to a physical base of territory and population, institutional expressions, and the idea of the state, a notion of its ultimate and legitimizing purpose (Buzan 1991: Ch. 2). The territorial extension of states is usually well defined. The institutional structure is well known, historically evolved, containing and expressing values that are closely associated with the historical development of the state. Defining the idea of a given state may well be the most problematic aspect, but it's indisputable that for the state to maintain a political community, there has to be some kind of accepted ideological principle involved. Putting the concept into the context of Europe, and the policy-making of the EU, is more problematic. The physical base is not fixed, but expanding through the on-going process of expansion. The institutional expressions of the union are, as testified by the process of revision of the founding treaties, in a state of constant flux and development. The idea, finally, to the extent that it can be discerned at all, is highly contested.

Essentially contested or not (Smith 2005: 27–8), security is the central value at the heart of any political community, i.e. a voluntary association of people for the pursuit of common ends. In fact, the concept of security is closely interrelated with notions of community as well as collective identity. If we have an impulse to think and talk in terms of European security this is because we have a corresponding impulse to think and talk about 'Europe', not just as a geographical or cultural entity, but also as a – at least potential – political community.

The LT was intended to provide a more coherent European Union. The extent to which this can be accomplished depends not only on the efficacy of the institutional structure created by the treaty, but also on the symbolic values attached to it. Accordingly, all kinds of social and political institutions make claims of intelligibility; they must, as a matter of course, convey reason and legitimacy. Hence institutions can fail not only by not performing their ostensive tasks, by not delivering intended or expected outcomes; they may also fail by simply not making sense, through an incapacity to – in their practices – communicate reason and rationale for what they do. By putting the argument in this way, I am indicating a complex interplay between ideas and practices in the rise and fall of institutions. It is a characteristic of stable institutions that the links between actual practices and motivating ideas are obvious, to the point of being invisible. That is to say, we ideally understand and condone a given institution since the activities that emanate from it need no further explication or justification; the manifestations of institutional practice comes across as perfectly intelligible. However, ideas and practices are frequently at variance, as Charles Taylor notes in a rather different context, but the gist of argument is relevant to the present discussion:

> Ideas and practices may come to be out of true with each other, because one or the other fails to reproduce itself properly. Some of the original rationale may be lost, just through drift or through the challenge of some new insight; or the practice may alter as it is inadequately handed down (Taylor 1989: 205).

The point is that the exchange between ideas and practices may be disrupted for several reasons, all with the effect of potentially rendering an institution not merely dysfunctional, but in point of fact unintelligible.

Implied in this discussion is the contention that social institutions have a textual quality, that we understand institutions as we understand complex texts, by assuming different levels of reference and requiring congruence between these in order for the text as a whole to make sense, that institutions are for reading. Likewise, any legitimate institution needs to make sense as a whole, not in parts and aspects. With a Wittgensteinian take we might say that the grammar of the word institution makes us look in the wrong places when contemplating the nature of institutions. 'Grammar tells us what kind of object anything is' (Wittgenstein 1958, 1: 373) and hence controls the ways in which words and expressions can be used (cf. Danford 1978: 111–12). Thus we talk and think about social and political institutions as if they were objects, made up of other 'objects' (norms, activities, rules, procedures, and so on), and this makes us look for (or think and talk of) more comparable 'thingish' phenomena to fill out the meaning of our concept. But it may also be contended that human institutions essentially are symbolic systems, both defined by and defining forms of communal life:

> Social and political institutions ... are not objects, though that is how we often talk about them, but complex sets of understandings, relations, and activities. They are ways of talking that can be learned and understood, and they play their part in constituting a world (White 1984: 11).

Institutions ought to be thought of not as social or cultural or political objects, but as systems of language, because

> ... their claims of authority in the end work like the claims made by a language: they offer us ways of thinking and talking not otherwise available, through which we can express ourselves and establish relations with others; one must comply, however, with the sets of expectations by which they work, on pain of exclusion from the community they define, and our acquiescence in them may lead by stages to consequences we cannot imagine (White 1994: 223).

So there appears to be a hermeneutical twirl involved in how we relate to institutions. On the one hand, the institutions of political life reflect our understanding of ourselves; on the other hand, these same institutions significantly condition this self-understanding. Claiming authority for an institution entails making use of the moral language that it constitutes, hoping that it will make sense, and thereby giving oneself up to this language and the unforeseen consequences it may generate. Complying with this authority entails taking on its language and worldview, which may affect, in ways that we cannot foresee, how we perceive others and ourselves. To comply is therefore a matter of recognizing rules, which not only proscribe behaviour, but also in fact define the terms of community. From this perspective, the LT can be viewed as a deeply constitutive document, and I use the expression 'deeply' to indicate that the true meanings and impacts of this or any other international treaty is likely to reach beyond the letter of the documents and beyond the institutional arrangements which are thereby set up.

In this context, the visions of European security that are related to, or expressed by, the treaty take on a particular importance. The counterpart of security is community, and policies of security are closely associated with processes of self-interpretation and self-understanding. Hence it is difficult to understand the development and future prospects of a European polity without an understanding of collective identity formation in Europe. Identity is, of course, in itself an extremely complex and embattled notion, but there is some basis for saying that collective identities depend on or are associated with notions of security. A purely negative form of this argument would claim that security issues are the very essence of collective or political identities, that communities are formed as self-conscious entities through the process of discerning external threats, a sense of otherness and difference (Campbell 1992). A moderate version of the argument would be that collective identity is determined both by discourses of otherness and affinity; the process is not just one of 'making foreign', but of recognizing – identifying – with societies and cultures on the basis of shared values, worldviews, and destinies. Indeed, it would seem that a discourse on European security inevitably would touch the issue of 'European exceptionality', the idea that contemporary Europe in its relations with the world is *different* from other powers. This line of thinking is, of course, implied in Cooper's distinction between the postmodern and other worlds, in Robert Kagan's claim that Europeans are from Venus (Kagan 2003), and in the literature on Europe as a civilian or normative power (Manners 2002, 2008; Tocci 2008).

It is important to point out the political nature of this discussion. In a sense I am using the security perspective to approach essential questions about European identity and in particular the coherence and authority of Europe as a political community. What the concept of security adds to a political analysis is precisely giving attention to the ways in which *space* is delimited, defined, and organized politically. Space denotes that political organization and structuration involves an aspect of extension, of scope and domain, which is not restricted to a physical or territorial dimension. Some years ago Yale Ferguson and Richard Mansbach made a signal effort to invigorate the concept of polity, in order to develop our tools for understanding the forms of political organization in a long-term historical perspective (Ferguson and Mansbach 1996). They did so from a distinctly political science point of view emphasizing the significance of political authority. A polity must have an identity, a quality that can foster a sense of 'we-ness', capacity to mobilize people for political purposes, i.e. there must be an element of political authority; and a polity must have an identifiable hierarchy with roles that provide institutional continuity. A polity, an organized political authority, is only in part a physical entity; political space comprises ideological and moral dimensions as well. There is a parallel here to Barry Buzan's analysis referred to above: the state has different components of which *the idea* of the state is the most important one, since this is the main fount of national identity (Buzan 1991). A polity lives primarily in the minds of people, as an imagined community (Anderson 2006), and even though territorial extension and institutional structures may be the tangible and thus desirable expressions of political identity, a political community may well survive without these assets.

This means that I take security to be a concept that is directly linked to the fundamental questions of political analysis: how do people organize themselves in order to achieve common ends? How do structures of authority, i.e. legitimate power, arise and change over time? How do people living in political communities understand and account for their social circumstances? These questions arise if we accept that security is immediately linked to a sense of community: problems of security (threats) and ideas about how these can be effectively (and legitimately) countered rest on an idea of belonging and shared identity. The point is that perceptions of security are subject to political change. The meaning of security will change, not only in response to new sources of threats in the international or global environment, but as the basic forms of political organization develop. Again using Cooper's conceptual ideas, a movement towards postmodernity – inter alia a re-evaluation or re-orientation of traditional sovereignty; the distinction between domestic and foreign affairs becoming increasingly irrelevant; a premium on openness and transparency – will obviously change the very idea of security and notions of security policy-making fostered by elites as well as the public. The relevant question about the LT is perhaps not whether the institutional reforms make the EU a more efficient international actor, but if the treaty in the long run pushes the union towards a European state or some other logic of political organization. Whatever the outcome will be, there will be consequences for how we understand European security, and the kind of institutions and policies needed to ensure security. Thus, from a political point of view, security is closely connected to questions of legitimacy. For European security to make sense, there must be a European polity, which not only has the resources and institutional clout to provide effective external actions, but which commands legitimacy, a capital of trust.

Lisbon and European security

If the LT is viewed as a deeply constitutive document, the overall arrangement of the treaty comes into view as an object of interpretation. Obviously, what is *not* included or dealt with forms part of this picture. The object here is not, however, an overall interpretation. For the purpose of this discussion I will merely take note of two striking facts. First, that issues concerning external relations of the EU are evidently central elements of the LT. Most of the more visible reforms, such as the creation of a permanent Presidency and a High-Representative for Foreign Affairs, as well as the affirmation of the legal personality of the EU and setting up of an External Action Service, address the actor-capability of the Union vis-à-vis its international environment. Almost half of the amendments made to Treaty of the European Union (TEU) concern the field of security, defence and foreign policy (Alecu de Flers 2008: 1). Second, that a main outcome of the treaty is that precisely those aspects of European integration, which appear most salient to address, are the ones least affected by a continued process of unification. In this context, a brief overview of expert evaluations may suffice to make the point that from the perspective of institutional arrangements and policy-making prospects, the LT is at least difficult to evaluate.

Thus, from a crisis management perspective, Blockmans and Wessel (2009) conclude that it is doubtful if the institutional innovations concerning foreign and security policy will have any effect on leadership and decision-making in this regard, due to the continued principle of unanimity in CFSP/ESDP and uncertainties about the working relationship between the High Representative and the President of the European Council in matters of foreign affairs. Wessels and Bopp (2008) find two possible interpretations: the LT as a major step making the EU a more unified and efficient international actor, or a continued refinement of the intergovernmental structures. Overall, there are clear deficiencies in the CFSP, but remarkable institutional innovations, which, however, remain to be tested. Much along the same lines, Alecu de Flers (2008) sees visible progress, but concludes that the parties to the treaty 'remain "masters" of their actions in the field of foreign, security and defence policy' (Alecu de Flers 2008: 19). Focusing on the EU as an actor in the UN, Laatikainen and Degrand-Guillaud (2010) claim that while the LT reforms may have created a great deal of consistency in EU external policies in the Brussels context, the result in the special environment of UN policy-making is restricting.

Inevitably these comments raise the spectre of the 'capability-expectation gap' (Hill 1993). With reference to the LT, concern has been expressed about the distance between EU rhetoric and capacity for practical action. Laursen concludes that there is a continued discrepancy between the rhetoric of the EU treaties, and the actual actor capacity of the Union (Laursen 2010: 19). But in a sense, and perhaps counter-intuitively, it may be argued that politics is made precisely in these lofty, rhetorical phrases. Michael Walzer, quoted at the beginning of this essay, points out in the same context that politics is 'an art of unification'. This may serve as a corrective to the prevailing view that symbolic action, and rhetoric for that matter, is the opposite of 'real' action. It may even be contended that symbolism and ritual processes are essential ingredients of political life (Kertzer 1988). Politics is not only about conceiving actions in order to shape and direct collective destinies, but also equally about accounting for and making sense of circumstances in which a community of people find themselves situated. The power of political symbols and ritual practices rests to a considerable degree in providing *recognition*, a stable pattern of significance onto which current events and new developments can be plotted. In this context, it is of some interest that a group of member-states found reason to declare the continued symbolic significance of the 'Ode to Joy' anthem, the motto 'United in diversity', the euro as the currency of the EU, and the Europe Day on 9 May, to 'express the sense of community of the people in the European Union and their allegiance to it' (Consolidated 2010, Declaration 52).

Social scientists frequently express the fundamental importance of social and political institutions in the dictum institutions matter (March and Olsen 1989). But institutions matter for many and variegated reasons, notably by providing hierarchy, which preferably reflects legitimate authority; a sense of continuity in enshrining and maintaining central values, even a sense of collective identity; and not least important, visibility. The latter point indicates that good institutions virtually represent and symbolize the values and ideas upon which they have been built. The 'efficiency' of political institutions is not just a matter of their capacity to fulfil specific tasks and perform certain policies; it is also a question of the *image* of community that they convey, to what extent they serve as 'units of feelings around which emotions of loyalty and assurance can cluster' (Walzer 1992: 67). The European institutions and the treaties on which they are based are perhaps unlikely to raise fervent enthusiasm and feelings of collective belonging, but they do provide a growing sense of continuity, which over time may translate into authority.

Concluding remarks

Walzer's observation on the state's essential invisibility and consequent need for reifying practices certainly holds true for the European polity. Europe cannot be understood, or accepted, as a political community without the appropriate symbolic underpinnings. And it may be argued that the need to establish a coherent notion of political community, a firm identity, still haunts the European project. But as indicated above, the state may not be an appropriate model for continued institutional reforms, nor as an analytical tool. Cooper makes the first point succinctly:

> It is curious that having created a structure that has transformed the nation state into something more civilized and better adapted to today's world, there are still enthusiasts who want to replace it with something more old-fashioned. If the nation state is a problem, then the super-state is certainly not a solution (Cooper 2003: 37).

As for the second point, the state (as a concept and thus as a model of thought) signifies an *end*-state, i.e. we can envisage the properties, which together constitute a fully developed political community. And applied to Europe, it does not leave much hope for attaining security, first of all because the European 'state' does not have a clearly defined physical base. On the contrary, the idea of successive expansion and inclusion has been the defining theme of the project; the notion that Europe is *not* to be delimited by fixed ideas of political and cultural frontiers. At the same time, this flexible territorial attitude has been a source of concern, and in recent years the European Neighbourhood Policy (ENP) can be understood as an attempt to demarcate the ultimate borders of Europe, offering a periphery of states 'everything but institutions', i.e. extensive partnership, barring actual membership (Browning and Christou 2010). But the original problem remains. The lack of a clearly defined physical base makes Europe an unfocused object of security. The European institutions are well established and constantly evolving, and it may well be that this is the most developed aspect of the European state. The central issue is, however, the idea of the state, which is inherently intractable, subject to efforts of strategic construction and political persuasion.

The proper concept, both for thinking about the future European order, and in particular addressing its security situation, may be that of polity. The concept of polity brings out the indeterminacy of the process of political organization. Security in one form or another is always present as a driving force, inducing people to develop community and organization for dealing with mutually experienced threats, but the modern state is evidently just one historically determined formula for meeting these demands. The path of European institutional development is a case in point, demonstrating the essentially open-ended process of political organization, and the limitations of strategic planning in this regard: once set in motion, the process of institutional development acquires a dynamic of its own. This also means that the LT appears as situated in the flow of time, not just a step in the European process of integration, but also in the historical process of political organization, the ways in which people organize themselves for the political purposes. In this context, the LT may appear as a minor and rather insignificant event.

The ways in which a polity deals with issues of foreign and security relations may be revealing as to its sense of identity and community. On the one hand, what may be thought of as an institutional inconsistency in the organization of Union policy-making, may also be taken as a major indication of the status of political cohesion and authority, and ultimately the amount of trust which the member states and their constituencies are willing to invest in the European polity. On the other hand, estimates of the possible or actual effects of the LT on the external action capability of the Union differ, and in any event it may be premature to make any kind of firm assessment in this regard.

However, one possible conclusion is that nothing much has changed in terms of European security. Europe continues to develop as a postmodern system. It is in the nature of things that the path of institutional development is undetermined and unpredictable, but in the general direction of an 'ever closer' union. In this regard, Lisbon has added a set of structures which potentially may change both the way in which the surrounding world perceives Europe as an actor in international affairs, and the European self-image. The EU and its policies do have an impact on the world. The problem is that the normative effects of policy-making are not fully controllable. The question is not just whether Europe does indeed pursue normatively guided policies, because all politics is founded on values and norms, in particular policies which explicitly claim the opposite, but what impact these policies do have on the international environment, and how these understandings in turn reflect back on European self-perceptions.

It may well be contended that the LT has augmented European security, not by providing the centralized framework for external action, but by reinforcing the cooperative institutions of the EU and thus in fact the sovereignty of the members, to whom the meaning of sovereignty has changed and is still changing. But the underlying pattern of development is unaffected, and thus also the particular dilemma of European security: Europe continues to develop as a security community, but needs to interact with a largely modern, and to some extent pre-modern, world.

From the policy and institutional perspective, it appears difficult to assess the effects of Lisbon. As indicated above, questions pertaining to CFSP and CSDP are prominent in the reform process, but no dramatic consequences are to be expected in terms of how policy is conducted in the fields of foreign, defence and security policy. The symbolic effects may, however, be considerable. To repeat, the significance of a treaty may not consist in the actual paragraphs and provisions of the treaty text as such, but is ultimately a question of self-appraisal, and of shared understanding as to the character of the parties and their relationship to each other, as well as the surrounding world. As a communicative act, treaty making is also an open-ended and undetermined activity. The effects, in terms of interpretations and understanding of the treaty, as an act and a staged performance, as well as a formal document to be transformed into joint or individual actions of institutional implementation, may well supersede the intentions and original understandings of those immediately responsible. As the treaty, hence understood as a complex communicative event, enters into the quotidian flow of political discourse, through bureaucratic processes, in media reporting, in educational settings, etc., it is constantly subjected to new readings and re-interpretations, giving rise to collective perceptions which may deplete as well as reinforce whatever meanings were originally intended. If Lisbon in the long run turns out to signify a milestone in the way in which elites as well as the European public at large conceive the European polity (or come to conceive Europe *as* a polity), this will highlight the European space as an object of security.

A final note concerns the individual human being as located in political structure. Europe is obviously caught up in a global development where internal security for individual citizens and societies is just as salient as external security towards other international actors; where the soft security issues in terms of economy, climate change, mass migrations, crime, and pandemics are becoming just as, or more important than hard, military ones. A question is, of course, to what extent the European security institutions before or after the Lisbon reforms are capable of responding to these challenges. At the same time as the traditional distinction in international politics between inside/outside, internal and external security, is becoming more difficult to uphold, the postmodern condition holds the prospect of a widening security agenda, including the various aspects of social security. In this context, finally, we also need to remind ourselves that from the individual citizen's point of view, not to speak of that of the displaced person or refugee, the state and the European polity at large may still well constitute a security threat of the first order.

References

Adler, E. and M. Barnett (eds). 1998. *Security Communities*. Cambridge: Cambridge University Press.

Alecu de Flers, N. 2008. The Provisions on CFSP and CSDP in the Lisbon Reform Treaty: Stumbling Blocks or Milestones? *Hebrew University International Law Research Paper* No. 08–08. http://papers.ssrn.com/sol3/papers.cfm?abstract_id=1262921#%23

Anderson, B. 2006. *Imagined Communities: Reflections on the Origin and Spread of Nationalism*. Rev. edn. London: Verso.

Blockman, S. and A.W. Ramses. 2009. The European Union and Crisis Management: Will the Lisbon Treaty Make the EU More Effective? *Journal of Conflict & Security Law*, XIV(2), 265–308.

Browning, C.S. and G. Christou. 2010. The Constitutive Power of Outsiders: The European Neigbourhood Policy and the Eastern Dimension. *Political Geography*, 29: 109–18.

Burgess, J.P. 2009. There is No European Security, Only European Securities. *Cooperation and Conflict*, 44(3), 309–28.

Buzan, B. 1991. *People, States, and Fear: An Agenda for International Security Studies in the Post-Cold War Era*. New York & London: Harvester Wheatsheaf.

Campbell, D. 1992. *Writing Security: United States Foreign Policy and the Politics of Identity*. Manchester: Manchester University Press.

Checkel, J.T. and P.J. Katzentstein (eds). 2009. *European Identity*. Cambridge: Cambridge University Press.

Consolidated versions of the Treaty on European Union and the Treaty on the Functioning of the European Union. 2010. *Official Journal of the European Union*, LIII, Notice No 2010/C 83/01.

Cooper, R. 2003. *The Breaking of Nations: Order and Chaos in the Twenty-First Century*. New York: Grove Press.

Danford, J.W. 1978. *Wittgenstein and Political Philosophy: A Re-examination of the Foundations of Social Science*. Chicago: University of Chicago Press.

Deutsch, K. et al. 1957. *Political Community and the North Atlantic Area*. Princeton: Princeton University Press.

Ferguson, Y.H. and R.W. Mansbach. 1996. *Polities: Authority; Identities, and Change*. Columbia, SC: University of South Carolina Press.

Gallie, W.B. 1962. Essentially Contested Concepts, in *The Importance of Language*, Max Black (ed.). Englewood Cliffs, NJ: Prentice Hall, 121–46.

Hill, C. 1993. The Capability-Expectation Gap, or Conceptualizing Europe's International Role. *Journal of Common Market Studies*, 31(3), 305–28.

Kagan, R. 2003. *Of Paradise and Power: America and Europe in the New World Order*. New York: Vintage Books.

Kertzer, D.I. 1988. *Ritual, Politics, and Power*. New Haven and London: Yale University Press.

Laatikainen, K.V. and A. Degrand-Guillaud. 2010. Two Logics, One Treaty: The Lisbon Treaty and EU Foreign Policy in Brussels and at the UN. *Studia Diplomatica*, 63(1), 3–22.

Laursen, F. 2010. The EU as an International Political and Security Actor after the Treaty of Lisbon: An Academic Perspective. *Dalhousie EUCE Occasional Paper* No. 9. http://euce.dal.ca/Files/Finn_Laursen_occasional_paper_No_9_2010.pdf

Manners, I. 2002. Normative Power Europe: A Contradiction in Terms? *Journal of Common Market Studies*, 37(3): 235–58.

Manners, I. 2008. The Normative Ethics of the European Union. *International Affairs*, 84(1), 65–80.

March, J.G. and J.P. Olsen. 1989. *Rediscovering Institutions: The Organizational Basis of Politics*. New York: The Free Press.

Smith, S. 2005. The Contested Concept of Security, in *Critical Security Studies*, Ken Booth (ed.). Boulder and London: Lynne Rienner.

Taylor, C. 1989. *Sources of the Self: The Making of the Modern Identity*. Cambridge: Cambridge University Press.

Tocci, N. (ed.). 2008. *Who Is a Normative Foreign Policy Actor?: The European Union and Its Global Partners*. Brussels: Centre for European Policy Studies.

Walzer, M. 1992. On the Role of Symbolism in Political Thought, in *The Self and the Political Order*, Tracy B. Strong (ed.). Oxford: Blackwell, 66–76.

Wessels, W. and F. Bopp. 2008. The Institutional Architecture of CFSP after the Lisbon Treaty: Constitutional Breakthrough or Challenges Ahead? *CEPS, Research Paper* No. 10. http://new.ceps.eu/system/files/book/1677.pdf

White, J.B. 1984. *When Words Lose Their Meaning: Constitutions and Reconstitutions of Language, Character, and Community*. Chicago: The University of Chicago Press.

White, J.B. 1994. *Acts of Hope: Creating Authority in Literature, Law, and Politics*. Chicago: The University of Chicago Press.

Wittgenstein, L. 1958. *Philosophical Investigations*. Transl. by G.E.M. Anscombe. Oxford: Basil Blackwell.

Chapter 6

The Reinforcement of Fundamental Rights in the Lisbon Treaty

Cristina Blasi Casagran

Introduction

Human rights are fully integrated in our current society to the point that they have become an essential element of it.

Indeed, today all Constitutions of Member states of the European Union (hereinafter, EU) classify such rights as 'citizens' fundamental rights' within their own basic laws.

In order to be effectively respected, these human rights have to be legally recognized. Nevertheless, several examples could be named of countries around the world where their Constitutions formally respect such human rights by their national authorities, but in practice they are just mere declarations manipulated at their whim.

In order to counteract this phenomenon, initiatives have been recently taken in pursuit of fighting increasing violations of human rights. The EU has participated actively too, incorporating projects within the European framework with the aim of stressing the importance of these inherent rights from a supranational perspective as well.

The goal has not been easy, since the initial EEC was created with a clear economic aim, avoiding external political issues; but as long as the EU has been moving forward, the equal importance of incorporating other policies has been noted.

The Maastricht Treaty of 1992 opened a door establishing citizenship within the EU, and with it a range of guarantees and rights for the citizens of EU Member states were offered. Since that moment, every amendment project of the Treaties in the last decade has put on the table the human rights issue.

Before the Lisbon Treaty, the jurisprudential task carried out by the European Court of Human Right (hereafter ECtHR) as well as the European Court of Justice (hereinafter the ECJ) and the Constititional Courts of Member States was laudable because they made an effective protection of such rights for EU citizens possible both at the national and European Community level, despite the fact that the Charter of Fundamental Rights was not binding.

Since the 50s, these Courts have ruled seeking the protection of human rights, and they have had a fundamental role during the first period of the European Community, when a legislative silence regarding human rights prevailed.

Since Maastricht, the legal value of those rights within the Treaty has been increased, thus reinforcing the internal role of national Constitutions, as well as the *acquis communautaire* set up in those days.

Due to the Treaty of Maastricht and the Charter of Fundamental Rights (hereinafter, the Charter) within the framework of the EU, the influence of human rights in rulings by the ECJ, as well as the ECtHR[1] has increased.

After the adoption of the European Constitution in 2005 failed, it was decided to slow down the integration of the Member states within the EU, elaborating this time a Reform Treaty, then called 'Treaty of Lisbon'. This Treaty came into force on the 9 December 2009, and with it, many institutional, political and social changes.

The present study analyses the transformations stemming from the new provisions of the Lisbon Treaty concerning human rights. My intention is to present all and every single amendment incorporated by the Treaty, with regard to respect of the human rights.

At first sight, the fact that the Charter gets the same legal value as the Treaties, as well as the accession of the EU to the European Convention of Human Rights (hereinafter ECHR) seem to be the main amendment. For this reason, in the first part of my work, both these innovations are examined.

However, my efforts aim to be a bit more ambitious, and although the first part of the work deals with the main changes regarding the better protection of human rights from the majority of observers, I will try to go further and analyse what other changes will entail, in any direct or indirect way, an improvement of the human rights protection. In this sense, I will study changes in the legal basis, as well as the new provisions with regard to the guarantee and control schemes.

Considering that the Lisbon Treaty has only recently come into force, many of its innovations have not yet been put into practice. The real effects of these will therefore only be determined once the ECJ rules and develops jurisprudence under the new legal basis.

Nevertheless, I hope my contribution helps in some way to reveal what is the true role of human rights in the European legal system, and what is the impact of the Lisbon Treaty in the current situation.

The Lisbon Treaty and the Charter of Fundamental Rights

Initially, there was no reference to fundamental rights in the Treaties, and the only way to regulate them was through jurisprudence.

---

1 For a recent and detailed study of the Charter, see Mangas Martín, Araceli. Carta de los derechos fundamentales de la Unión Europea: comentario artículo por artículo. Fundación BBVA, 2008, 880 pp.

The first constitutionalizing narrative on fundamental rights came to a head with the debate on the Charter of Fundamental Rights of the EU. The main objective of the Charter was to create polity support by bringing the EU closer to the citizen through a bill of rights, facilitated by a relatively public and participatory drafting process through the Convention (Smismans 2010: 50).

In 1999, the Cologne European Council adopted the decision of elaborating the Charter. Initially, criticism was raised against the initiative, but as stated in the European Council[2]:

> There appears to be a need, at the present stage of the Union's development, to establish a Charter of fundamental rights in order to make their overriding importance and relevance more visible to the Union's citizens.

Thus, the Heads of State and Government decided to set up a convention with the former president of Germany, Roman Herzog, as president. Roman Herzog established a basis to create a reflection group, called 'Citizen and EU', which would be in charge of the Charter elaboration and constituted an organ ad hoc composed of delegates of Heads of Government, the president of the Commission, some members of the European Parliament (MEPs) as well as some members of national parliaments. Moreover, the ECJ participated as an observer, and other institutions and bodies such as the European Economic and Social Committee, the Committee of Regions and the European Ombudsman could give their opinion. The Charter was first called 'Convention'.

The Charter included two big categories of rights: civil and political rights, and economic, social and cultural rights. Furthermore, it was structured according to the subjects, such as dignity (Arts 1 to 5), freedoms (Arts 6 to 9), equality (Arts 20 to 26), solidarity (Arts 27 to 38), citizens' rights (Arts 39 to 46) and justice (Arts 47 to 50). As Article 51 stipulated, the EU institutions would be able to invoke the rights of the Charter as long as the principle of subsidiarity is respected.[3]

Legal value of the Charter

Initially the Charter was not mandatory. It was adopted on December 2000, and at that time the Cologne European Council left open the question of the 'legal value', aware of possible debates at issue.

Thus the Convention worked 'as if' the Charter had binding value, but finally a division of opinion was inevitable: the Commission and the European Parliament wanted it to be binding, whereas some Member states were in favour of an exclusive political value, since they argued that they had already the national

2 Presidency Conclusions – Cologne European Council (3 and 4 June 1999).

3 OJ C 364, 18.12.2000: 1–22.

Constitutions and the ECHR dealing with those rights, and the legal loopholes were already covered by the ECJ jurisprudence.

Therefore, the Charter was finally adopted as a document with political value and a merely declarative character, without legally contributing to reinforce the protection of human rights within the EU. It could be interpreted as a clear sign of the increasing constitutionalization of the EU, since it reinforced the existing national standards and 'went beyond' them, but at the same time it could produce results more complex and troubling for the ensemble of core political values than some simple and cost-free 'freedom dividend' (Walker 2003: 52).

The initial adoption of the Charter as a mere declarative document disappointed some observers, since it was closer to what is well known as '*memoranda of understanding of gentlemen's agreements*' (Pastor Rigruejo 2008: 327); however, there were some optimists who saw the Charter as a source of inspiration that could carry an indirect legal value, operating as a tool of interpretation by the ECJ.

Indeed, the Charter was used by several national courts, by Advocate Generals of ECJ, by the General Court (case Jegó-Queré, 3 May 2002) and also by the Spanish Constitutional Court as an interpretative element (Pastor Ridruejo 2008: 328). But the principal case to be pointed out is the 'Family Reunification' judgment[4], in which the European Parliament invoked before the ECJ a violation from the Council Directive 2003/86/EC, of 22 September 2003, of Arts 7 and 21.1 of the Charter (family life and non-discrimination principles).

The ECJ ruled using the Charter in an innovative way, as established in paragraph 38 of the judgment:

> While the Charter is not a legally binding instrument, the Community legislature did, however, acknowledge its importance by stating, in the second recital in the preamble to the Directive, that the Directive observes the principles recognized not only by Article 8 of the ECHR but also in the Charter.

One of the main debates of the Convention was the relationship between the ECHR and the Charter, because there was a fear of a possible dual system with two different levels.

However, this concern was clarified with Art. 52.3 of the Charter, which set up peaceful coexistence between both systems:

> In so far as this Charter contains rights which correspond to rights guaranteed by the Convention for the Protection of Human Rights and Fundamental Freedoms, the meaning and scope of those rights shall be the same as those laid down by the said Convention. This provision shall not prevent Union law providing more extensive protection.

---

4 ECJ judgment European Parliament v. Council of the European Union, case C-540/03, 27.06.2006.

It shows the existence of independence between both courts: the ECHR would operate guaranteeing a minimal standard of protection, while the Charter could not reduce it but it could always go beyond. In addition, the objectives were not the same: the ECHR establishes a catalogue of rights with the aim of protecting human rights, whereas the Charter was not limited to protecting civil and political rights, but also economic, social and citizens' rights.

We know that to date both the ECtHR and the ECJ have lived together without overlaps in their resolutions.

The Charter since the Lisbon Treaty

With the Lisbon Treaty, all debates about the value, the binding elements and the discussion about the Charter as a merely declarative text found their response: the Lisbon Treaty establishes in its Art. 6 TEU that

> The Union recognizes the rights, freedoms and principles set out in the Charter of Fundamental Rights of the European Union of 7 December 2000, as adopted at Strasbourg, on 12 December 2007, which shall have the same legal value as the Treaties.

Hence, the Charter becomes part of the *acquis communitaire* and also an element legally binding within the EU, obligatory for EU institutions as well as for the Member states, as long as they execute European law.

Likewise, the ECJ, the General Court and national courts will use the Charter every time they are dealing with cases concerning the protection of human rights. The ECtHR will also refer to it, but just for the interpretation of the ECHR.

In 2001, when the European Constitution was being prepared, the European Council of Laeken questioned the possibility of integrating the Charter into the Treaty. Three different options were considered: the first consisted of fully integrating the Charter into the Treaty, the second possibility proposed was to include just a reference to the Charter in an Article, and the last one was based on an indirect reference to the Charter, which would be binding but without any constitutional status. The Lisbon Treaty finally established the second option above-mentioned (a reference clause).

Pursuant to Art. 6 TEU, the Charter becomes positive law and it is not just an interpretative element. It grants legal certainty for all European citizens too.

However, the United Kingdom, Poland and the Czech Republic enjoy a special regime with regard to the Charter: Poland has two Declarations attached to the Treaties (Declarations 61 and 62) which exclude the ability of the Charter

> to legislate in the sphere of public morality, family law, as well as the protection of human dignity and respect for human physical and moral integrity. Poland also highlighted that 'having regard to the tradition of social movement of

'Solidarity' and its significant contribution to the struggle for social and labour rights, it fully respects social and labour rights, as established by European Union law, and in particular those reaffirmed in Title IV of the Charter of Fundamental Rights of the European Union (Declaration 62).

Likewise, United Kingdom as well as Poland have a special Protocol[5] that states the Charter does not extend the ability of the Court of Justice of the European Union, or any court or tribunal of Poland or of the United Kingdom, to find that the laws, regulations or administrative provisions, practices or action of Poland or of the United Kingdom are inconsistent with the fundamental rights, freedoms and principles that it reaffirms.

With regards to the Czech Republic, an opt-out was agreed at the end of 2010, and a new Protocol regulating its special regime is expected to be included in the near future.

However, we will have to see what effects these exceptional measures will have in practice, and how they will be applied by the ECJ as well as national courts (Campos Sánchez-Bordona 2009: 23).

The EU accession to the ECHR

This section shows the historical evolution, examining some important rulings by the ECtHR as well as the Opinion 2/94 by the ECJ, and culminating with a thorough analysis of the new legal basis since the Lisbon Treaty.

The control of respect of human rights within the Community framework by the ECtHR: Matthews and Bosphorus cases.

In the Matthews case,[6] a Gibraltarian citizen filed a lawsuit before the ECtHR against the United Kingdom on 7 April 1994 for an alleged violation of Art. 3 Prot. 1 ECHR,[7] due to the absence of direct elections in Gibraltar to the European Parliament.

The ECtHR decided that, indeed, there was a violation of the right to free elections by the United Kingdom, since the country should have implemented the European Act in accordance with the ECHR. Specifically, the Court stated that notwithstanding the transfer of competences to the European Community,

5 PROTOCOL (No 30) ON THE APPLICATION OF THE CHARTER OF FUNDAMENTAL RIGHTS OF THE EUROPEAN UNION TO POLAND AND TO THE UNITED KINGDOM.

6 Matthews v. United Kingdom, 18.02.1999, ECtHR/1999/9.

7 Right to free elections: 'The High Contracting Parties undertake to hold free elections at reasonable intervals by secret ballot, under conditions which will ensure the free expression of the opinion of the people in the choice of the legislature'.

contracting states remain responsible for ensuring that Convention rights are guaranteed.

Subsequently, a debate arose about the duality of human rights protection between ECtHR and the ECJ. In the particular case, there was a complementary relationship between them, since the ECJ has no competence to judge its own Treaties.[8] Nevertheless, fears spread with regard to the possible case in which the national court issued a preliminary ruling before the ECJ and, once the national judicial procedure was exhausted, the ECtHR ruled contrary or with a different interpretation than the ECJ.

Six years later, in 2000, another case was issued before the ECtHR, in which the duality question was considered again. It was the *Bosphorus case*[9] and its application was brought against Ireland by an airline charter company registered in Turkey. Ireland had leased one of the Bosphorus' aircrafts under the EC Council Regulation 990/93, which implemented UN sanctions against the Federal Republic of Yugoslavia. The supreme court of Ireland issued a preliminary ruling to the ECJ, which ruled that the restrictions were justified, because they followed an objective of general interest.

After exhausting the domestic courts, the case was referred to the ECtHR, concerning a violation of Art. 1 of Prot. 1 ECHR, which concerns the protection of property.

Unlike the *Matthews* case, in *Bosphorus* the EU Council Regulation did not leave any margin of appreciation in implementation by member states, so this time the ECtHR clearly established its relationship with the ECJ. Thus, the Court stated that when a State does no more than implement its legal obligations flowing from its membership of an International Organization, which offers an equivalent protection, it would be presumed that the state complies with the legal obligations of the ECHR. In addition, the Court established that this presumption of conformity would just be rebutted in situations of manifestly deficient protection.[10]

Opinion 2/94

However, neither the *Matthews* case nor the *Bosphorus* case referred to the matter of the appropriate legal basis with regards to the future accession of the Community to the ECHR. The proposal goes back to 1996, when the ECJ issued Opinion 2/94 in relation to the accession by the Community to the ECHR. The

8 The ECtHR established that 'The Court observes that acts of the EC as such cannot be challenged before the Court because the EC is not a Contracting Party. The Convention does not exclude the transfer of competences to international organizations provided that Convention rights continue to be "secured". Member States' responsibility therefore continues even after such a transfer' (Par 32, Matthews v. United Kingdom).

9 Bosphorus Hava Yollari Turizm ve Ticaret Anonim Sirketi v. Ireland.30.06.2005. JUR\2005\174046.

10 Ibid., par. 155 and 156.

ECJ concluded that, at the time, the Community legal order had no competence to accede to the ECHR, since there were no provisions in the Treaty that conferred powers, and the only available way would be the so-called 'flexibility-clause' (ex-Art. 235 TCE, current Art. 352 TFEU). This clause is designed to fill the gap where no specific provision of the Treaty confers to the Community institutions express or implied powers to act, and it is necessary in order to carry out objectives of the Treaty. However, the flexibility clause could not be used for this matter, since any accession to the ECHR would carry a substantial change in the current regime only achievable with an amendment to the Treaties.

Thus the ECJ closed the debate about the accession, but left open the possibility of subjecting community institutions to an external control in order to guarantee the protection of fundamental rights.

New legal basis in the Lisbon Treaty

Art. 6.2 of the new TEU establishes the necessary legal basis in order to make the accession of the EU to the ECHR possible. The EU becomes thus the contracting-party no. 48 of the ECHR, although it will not be a member of the Council of Europe. With the aim of appeasing the Member states, this Art. 6.2 also states that '*The Charter shall not extend in any way the competences of the Union*'. Likewise, par. 3 of Art. 6 foresees that the fundamental rights regulated in the ECHR result from the constitutional traditions common to all Member states, and that they are equal to the general principles.

The Lisbon Treaty also includes a Declaration on Art. 6(2), which reinforces the complementarity between the ECtHR and the ECJ, and the Protocol Number 8, which states that the accession will not be pure and simple, but an agreement will be adopted (Pastor Ridruejo 2007). In fact a draft agreement on the Accession of the EU to the European Convetion on Human Rights was published by the Steering Committee for Human Rights of the Council of Europe on 14 October 2011. After it will be adopted, the ratification by all Member states in the EU as well as ratification by all Contracting-parties of the ECHR will be needed.

Due to the accession, European citizens will enjoy, besides the control of human rights by the ECJ, an external protection by the ECtHR. In addition, some exiting loopholes will be covered, since Member states will no longer be responsible for the execution of European Acts; and the EU will continue to enjoy a presumption of conformity (Gordillo Perez; Canello Arrillaga 2008: 56).

Regarding the question of whether to appeal, or not, once the internal courts have been exhausted, where both Courts have jurisdiction, the majority of scholars are of the opinion that the individual could only lodge a complaint before the ECtHR after an appeal before the ECJ, as the latter is the guardian within the EU. Therefore, the accession of the EU to the ECHR will not create any overlap between the Courts, since they have no hierarchical relationship (Jiménez de Parga 2003: 135).

Finally, it is important to point out that when Opinion 2/94 was issued, only accession by the European Communities could be examined, but since the Lisbon Treaty the EU enjoys legal personality and hence it has competence to make international agreements. However, Art. 218 par. 8 TFEU establishes a specific procedure for the accession to the ECHR, which may cause delays and difficulties, because it has to be approved by all Member states.[11]

New legal basis reinforcing data protection in the Lisbon Treaty

Pre-existing legislation

Before the Lisbon Treaty, legislation concerning data protection could be divided into two big groups: Data collected and administered by the EU Institutions and data within the framework of the internal market.

In the first instance, the EU had the legal basis in Art. 286 TEC, as well as the protection offered by the Council of Europe in its Convention no. 108,[12] and Art. 8 of the Charter of Fundamental Rights. Lastly, with regards to legislative acts on the EU, the Regulation (EC) 2001/45 regulates the protection of individuals with regard to the processing of personal data by the Community institutions and bodies and on the free movement of such data.[13]

Regarding the data within the context of the internal market, four Directives[14] under the basis of Art. 95 TEC (current Art. 114 TFEU) were adopted, with the aim of harmonizing protection among the Member states. Moreover, in 2008, a Framework Decision, under the former third pillar, was adopted.[15]

---

11 Art. 218.8 moves away from the drafting in the European Constitution, which foresaw in its Art. 328.8 that the Council would act by qualified majority voting during the procedure.

12 OJ L246, 29/08/1981: 31.

13 OJ L8, 12.01.2001: 1–22.

14 Directive 95/46/EC on the protection of individuals with regard to the processing of personal data and on the free movement of such data (OJ L281, 23.11.1995: 31–50); Directive 97/66/EC concerning the processing of personal data and the protection of privacy in the telecommunications sector (OJ L24, 31.01.1998: 9–30); Directive 2002/58/EC concerning the processing of personal data and the protection of privacy in the electronic communications sector (OJ L201, 31.07.2002: 37–47); and Directive 2006/24/EC on the retention of data generated or processed in connection with the provision of publicly available electronic communications services or of public communications networks and amending Directive 2002/58/EC (OJ L105, 13.04.2006: 54–63).

15 Framework Decision 2008/977/JAI on the protection of personal data processed in the framework of police and judicial cooperation in criminal matters (OJ L353, 30.12.2008: 60).

The Passenger Name Record problem

As a direct result of the terrorist attacks of 11 September 2001, US authorities adopted measures, which obliged airlines taking off, landing or flying through US territory to facilitate all booking and departure data. They were called '*Passenger Name Record*' or PNR data.

The EU recognized the security interest of such measures but in 2002 it informed the US that they might be contrary to Community legislation as well as being contrary to Member states' domestic legislation. However, that did not stop the US decision, which just postponed the law's implementation to 2003, and expressly manifested the intention to impose sanctions to those airlines which did not comply with the new rules.

Within the EU framework, two Decisions under the basis of Art. 95 were adopted: Council Decision 2004/496/EC[16] and Commission Decision 2004/535/EC.[17] The reason for the legal basis chosen was, in fact, to avoid the adoption of 27 different agreements, which could carry comparative advantages among Member states, creating a distortion in the market.

Hence, the European Parliament appealed for the annulment of the Decisions before the ECJ, arguing that they were adopted on the wrong legal basis, since it was not an issue concerning the internal market, but it was a matter of public security and criminal law (former third pillar).

On the contrary, the European Commission justified the basis chosen, considering that booking a flight implied a provision of service, so it carried a commercial activity.

The ECJ, in May 2006, finally ruled the annulment of the Decisions, since it found that they were more closely related to a matter of public security and therefore they had to be adopted under the third pillar, by unanimity by all Member states.

The direct consequence was the adoption of a new PNR agreement in October 2006, this time under the scope of the third pillar, culminating with the Council Decision 2006/729/CFSP/JHA.

Consequently, similar PNR schemes were established between the EU and Canada as well as the EU and Australia.

In addition, since 2007 negotiations between the Commission and the US, Australia and Canada have been carried out, in order to compose a new Directive regarding the PNR strategy.[18] Almost four years later, in February 2011, the Commission finally launched the proposal,[19] this time under the legal basis of the Treaty of Lisbon, which enhances the competences of the European institutions.

---

16 OJ L183, 20.05.2004: 83.

17 OJ L235, 06.07.2004: 11.

18 COM(2007) 654 final, 06.11.2007.

19 Proposal for a Directive of the European Parliament and of the Council on the use of Passenger Name Record data for the prevention, detection, investigation and prosecution of terrorist offences and serious crime, COM(2011) 32 final, 2.2.2011.

Later, the European Data Protection Supervisor (hereinafter, EDPS) as well as the European Agency of Fundamental Rights (hereinafter, FRA) adopted Opinions[20] in which it argued that the Proposal did not comply with the requirements of necessity and proportionality.

It remains to be seen what will happen with this PNR Directive and whether it will finally be approved by the Council and the Parliament. What is clear is that a new PNR Directive would harmonize existing PNR agreements and the current difference with regard to their data retention periods.

The Directive 2006/24/EC and the new line of cases

As expected, the use of Art. 95 as the legal basis was also the issue at stake when Ireland lodged a lawsuit for the annulment of Directive 2006/24/EC[21] before the ECJ.

In July 2006, Ireland argued that the legal basis for adopting EU acts concerning data protection was wrong.

Nevertheless, surprisingly the ECJ did not follow its jurisprudence and ruled this time in favour of the Commission, stating that it was a Directive of services, which fell within the scope of the internal market.

Hence, it can be highlighted that the border between the scope of the first and third pillars was not completely clear, not even for the ECJ. Therefore, this decision, together with the previous PNR case, had a direct impact on the necessity to change the focus of the legislation from the internal market basis to criminal law.

Data protection within the former third pillar

As mentioned above, the protection concerning data protection has been much higher when the competence to regulate fell under the scope of the first pillar, than when Member states, under the scope of the third pillar, were in charge of the protection of fundamental rights, because more political interests were involved.

However, that does not mean that there are no steps forward: despite the reluctance of the EDPS in November 2008[22] in adopting the Framework Decision 2008/977/JHA, it was finally adopted.

---

20 Opinion of the European Data Protection Supervisor on the Proposal for a Directive of the European Parliament and of the Council on the use of Passenger Name Record data for the prevention, detection, investigation and prosecution of terrorist offences and serious crime, 25.03.2011; and Opinion of the European Union Agency for Fundamental Rights on the Proposal for a Directive on the use of PNR data for the prevention, detection, investigation and prosecution of terrorist offences and serious crime, 14.06.2011.

21 OJ L 105, 13.04.2006: 54–63.

22 11th Conference on Data Protection and Data Security – DuD 2009. Berlín, 8 de Junio de 2009. 'Data Protection in the Light of the Lisbon Treaty and the Consequences for Present Regulations. Peter Hustinx.

Apart from the Framework Decision, on 30 November 2009 (one day before the entry into force of the Lisbon Treaty) the Council signed the so-called SWIFT agreement with the US authorities in order to allow access to the European bank data, with the aim of fighting against terrorism. The Belgian company SWIFT (*Society for Worldwide Interbank Financial Telecommunication*) is the link between the US government and the EU.

The agreement came into force on 1 February 2010 and was supposed to be applied temporarily until the 31 December 2010. However, on 11 February 2010, the European Parliament rejected the adoption, arguing a lack of protection of personal data.

Hence, the Commission composed a new draft agreement (SWIFT II), this time approved by the European Parliament in July 2010.

Nevertheless, even this new SWIFT agreement between the EU and the US being an attempt to balance security/law enforcement objectives with data protection[23] has been controversial. The EDPS pointed out in an Opinion,[24] among other concerns, that bulk transfer of personal data should be replaced by a filtering mechanism in the EU, transferring only relevant and necessary data to the US and that the retention period of five years was too long. Likewise, the EP[25] raised concerns in March 2011, since Europol, which is in charge of checking US compliance with the agreement, did not provide any updated written information about the requests from the US Treasury Department and its compliance with European data protection standards.

The legal basis in the Lisbon Treaty

Since the Lisbon Treaty and the removal of the pillars, the criteria and standards of protection between the first and the third pillar have become equal.

Moreover, a unique legal basis is established regarding data protection: Art. 16 TFEU.

In particular, pursuant to Art. 16.2 TFEU

> The European Parliament and the Council, acting in accordance with the ordinary legislative procedure, shall lay down the rules relating to the protection of individuals with regard to the processing of personal data by Union institutions, bodies, offices and agencies, and by the Member States when carrying out activities which fall within the scope of Union law, and the rules relating to the

23 Marise Cremona, "Justice and Home Affairs in a Globalised World: Ambitions and Reality in the tale of US-EU SWIFT Agreement," *Institute for European Integration Research*, Working Paper no. 04/2011, Vienna, 19.

24 OJ C 355, 29.12.2010, p.10.

25 Press release, "SWIFT implementation report: MEPs raise serious data protection concerns," Committee on Civil Liberties, Justice and Home Affairs, March 2011.

> free movement of such data. Compliance with these rules shall be subject to the control of independent authorities.

Hence, with regards to this new legal basis, data protection falls not only under the scope of the former first pillar, but also what used to belong to the third pillar, and thus competence by Member states.

Likewise, Art. 39 TUE foresees the processing of personal data by the Member states on the activities which fall under the common foreign and security policy (CFSC) matters.

Nevertheless, the Lisbon Treaty added Declarations 20 and 21 for special regimes or possible exceptions. Thus, in case that national security is affected, it is possible to apply specific characteristics, and other specific rules can be adopted concerning the fields of judicial cooperation in criminal matters and police cooperation.

In conclusion, the Lisbon Treaty closes the existing loopholes regarding data protection in the EU, and ends the risk of adoption of 27 different bilateral agreements. Under the new legal basis, just one agreement will be sufficient, applying the ordinary legislative procedure, by co-decision between the Council and the European Parliament.

Other amendments in the legal basis since the Lisbon Treaty

Procedural amendment of Article 7 TEU

Art. 7 TEU gives to the EU institutions the necessary means to guarantee respect of common values in Art. 6 TEU. In particular, this article establishes a mechanism in the event that one of the Member states commits a serious breach of these values.

Since the Treaty of Amsterdam, the wording is as follows:

> The Council[…] acting by unanimity on a proposal by one third of the Member States or by the Commission and after obtaining the <u>assent</u> of the European Parliament […].

With the Lisbon Treaty, the word 'assent' is replaced by the word 'consent', turning the text into:

> The European Council, acting by unanimity on a proposal by one third of the Member States or by the Commission and after obtaining the <u>consent</u> of the European Parliament […].

It is in fact just a formal amendment, which aims to unify terminologies when the same procedure is referred to. Furthermore, new Art. 354 TFEU foresees that the Member state in question will not take part in the vote.

Notwithstanding that Art. 7 has never been used to date, it presupposes a new guarantee which reinforces fundamental rights within the EU.

Legal basis on external action

The Lisbon Treaty establishes more clarity and coherence between the external action from a political perspective, which is regulated in the Title V TEU[26]; and the external action concerning economic issues, which is set out in Part 5 TFEU.[27]

In particular, it should be pointed out that in Art. 21 TEU human rights are also protected, when it establishes respect of the principles of

> democracy, the rule of law, the universality and indivisibility of human rights and fundamental freedoms, respect for human dignity, the principles of equality and solidarity, and respect for the principles of the United Nations Charter and international law.

Therefore, it can be stated that the Lisbon Treaty reinforces the clarity and coherence of external action, which will have to be based on basic values such as democracy, rule of law and respect for human rights and fundamental freedoms.

Legal basis on non-discrimination

The new Treaty consolidates the existing measures against all kinds of discrimination. As main new features, the Treaty incorporates Arts 2 and 3 TEU. The first one foresees the EU values, establishing that

> These values are common to the Member States in a society in which pluralism, non-discrimination, tolerance, justice, solidarity and equality between women and men prevail;

while the latter amends the ex-Art. 2 and adds, among other objectives of the EU, to combat social exclusion and discrimination, to promote social justice and protection, equality between women and men, solidarity between generations and protection of the rights of the child.

Regarding the TFEU, Art. 10 establishes that the EU will execute its policies, aiming to

> combat discrimination based on sex, racial or ethnic origin, religion or belief, disability, age or sexual orientation.

---

26 Title V: General Provisions on the Union's External Action and Specific Provisions on the Common Foreign and Security Policy.

27 Part five: The Union's External Action.

Finally, it is worth highlighting that non-discrimination protection has its own heading in the Second Part, Title I, with the name of '*Non-discrimination and citizenship of the Union*'.

Amendments on guarantee and control mechanisms

Jurisdictional procedures

The Lisbon Treaty increases the legitimacy enjoyed by natural and legal persons before the ECJ.

In the previous Treaties, the amendment of an appeal system whereby the individuals were able to appeal against European legislation remained pending. Till then, European citizens interested in defending their rights and lodging an appeal for annulment had to breach first the European law, get a sanction by their national authorities, and only once they were sanctioned, could they appeal before European courts. Hence, an appropriate legal protection was necessary.

During the preparatory phase of the Constitution for Europe several proposals were launched. One of them was the idea of establishing a mechanism similar to the Spanish '*recurso de amparo*' or the German '*Verfassungsbeschwerde*', offered in domestic law by their Constitutional Courts.

However, the idea of creating an Amparo law at the European level caused some fears about the possible use of such a mechanism on grounds other than the ones within the scope of human rights violations.

The Lisbon Treaty is not so ambitious, but it incorporates relevant amendments in its current Art. 263 TFEU (Piris 2006). Pursuant to this provision, any natural individual is able to appeal either a National law or a European law which violates their human rights, through an appeal before national courts or even a direct appeal before the ECJ, whenever this individual challenges an act which is addressed to him and, hence, he has a direct and individual concern. Likewise, any individual is able to appeal against a regulatory act,[28] providing that a direct concern exists (the individual concern is not required here).

Moreover, the new Art. 263 TFEU also contributes to increasing control mechanisms with the establishment of protection against acts of bodies, offices and agencies of the EU. Unlike the former Art. 230 TEU, which only permitted a control of acts adopted by EU institutions, the Lisbon Treaty incorporates an extension to all those other organisms and organizations which may have an implied 'decision making power' in the EU, since there are important sources of documentation and studies which the European Commission aims to regulate.

Recently, there have been criticisms raised because of the perceived lack of access to the information of these agencies, bodies and offices, whether because of

28 A regulatory act has to be understood as any 'infra-legislative act', differing from legislatives acts.

the small number of languages that they are using, or for the lack of transparency in general (Vos 2000: 1128).

It is for the reasons stated above that these new control mechanisms, established under the Lisbon Treaty, make increased legitimacy possible in an appeal before the ECJ, and such an extension may apply to the scope of the former second and third pillars as well, since the pillar structure has been abolished.

Non-jurisdictional procedures

On the one hand, the new legal basis with regards to the European Ombudsman can be highlighted. Even though it is true that the new Art. 228 TFEU does not amend in content what the ex-Art. 195 TEC established in terms of maladministration cases, there are many cases in which such maladministration is linked to human rights violations.[29] For instance, there have been more than a few cases concerning the lack of access to administrative registers or public information, or cases relative to the inappropriate use of data by the institutions (Cotino Hueso 2005: 741).

As mentioned, in the Lisbon Treaty the Ombudsman's functions remain, but its control is extended to the bodies, offices and agencies of the EU. Before the Lisbon Treaty, the General Court was the only competent organism to control them (Ikonen 2002: 374). Now, since the reform Treaty, the Ombudsman is in charge of this control, relieving the General Court from great amounts of pending cases.

However, the role exercised by the Ombudsman within the EU is still very limited (Diamandouros 2006: 227–8), and although there have been attempts to enhance its competences and attain a role in human rights comparable to that of the EDPS concerning data protection (the latter is in charge with studies, data and reports regarding data protection), this has not yet been achieved. Therefore, all decisions by the Ombudsman will remain non-binding, used at the most as a way of inspiration and interpretation for the European courts.

On the other hand, the new legal basis in Art. 16 TFEU may entail an extended role for the EDPS, covering the scope of the area of police and judicial cooperation. Moreover, a more independent supervision by the EDPS is established, and the new provision brings an obligation to the Council as well as the European Parliament to adopt legislation according data protection.

Although the current supervisor, Peter Hustinx, has already expressed his satisfaction on this issue,[30] the real consequences stemming from this new legal basis are yet to be seen.

29 In the Annual report in 2007, the Ombudsman pointed out that several applications (the 28 per cent) were issued because of a lack of transparency of the EU institutions.

30 9th Data Protection Conference, Berlin 6 May 2008, 'Strategic Challenges for Data Protection in Europe', Peter Hustinx: 2.

Conclusions

The Lisbon Treaty entails many changes in its new legal basis, which in one way or another reinforce the protection of fundamental rights within the EU.

One of the most relevant amendments is the new nature of the Charter of Fundamental Rights, which becomes a new source of law, equal to the Treaties.

Secondly, the accession of the EU to the ECHR is worth pointing out, since it will establish an external level of protection of the human rights stipulated in the Convention, controlling not only the Member states of the EU but also the EU institutions.

Thirdly, the EU enjoys a new legal basis regarding data protection, necessary to unify the existing legislation in this field as well as to the current and future international agreements adopted concerning access to the personal data of the European citizens.

Finally, there is a better control of the legislative and regulatory acts by the European courts, and new jurisdictional and non-jurisdictional mechanisms against possible violations of human rights by bodies, offices or agencies of the EU are established.

References

Alonso García, R. and D. Sarmiendo. 2006. *La Carta de los Derechos Fundamentales de la Unión Europea. Explicaciones, Concordancias, Jurisprudencia*. Navarra: Editorial Aranzadi S.A.

Arenas M. and E. Miguel. 2008. Algunas Reflexiones en torno al papel del Defensor del Pueblo Europeo en la protección de los Derechos Fundamentales de los ciudadanos en la Unión Europea. Los Tratados de Roma en su cincuenta aniversario. *Perspectivas desde la Asociación Española de profesores de derecho internacional y Relaciones Internacionales*. Madrid: Marcial Pons.

Arenas Ramiro, M. 2006. *El Derecho Fundamental a la Protección de datos personales en Europa*. Valencia: Editorial Tirant Lo Blanch.

Ballester, P. and M. Amparo. 2009. Los derechos sociales en la Carta Comunitaria de derechos fundamentales y en el Tratado de Lisboa. *Actualidad laboral*, no 15.

Campos Sánchez-Bordona, M. 2009. *Los jueces nacionales ante la Carta de derechos fundamentales de la Unión Europea: algunas cuestiones que suscita el Título VII de la Carta*. Noticias de la Unión Europea, no. 291.

Cotino Hueso, Lorenzo. 2005. *El nuevo derecho fundamental europeo al acceso a los documentos, transparencia e información pública*. Libro homenaje a D. Iñigo Cavero, Tirant lo Blanch (ed.). Valencia.

Cremona, Marise. 2011. *Justice and Home Affaires in a Globalised World: Ambitions and Reality in the tale of US–EU SWIFT Agreement*, Viena: Institute for European Integration Research, Working Paper no. 04/2011.

Decher, F. and M. Höreth. 2009. *Die Verfassung Europas. Perspektiven des Integrationsprojekts*. VS Verlag für Sozialwissenschaften.

Diamadouros, N. 2006. La millora de la protecció dels drets dels ciutadans europeus: Les relacions de cooperació entre el defensor del poble europeu i els ombudsman estatals i regionals. 20è Aniversari de la llei del Síndic de Greuges de Catalunya Terceres Jornades, l'expansió de l'Ombudsman: Diferents models. Barcelona: Sindic de Greuges de Catalunya.

Díaz Barrado Cástor, M. 2006. *Los derechos humanos en la acción exterior de la Unión Europea*. Derecho internacional y Tratado Constitucional Europeo. Madrid: Marcial Pons.

Erkelens, C. and P. Van De Velde. 2007. PNR Agreement: EU and US reach agreement but controversy remains. *Data protection & policy*, 4(10).

Feanzius, C. 2008. Der Vertrag von Lissabon am Verfassungstag: Erweiterung oder Ersatz der Grundrechte? *Zentrum für Europäische Rechtspolitik an der Universität Bremen*. Papier 4/2008.

Garzón Clariana, G. 2005. *Holding the administration accountable in respect of its discretionary powers: the roles and approaches of the Court, the Parliament and the European Ombudsman. The European Ombudsman – Origins, establishment, evolution*, Commemorative volume published on the occasion of the 10th anniversary of the institution. Belgium.

Guerrero Picó, M. del Carmen. 2007. Operadores privados y seguridad pública: la retención de los datos de tráfico a la luz de la 'sentencia PNR'. *Revista Española de Protección de Datos*, no. 2.

Hellmann, V. 2008. *Der Vertrag von Lissabon. Vom Verfassungsvertrag zur Änderung der bestehenden Verträge – Einführung mit Synopse und Übersichten*. Heidelberg: Springer-Verlag Berlin.

Ikonen, A.-M. 2002. Las Agencias y su función en la Unión Europea ampliada. *Revista de Derecho de la Unión Europea*, no. 3.

Jiménez de Parga, M. 2003. La adhesión de la Unión Europea al Convenio Europeo de Derechos Humanos. Une communaité de droit. *Festschrift für Gil Carlos Rodríguez Iglesias*. Berlin.

Kuhlmann, J. 2008. Kompetenzrechtliche Neuerungen im europäischen Energierecht nach dem Vertrag von Lissabon. *Working Papers*, no. 79, Europainstitut.

Longo, M. 2006. Constitutionalising Europe. Processes and Practices. *Federalism studies*.

Mangas Martín, A. 2008. *Carta de los derechos fundamentales de la Unión Europea: comentario artículo por artículo*. Fundación BBVA.

Maurin de Fariña, C. 2008. *La Carta de Derechos Fundamentales de la Unión Europea: implicaciones para la integración europea*. Madrid: Ciudadanía y Valores Fundación.

Ortega Álvarez, L. 2003. Los Derechos Fundamentales de la Constitución Europea. *Revista Derecho Privado y Constitución* no. 17.

Palacios González, J. 2009. La protección de los Derechos Fundamentales por el Tribunal de Justicia de la UE: alcance y consecuencias de la futura adhesión de la UE al Convenio Europeo. *Cuadernos europeos de Deusto*, no. 40 (Ejemplar dedicado a: El Tratado de Lisboa (II)).

Pastor Ridruejo, J.A. 2008. Las relaciones entre el Tribunal de la Unión Europea y el Tribunal Europeo de Derechos Humanos tras la entrada en vigor de la Constitución para Europa. Los Tratados de Roma en su cincuenta aniversario. *Perspectivas desde la Asociación Española de profesores de derecho internacional y Relaciones Internacionales*. Madrid: Marcial Pons.

Passos, R. 2007. *Le système jurisdictionnel de l'Union. Genèse et Destinée de la Constitution Européenne. Commentaire du Traité établissant une Constitution pour l'Europe à la lumiere des travaux préparatoires et perspectives d'avenir* . Brussels: Buyland.

Pi Llorens, M. 2001. *La Carta de los Derechos Fundamentales de la Unión Europea*. Publicacions de la Universitat de Barcelona. Barcelona.

Pi Llorens, M. 2007. La Agencia de los Derechos Fundamentales de la Unión Europea.: ¿Un avance u oportunidad perdida?' *Revista de Derecho Comunitario Europeo*, no. 27.

Rideau, J. 2009. *Les droits fondamentaux dans l'Union européenne. Dans le sillage de la Constitution européenne*. Collection Droit de l'Union Européenne dirigée par fabrice Picod, Bruylant.

Ruiz-Jarabo, P. 2002. La Carta de Derechos Fundamentales de la Unión Europea y su renuncia a regular la competencia de los tribunales Comunitario y de Derechos Humanos: ¿Virtud o defecto?', *Noticias de la Unión Europea*, no. 207.

Sánchez Patron, J.M. 2008. *El sistema judicial comunitario y la protección de los Derechos Fundamentales. Los Tratados de Roma en su cincuenta aniversario. Perspectivas desde la Asociación Española de profesores de derecho internacional y Relaciones Internacionales*. Madrid: Marcial Pons.

Smismans, S. 2010. The European Union's Fundamental Rights Myth. *Journal of Common Market Studies*, 48(1): 45–66.

Sobrino Heredia, J.M. 2009. El Tratado de Lisboa o la capacidad de Europa para reinventarse constantemente. *Revista general de Derecho Europeo*, 19.

Vos, E. 2000. Reforming the European Commission: What role to play for EU Agencies? *Common Market Law Review*, 37(5).

Walker, N. 2003. *Postnational constitutionalism and the problem of translation*, in European constitutionalism beyond the state, edited by M. Wind and J.H.H. Weiler. Cambridge: Cambridge University Press.

Weiler, J. 1999. *The Constitution of Europe – 'Does the New Clothes have an Emperor?' and other Essays on European Integration*. Cambridge: Cambridge University Press.

Weiler, J. 2002. A Constitution for Europe? Some Hard Choices. *Journal of Common Market Studies*, 40(4).

Chapter 7
Enhanced Cooperation under the Lisbon Treaty

Nico Groenendijk

Introduction

Provisions regarding closer cooperation between EU Member States appeared for the first time in the 1997 Treaty of Amsterdam. Three years later these provisions were augmented and restated by means of the Treaty of Nice, now using the term enhanced cooperation. The Lisbon Treaty has once again made some minor changes to the conditions under which Member States can engage in enhanced cooperation.

Put briefly, as Articles 20 and 326–34 of the Treaty on the functioning of the European Union (TFEU) state, enhanced cooperation is regarded as a measure of last resort and applicable only if the Council establishes that certain objectives cannot be obtained within a reasonable period of time by the Union as a whole. At least nine Member States have to participate in the enhanced cooperation, which can only deal with policies within the framework of the Union's non-exclusive competences. The enhanced cooperation is open to all Member States at any time. Acts adopted within the framework of enhanced cooperation do not become part of the general accession *acquis*.

Until recently, the possibility for closer or enhanced cooperation had not been used, even though more informal ways of flexible integration have been used in abundance (Groenendijk 2007). Recently however, enhanced cooperation has been put forward as a feasible option in two specific policy fields. In the field of *patents* eleven Member States will go ahead to implement a single patent, leaving Member States like Spain and Italy behind. In the field of *divorce law*, enhanced cooperation has been established by fourteen Member States, in June 2010.

This chapter analyses the pros and cons of the use of enhanced cooperation under the Lisbon Treaty, both in a general way and by looking specifically at these two cases.

The chapter is structured as follows. In section 2 we discuss the concept of flexible integration and the various forms it can take, with an emphasis on alternative integration and differentiated integration. Section 3 gives an overview of the procedural and substantive requirements to use the enhanced cooperation mechanism. Section 4 deals with the pros and cons of enhanced cooperation as compared to unitary integration and alternative integration. Section 5 focuses on the two current cases of actual enhanced cooperation (patents and divorce law). Section 6 concludes.

Flexible integration

Types of flexible integration[1]

Flexible integration (or sub-integration) refers to an instance of integration that takes place among some but not all members of an already existing (larger) integration scheme (*in casu* the European Union). It can take different shapes. The first typical feature is whether flexible integration takes place within the EU institutional and decision-making framework or not. The second typical feature refers to the policies involved. Flexible integration can deal with policies that are within the EU policy domain (as marked out by the relevant EU Treaties) or outside the EU policy domain.

If flexible integration uses another institutional framework than the EU framework it can either be labelled new integration or alternative integration.[2] *New integration* refers to flexible integration outside the EU institutional framework dealing with policy areas that are not part of the EU policy domain. Integration outside the EU institutional framework, concerned with policy areas that are within the EU domain, is called *alternative integration*. In both cases, because the EU institutional framework is not used, it is possible to cooperate with EU Member States as well as with outsiders (third countries).

If flexible integration occurs within the EU institutional framework, there are again two possibilities. One may be called the *odd integration*, flexible integration that employs EU institutions but deals with policies outside the EU domain. The term *differentiated integration* concerns flexible integration taking place both within the institutional framework and within the policy domain of the EU. Table 7.1 shows the four basic types of flexible integration.

Table 7.1 Four basic types of flexible integration

	Use of EU framework	*Use of alternative framework*
Policies within EU domain	Differentiated integration (including enhanced cooperation)	Alternative integration
Policies outside EU domain	Odd integration	New integration

In the literature on integration, a large variety of concepts and terms has been put forward to denote certain types of 'flexibility': *inter se* agreements, partial

1 See Groenendijk (2007) for a more elaborate discussion.

2 The distinction between the four types of (sub-)integration is based on but different from Su (2007), who uses the terms opt-out integration (rather than alternative integration) and alienated integration (rather than odd integration).

agreements, parallel procedures, two-speed Europe, multi-speed Europe, multi-speed integration, European vanguard, *avant-garde* group, *directoire*, pioneers' clubs, pioneers and followers, core Europe, *Kern Europas*, *Harter Kern*, *noyau dur*, *centre de gravité*, centre of gravitation, variable geometry, *géometrie variable*, Europe à la carte, pick-and-choose, differentiated Europe, *Abgestufte Integration*, two-tier Europe, multi-tier Europe, *plusiers niveaux*, concentric circles, *cercles concentriques*, magnetic fields, hub-and-spoke-Europe, eccentric ellipses, opt-in arrangements, opt-out arrangements, constructive abstention, declaratory abstention, positive abstention, active abstention, transition periods, special treatments, derogations, exemptions, flying geese, breakaway riders and pelotons.[3]

In the remainder of this section we will try to make some sense of these different concepts and terms by focusing on two types of flexible integration: alternative integration and differentiated integration.

Alternative integration

Europe is replete with integration outside the EU framework. After all, EU membership does not imply that countries have given up all other treaty-making authority, which is exercised in relation with third countries or fellow Member States. Such agreements are called *inter se agreements*, *partial agreements*, or *parallel procedures*. Some examples of alternative integration are: the Benelux cooperation between Belgium, the Netherlands and Luxembourg; the monetary union between Belgium and Luxembourg (now incorporated into the EMU); the Nordic cooperation between Denmark, Norway, Finland and Sweden, the Faroe Islands, Greenland and Åland; the Schengen cooperation based on an Agreement signed in 1985 (part of the EU framework since the Treaty of Amsterdam); the Common Travel Area between the UK and Ireland; the Bologna Process dealing with higher education, which now involves 47 European countries; the European Patent Organization; the cooperation within the framework of NATO and the Western European Union (WEU); the cooperation within the OECD, and various other bilateral or multilateral treaties on a multitude of issues.

In some of these cases (for example the Benelux and the Nordic cooperation) the term alternative integration as a form of flexible integration may be misleading, because the 'alternative' cooperation was already there before the larger integration within the EU framework came about (Benelux: 1944; Nordic cooperation: 1952). The EEC Treaty specifically did not put an end to existing bilateral or multilateral treaties, a line which has been held with the various accession treaties.

Besides, some of these forms of cooperation do not so much or exclusively deal with specific policy areas (functional cooperation) but have developed into forms of structured coordination of views in order to maximize influence on

3 See inter alia Wallace and Wallace (1995), Lansdaal (2002), and Federal Trust (2005) for overviews of concepts of flexibility.

collective decision-making within the EU. Again, the Benelux is an example of such a structured coordination, as is the Nordic cooperation.

Interestingly, it appears that alternative integration has more than one potential advantage. First, with parallel agreements it is possible to cover a larger part of Europe than just the EU-27 (or before 2004: the EU-15), with Norway, Iceland, Liechtenstein and Switzerland as the 'usual suspects' when it comes to cooperation with third countries.

Secondly, alternative integration may be beneficial because the EU framework imposes various constraints (in terms of decision-making, legislation, democratic accountability etc,). This should especially explain instances of alternative integration involving all EU Member States.

Thirdly, in cases where only some but not all EU Member States are involved, *inter se* agreements may be seen as a form of *de facto* enhanced cooperation between a relatively small subset of Member States, but without using the EU enhanced cooperation mechanism. Lack of consensus in a specific policy field, or perceived differences in implementation capacity and speed, is at the root of this kind of alternative integration. As the Schengen and Bologna cases show, such alternative integration by a vanguard group can easily become a catalyst for all EU Members, eventually spilling-over to the entire EU. Alternative integration can thus be used as leverage to speed up EU integration in a specific area.

The main disadvantage of alternative integration is of course that the EU institutional and legal framework is not used, resulting in a relatively high level of transaction costs, both in terms of preparation and negotiation of a multitude of bilateral agreements as in terms of enforcement and uniform application.

The success of alternative integration can be seen as posing varying degrees of antagonism to EU-wide integration. One, to a certain extent, manifold alternative integration could be interpreted as the result of failure of integration within the EU framework. If Member States cannot satisfactorily deal with policy problems inside the EU, they will start looking for alternative arrangements. Similarly, alternative integration is sometimes perceived as a threat to the larger EU integration, and various possibilities for differentiated integration (i.e. flexibility *within* the EU institutional framework) have developed – especially since the Treaty of Maastricht – as an alternative to 'alternative' integration.

Differentiated integration

The starting point to discuss differentiated integration is the EU default mode of integration, which involves uniformity in time and matter, and which can be called monolithic integration or *unitary integration*. With unitary integration common EU-wide goals are set and are to be reached at a certain unique point in time by all Member States.

Departure from this default mode is possible along a number of dimensions:

1. Differentiation can refer to time only, as opposed to differentiation in time and matter. Put differently: to what extent should sub-integration eventually be an exclusive thing? If there is differentiation in time only, common EU-wide goals are retained but may be reached at different points in time by different Member States. Sub-integration in this sense is open to all, and indeed is successful only if eventually all members of the larger integration participate (after which the sub-integration is simply absorbed into that larger integration). If there is differentiation in time and matter, aiming at and attaining certain policy goals will be exclusive to the 'insiders';
2. Sub-integration may deal either with a single issue (or a few single, non-related issues) or with a multitude of (potentially interrelated) policy issues;
3. Sub-integration can differ as far as the size of the group of insiders is concerned (relative to the size of the group of outsiders);
4. The composition of the group of insiders can be steady across the range of policy areas in which sub-integration occurs, but can also vary (mixed coalitions);
5. Moreover, such coalitions can be more or less stable over time;
6. There can be a difference in influence in issues of the larger integration between those Member States inside and those Member States outside the sub-integration.

The closest thing to the default mode, i.e. unitary integration, is differentiation in time only, on a limited number of issues, and involving a limited number of outsiders. *Transitional arrangements, temporary derogations and/or exemptions* (to the *acquis communautaire*) are a clear example of this kind of flexibility. Such differentiation has always been part of the Treaties (and of numerous Protocols) and of specific Community Directives. *Constructive abstention (declaratory abstention, positive abstention, active abstention)* is yet another possibility, earlier restricted by the Treaty to specific measures taken as part of the Common Foreign and Security Policy, but now (under the Lisbon Treaty) expanded to (European) Council decision-making under the unanimity rule (Articles 235 and 238 TFEU). With constructive abstention a Member State can simply declare that it does not support the decision taken and will not apply it itself, but accepts that the decision commits the Union. Constructive abstention to a large extent resembles the more general idea of a (temporary and single-issue) *opt-out* clause, as for instance used by the United Kingdom and Denmark to be left out of the third stage of Economic and Monetary Union (EMU).[4]

If a larger number of Member States opt out, but these outsiders are still expected to catch up with the others at a later stage, such sub-integration can be

4 In the EU opt-out clauses are generally reserved for incumbent members. Candidate states are not being offered the opportunity to negotiate similar flexible arrangements; the European Council has made it clear on a number of occasions that acceding members will not be allowed opt-outs or others forms of flexible integration.

labelled *multi-speed Europe (two-speed Europe, multi-speed integration*). Here the idea is that European integration is driven forward by a sub-group of Member States, but no Member State is excluded in the long run nor can Member States exclude themselves indefinitely. Differentiation is allowed to exist temporarily only. A special case of multi-speed is what German commentators call *abgestufte Integration.* Member States agree on particular policy objectives, but specific timetables or stages of adoption by individual Member States are set. Differentiation is then a matter of (timing of) policy implementation rather than policy goals.

The multi-speed concept is rather similar to the idea of a *European vanguard group (avant-garde group, directoire, pioneers' clubs, pioneers and followers, pathfinders, breakaway riders*). Again, the final goal is to reach shared objectives, with the vanguard group breaking ground and shaping these objectives along the way.

Other forms of differentiated integration presuppose that differentiation is not necessarily temporary. The idea of a *core Europe* (*Kern Europas, Harter Kern, noyau dur*) assumes a highly restricted membership of that core, which is (potentially) permanently limited. The core countries get engaged in far deeper integration than Member States outside the core. The latter no longer constrain the former. The deeper integration does involve multiple related issues, and core countries do have a considerably larger overall influence than countries outside the core. The idea of a *two-tier Europe* is essentially the same, but uses another kind of visualization.[5] The related ideas of *concentric circles* (*cercles concentriques*) and of *multi-tier Europe* (*Europe de plusiers niveaux*) differ in that they presuppose the existence of more than just two groups (of insiders and outsiders).

Variable geometry (*géometrie variable*) is yet another concept of sub-integration. It also assumes a permanent state of sub-integration to be established, due to the fact that integrative capacities and desires will vary across the Union. Variable geometry envisages a series of different policy areas (in addition to the internal market), all of which would have varying membership (or policy consortia).[6] Contrary to the idea of a hard core, which puts a permanent set of Member States in the middle of integration, variable geometry starts from the internal market as core policy, around which various other policies have developed and will develop. This policy area configuration and the membership of the different policy consortia are, however, rather stable. The latter is not necessarily the case with *Europe à la carte* (or *pick-and-choose*, or *opt in/opt out*). Moreover, the policy core here is not a full-fledged internal market but a common trading zone.

The differences between the various forms of differentiated integration are gradual only, and it is hard to unambiguously label actual examples of differentiated integration. EMU, for example, can be regarded as an example of two-speed

---

5 The same goes for concepts like magnetic fields, centre of gravitation, and hub-and-spoke Europe.

6 The concept of eccentric ellipses (Gomes de Andrade 2005) is one way of visualizing this variable geometry.

Europe but it also resembles a vanguard group, it involves opt-outs, and it can also be concerned with the current and future EU core. However, the different types of flexibility are linked to certain views on how European integration should proceed, and in some cases can be linked to specific Member States. The idea of a Europe *à la carte* can be regarded as a mechanism to break federalist dynamism (Philippart and Sie Dhian Ho 2003: 5) and was put forward in 1994 by then UK Prime Minister John Major.[7] Ideas like the *noyeau dur*, *géometrie variable*, and *cercles concentriques* have been advocated by French politicians (Delors, Mitterrand, Balladur), assuming a Franco-German coalition at the heart and at the helm of Europe.[8] Interestingly, differentiated integration can be advocated from a position that favours deeper integration as well as from a position that aims at curbing federalist tendencies.

How do all these variants of flexibility relate to the formal mechanism of enhanced cooperation? As Su (2005) observes, the need to seriously discuss differentiated integration became imminent due to the eastern enlargement of the EU. In his analysis (partly building on Philippart and Sie Dhian Ho 2003), enlargement has been postponed time and time again, in order for the EU to reach consensus on mechanisms it could use to deal with diversity, which explains the emergence of opt-outs, the increased importance of subsidiarity, the embracing in 2000 of the open method of policy coordination, and – last but not least – of enhanced cooperation. When it became clear, quite early in the process, that the central and eastern European countries would not content themselves with association agreements but wanted full EU Membership, and EU leaders – pressured by Germany – had to give enlargement the green light (in Copenhagen, June 1993), a new and formal mechanism had to be found to make differentiation between EU Members possible: 'closer cooperation' or 'enhanced cooperation', to which we now turn.

Provisions for enhanced cooperation

Enhanced cooperation can be seen as a specific mode of flexible integration, with a particular legal basis which regulates (and constrains) it. Provisions regarding 'closer cooperation' appear for the first time in the 1997 Treaty of Amsterdam and were changed (now using the term 'enhanced cooperation') by means of the Treaty of Nice (which became effective on 1 February 2003). In the still-born Constitutional Treaty the Nice mechanism was subjected to further changes; the provisions on enhanced cooperation in the Constitutional Treaty were later fully incorporated into the Lisbon Treaty.

The closer cooperation mechanism of the *Treaty of Amsterdam* was a very cautious and rather general mechanism, allowing a group of willing states to

7 In his William and Mary Lecture given in Leyden in June 1994.

8 See Lansdaal (2002) for a more detailed discussion of joint Franco-German ideas in this field.

undertake closer cooperation among themselves while using the institutional mechanisms of the EU, but only if others would allow them to do so (De Witte 2004: 145). This mechanism was established in the first and third pillars, and contained an emergency brake procedure: the Council of Ministers had to decide on closer cooperation by qualified majority, but any Member State, for important and stated reasons of national policy, could refer the proposal to the European Council for a unanimous decision (thereby constituting a *de facto* veto right). Furthermore, closer cooperation had to be endorsed by a majority of Member States (smaller groups were not allowed).

The *Nice Treaty* did away with the emergency brake procedure (in the first and third pillar) and extended enhanced cooperation to the second pillar (CFSP) albeit with an emergency brake (i.e. *de facto* veto) procedure. In the first and second pillar, proposals for enhanced cooperation (put to the Council by the European Commission following a request from the Member States involved) were subject to a qualified majority vote. The number of Member States required for launching the procedure was changed from the majority to a fixed number of eight Member States.

The *Constitutional Treaty* and the subsequent *Lisbon Treaty* stripped the enhanced cooperation mechanism of some of the conditions mentioned in the Amsterdam and Nice Treaties (which were largely considered to be superfluous anyway; see Philippart 2003a, 2003b), but most provisions were retained, albeit rephrased. Following Philippart (2003b) we can distinguish between substantial, procedural and decision-making/operational provisions.

First, under the Lisbon Treaty, the *substantial provisions* for enhanced cooperation[9] are the following:

a. provisions that specify what enhanced cooperation should aim at. Enhanced cooperation is meant to aim at furthering the objectives of the Union, at protecting and serving EU interests, and at reinforcing the process of European integration. Still, enhanced cooperation is a last resort (i.e. it has to be established within the Council that the objectives of such cooperation cannot be attained within a reasonable period by the Union as a whole);
b. provisions referring to what enhanced cooperation should not entail. Enhanced cooperation must not undermine the internal market, should not undermine economic, social and territorial cohesion, and should not distort competition. It has to comply with the Union's Treaties and law. However, acts adopted and decisions taken within enhanced cooperation unions shall not become part of the Union *acquis* (which new EU Member States must adopt upon accession);
c. provisions referring to areas in which enhanced cooperation is simply forbidden. Enhanced cooperation should be established within the framework of the Union's non-exclusive competences, i.e. it cannot

9 We focus here on the general enhanced cooperation mechanism and refrain from discussing the special provisions for enhanced cooperation in the area of CFSP.

be established in areas where the Union has no powers or has exclusive powers (common policies);

d. several provisions that deal with the protection of Member States not participating in the enhanced cooperation. Enhanced cooperation must respect the competences, rights, and obligations of the outsiders. Acts adopted and decisions taken within enhanced cooperation unions are not binding on the outsiders, but EU Members wishing to join the enhanced cooperation at a later stage have to adopt the enhanced cooperation *acquis*.

Secondly, there are some *procedural provisions* for enhanced cooperation:

1. a participation threshold applies of nine Member States;[10]
2. the enhanced cooperation scheme should be open at all times to all EU Member States, provided new participants adhere to the enhanced cooperation *acquis*;
3. the Council grants authorization to proceed with enhanced cooperation by a European decision, upon a proposal from the Commission, and after obtaining the consent of the European Parliament. The Council decides by qualified majority.

Finally, the following provisions deal with decision-making within the enhanced cooperation union and its operation:

4. the enhanced cooperation may make use of the Union's institutions;
5. it is possible for the Member States engaged in enhanced cooperation to decide (unanimously) to take decisions by qualified majority even if in the specific area unanimity is the rule;
6. all EU Member States are able to take part in deliberations, but only enhanced cooperation union members shall take part in the vote;
7. expenditure resulting from enhanced cooperation (other than administrative costs) shall be borne by the insiders only;

Both under the Nice Treaty and the Lisbon Treaty an important role is played by the European Commission.[11] First, the Commission is to pass a request for enhanced cooperation to the Council by means of a Commission proposal. Secondly, the Commission vets any later applications of Member States wanting to join the sub-group.

10 In this regard the Lisbon Treaty differs from the Constitutional Treaty, which used a general threshold of one-third of the number of Member States.

11 See Federal Trust (2005) for a discussion of the possible functioning of some other institutions under flexibility.

Pros and cons of enhanced cooperation

In the academic literature various pros and cons of differentiated integration, and more specifically of enhanced cooperation, have been put forward, though unfortunately not in very systematic way.

We should compare enhanced cooperation with two other possibilities:

a. unitary integration;
b. alternative integration (outside the EU framework).

Table 7.2 lists some aspects that are relevant in comparing unitary integration, enhanced cooperation and alternative integration.

Table 7.2 Comparison of uniform integration, enhanced cooperation and alternative integration

	Uniform integration	Enhanced cooperation	*Alternative integration*
1. Danger of distortion of competition, internal market infringements	No	Low	Low
2. Danger of decrease of cohesion	No	Middle	Possibly high
3. Transaction costs in general	Relatively low	Relatively low (if EU framework is used), relatively high (if EU framework is not used)	Relatively high
4. Procedural constraints	High	Middle (but mitigated if unanimity is replaced by majority decision-making)	Low
5. Democratic (input) legitimacy	High	High	Low
6. Use in fields of non-EU-competences	Not possible	Not possible	Possible
7. Position of outsiders	No outsiders	Relatively weak due to first-mover advantage Beneficiaries of path-finding	Relatively weak due to first-mover advantage Beneficiaries of path-finding
8. Involvement of third countries	Not possible	Not possible	Possible

One of the main possible disadvantages of flexibility in general, compared to unitary integration, is that it leads to less internal cohesion (in economic, social or territorial terms). In addition to this, often the dangers of distortion of competition and of distortion of the functioning of the internal market are mentioned. Whether flexibility indeed endangers cohesion and the internal market is a matter of judgment. It could be argued that the substantive conditions for enhanced cooperation (see b. and c. in the previous section) are rather restrictive and that they explicitly address these dangers. Actually, a closer look at these conditions shows that these conditions are rather general and merely repeat general obligations also to be found elsewhere in the Treaties (Philippart and Sie Dhian Ho 2003: 15). In that sense, compared to the possibility of unitary integration, enhanced cooperation does not entail a disadvantage. Moreover, compared to alternative integration, the conditions referring to the internal market, to competition, to cohesion and to the exclusive powers of the Union, do not really constitute a disadvantage to enhanced cooperation as Member States are not allowed to infringe EU Treaties in these respects as part of alternative integration schemes either. There is, however, the possibility that enhanced cooperation may lead to a permanent divide between insiders and outsiders, between a rich core and a poor periphery, which Martin and Ottaviano (1995) – in the context of possible enhanced cooperation in the field of company taxation – have labelled the 'agglomeration effect of multi-speed integration', which is increased if enhanced cooperation groups in different fields are stable (rather than mixed coalitions). As the decision to form such groups in the case of alternative integration is easier than in the case of enhanced cooperation, this danger is even greater in the case of alternative integration.

As far the general transaction costs are concerned, these are high in the case of alternative integration, but can be low in the case of enhanced cooperation if the EU administrative framework is used (and in that case these administrative costs are borne by the EU-27). Such use is, however, not compulsory.

Another issue is the extent to which procedural (decision-making) constraints play a part. Obviously, these are in principle high in the case of unitary integration, thereby creating the possibility of decision-making and integration deadlock. With enhanced cooperation these procedural constraints are less strict and can even be reduced if the enhanced cooperation group members decide (unanimously) to switch from unanimity (if that is the relevant decision-making rule) to majority decision making.

Related to this is the issue of democratic (input) legitimacy. The provisions on enhanced cooperation safeguard proper involvement of the European Parliament and –in terms of deliberative democracy – of outsiders. This is clearly different from the case of alternative integration, which is often fully intergovernmental, with limited involvement of (national) parliaments and no involvement of outsiders. In terms of legitimacy, a possible drawback of enhanced cooperation could be the impression it creates among citizens of a Union that is weak and permissive, making it possible for its member states to pick-and-choose.

Unitary integration and enhanced cooperation cannot deal with policy fields that are not in the realm of the EU. The prohibition of enhanced cooperation in fields where the Union has no powers clearly is a disadvantage of enhanced cooperation compared to alternative integration.

The position of outsiders is a complicated one. Enhanced cooperation (and the same goes for alternative integration schemes) creates a partial *acquis* resulting in a first-mover advantage (Bordignon and Brusco 2003; Bordignon 2005) as those member states that move first set the stage for later entrants. On the one hand, such an advantage could be an incentive for hesitant Member States to participate in the enhanced cooperation from day one, or even to promote direct moves forward for the EU as a whole without actual enhanced cooperation taking place. In the latter case the existence of the mere possibility of an enhanced cooperation mechanism can already break deadlock. As Philippart and Sie Dhian Ho (2003) argue, in a number of cases the 'threat' of starting enhanced cooperation has probably contributed to breaking deadlock situations.[12] On the other hand, the first-mover advantage could create rigidity at later stages. Although enhanced cooperation is open to all Member States at all stages, accession to the enhanced cooperation is restricted to those Member States willing to accept the *partial acquis* created by the first movers. Contrarily, one could argue that outsiders profit from the path-finding efforts of the first movers. The enhanced cooperation group paves the way for the countries temporarily left behind. Another possibility is that enhanced cooperation in one field, by one group of countries, will extend to other areas and will thus benefit other countries. This possibility has been put forward by, among others, Baldwin (1993), who uses the term 'domino-effect', by Pisany-Ferry (1995) who talks of a 'centripetal force' and by Gomes de Andrade (2005) who uses the term 'pull effect'.

Finally, alternative integration, compared to unitary integration and enhanced cooperation, offers the possibility of including third countries in the cooperation.

Patents and divorce law

Enhanced cooperation and the single community patent

Although there is the European Patent Organization (EPO), there is no single EU patent, which is in sharp contrast with, for example, the United States of America and is regarded as putting EU inventors and innovators at a significant competitive disadvantage.

12 They mention the unlocking (in 2000) of the deadlock on the regulation concerning the European Company Statute and the 2001 agreement on a European Arrest Warrant. In addition the Bolkestein Directive on services (2006) could be mentioned. This mechanism is similar to the one described in more general terms regarding the fear-to-be-left-out in international cooperation as an incentive for such cooperation, by Gruber (2000).

The EPO is an example of a parallel procedure (alternative integration). The EPO was preceded by the International Patent Institute (*Institut International des Brevets*, IIB), established in The Hague in 1947 by France and the three Benelux countries. Already in 1949 an international organization like the later EPO was advocated by the Council of Europe, modelled on the IIB. It would take until 1973 for the EPO to be established, by the Munich Convention (or European Patent Convention). Currently, the EPO has 38 Member States, including all 27 EU Member States.

The EPO provides a single patent grant procedure, not a single European patent. An *EPO-patent* can be obtained by filing a single application in one of the official languages of the European Patent Office (English, French or German) in a unitary procedure before the EPO and is valid in as many of the contracting states as the applicant cares to designate. An EPO-*patent* affords the same rights in the designated contracting states as a national patent granted in any of these states, but it is not a single, centrally enforceable, EU-wide patent. This can be expensive for the patentee in that enforcement must be carried out through national courts in individual countries, and for a third party in that revocation cannot be accomplished centrally once a certain opposition period has expired. That is why, since the 1970s, there has been concurrent discussion towards the creation of a Community Patent (ComPat) in the European Union. The ComPat is intended to solve both of these problems, and also to provide a patent right that is consistent across Europe, thus fulfilling one of the key principles of the SEM (as different patent rights in different countries present a distortion of the internal market principle). Although initially political agreement was reached, the Luxembourg convention on the Community patent of 1975 never entered into force.

In August 2000 the Commission proposed a regulation for a Community patent. In May 2004, however, discussions within the EU led to a stalemate (the language issue being the most notable obstacle) and the prospect of a single EU-wide patent receded. Even though the EPO-patent is far from perfect, there simply was no alternative available within the EU framework. Other legal agreements have been proposed –as with EPO: outside the EU legal framework – to reduce the costs of translation (of patents when granted) and litigation, namely the London Agreement (of 2000, signed by ten countries, of which seven are EU Members, but still waiting to be ratified) and the European Patent Litigation Agreement (EPLA, still under discussion).

After ten years of negotiations on the 2000 Commission proposal, in December 2010 it was concluded in the Competitiveness Council that unanimous agreement could not be reached on a joint approach of all Member States, as Spain and Italy strongly opposed the idea of using English, German and French as sole languages in patent granting. On 14 December 2010, the Commission, on request of twelve member States,[13] submitted a proposal for a Council Decision authorizing

13 Denmark, Estonia, Finland, France, Germany, Lithuania, Luxembourg, the Netherlands, Poland, Slovenia, Sweden and the UK.

enhanced cooperation in this field. On 15 February 2011 the European Parliament gave its consent to the use of an enhanced cooperation mechanism. The Council is expected to formally adopt the decision authorizing enhanced cooperation in March 2011. Subsequently, the Commission will put forward two proposals, one establishing the single patent and another on the language regime.

There are, however, indications that Spain and Italy will not let the case rest and may take the Commission and/or Council to the European Court of Justice. Their main argument is that the last-resort requirement is not fulfilled as it is not yet clear that the patent issue cannot be resolved by a joint approach.[14]

Enhanced cooperation and divorce law

Currently, in cross-border divorce matters (which potentially affect 16 million married couples in the EU, i.e. 13 per cent of total EU marriages), 20 Member States determine which country's law applies, based on factors such as nationality and long-term residence of the spouses. Seven Member States (Denmark, Latvia, Cyprus, Finland, Sweden and the United Kingdom) always apply domestic law, regardless of the nationality or residential history of the spouses. This lack of harmonization of choice-of-law in divorce matters has resulted in a rush-to-court phenomenon, with husbands or wives in international marriages taking action in these courts where they feel they will get the best divorce settlement.[15]

Following its 2005 Green Paper on Applicable Law and Jurisdiction in Divorce Matters (SEC(2005)331), the Commission in 2006 has proposed a Regulation (called Rome III) which aims at harmonizing choice-of-law rules in divorce matters. Due to the opposition of a number of Member States, including Sweden, the United Kingdom, Ireland and the Netherlands, Rome III was never endorsed. These countries want to be able to keep applying their own – relatively liberal – divorce laws.

Over the summer of 2008 nine[16] EU Member States proposed to then Commissioner Barrot to go ahead with harmonizing choice-of-law rules in divorce matters through the mechanism of enhanced cooperation. They argued that the draft legislation of Rome III had been stalled in the Council and that there was no other way to take it forward. In 2009 and 2010 other[17] Member States joined this request. Eventually, by 2010, 14 member States were backing the request for enhanced cooperation.

---

14 EUobserver, 15 February 2011.

15 Also known as forum shopping or litigation shopping.

16 Austria, Bulgaria, Greece, Hungary, Italy, Luxembourg, Romania, Slovenia and Spain. In 2010 Greece withdrew its 2008 request.

17 Belgium, France, Germany, Latvia, Malta and Portugal. The Netherlands, the United Kingdom, Sweden, Finland, Denmark, Estonia, Lithuania, Cyprus, Ireland, Poland, Czech Republic, Slovakia and Greece are the outsiders.

Following the request, the Commission, on 24 March 2010, announced a new proposal, similar to Rome III, but to be adopted by a limited number of Member States only. Commissioner Reding indicated that although the optimal solution would be one that would include all 27 Member States, the new proposal should be seen as a desirable midway solution. On 16 June 2010 the European Parliament gave its consent to the enhanced cooperation measures. After political agreement was reached on 3–4 June 2010 (with a comfortable qualified majority), on 12 July 2010 the Council formally authorized the 14 Member States concerned to establish enhanced cooperation between themselves. On 3 December 2010 the justice ministers of these 14 Member States reached a political agreement on the actual legislation, which was approved by the European Parliament on 15 December 2010. The enhanced cooperation legislation will enter into force 18 months after its adoption.

Conclusions

Both cases clearly show the use of enhanced cooperation due to its main advantage: bypassing the constraints of unitary integration in terms of unanimous decision-making which has led to decades of integration deadlock. Moreover, in both cases the EU administrative framework is used and democratic (input) legitimacy has been safeguarded by the involvement of the European Parliament.

However, these first actual cases of enhanced cooperation also show the possible weaknesses of the mechanism. First, one could argue that the case of enhanced cooperation in patents shows that the introduction of enhanced cooperation has brought about the danger that unanimous decision-making has *de facto* been done away with in the few fields that it is still relevant in. After all, the unanimity requirement can be bypassed by establishing, with a qualified majority, an enhanced cooperation. In that regard the possible involvement by Spain and Italy of the European Court of Justice to 'vet' the enhanced cooperation decision regarding the patent system could be a first test to see if the mechanism really holds.

Secondly, although it is too early to assess the risk of stable coalitions and agglomeration effects of enhanced cooperation, as we only have two cases of enhanced cooperation yet, it is interesting to see that in both cases France and Germany (being the most distinct advocates of a core Europe) are part of the enhanced cooperation groups.

Thirdly, the case of patents shows that the (majority of the) Council, the Commission and the European Parliament are not overcautious when it comes to application of the requirements on non-distortion of the internal market and competition. Enhanced cooperation in this field could lead to a split patent system, which is clearly at odds with the idea of common rules for a common market. On the other hand, it could be argued that having a split system is always better than having 27 different systems.

Finally, the case of enhanced cooperation in divorce law shows that the concept of a vanguard group is a relative one. The countries that are engaged in enhanced cooperation in this field may be 'path-breaking' as far the cooperation as such is concerned but not necessarily when it comes to the content of their divorce laws. Enhanced cooperation, through the first mover mechanism, can also be used to create a *fait accompli* in a specific policy field.

References

Baldwin, R. 1993. A Domino Theory of Regionalism. *NBER Working Paper No. W4465*. Cambridge: NBER.

Bordignon, M. 2005. Institutional aspects of EU organization: an economic analysis. *Paper*, CESifo-Delphi 2004 Conference.

Bordignon, M. and S. Brusco. 2003. On Enhanced Cooperation. *CESifo Working Paper No. 996*. Munich: CESifo.

Federal Trust. 2005. *Flexibility and the future of the European Union*. London: Federal Trust.

Gomes de Andrade, N.N. 2005. 'Enhanced Cooperation: the Ultimate Challenge of Managing Diversity in Europe'. *Intereconomics*, 40, 201–16.

Groenendijk, N. 2007. Enhanced cooperation: the way-out or a non-starter?, in *Unresolved Issues of the European Constitution – Rethinking the Crisis*, edited by N. Neuwahl and S. Haack. Montréal: Éditions Thémis, 263–90.

Gruber, L. 2000. *Ruling the World: Power Politics and the Rise of Supranational Institutions*. Princeton: Princeton University Press.

Lansdaal, A. 2002. Differentiation or Enhanced Cooperation. Formalizing Flexibility', in *Flexibility in constitutions: forms of closer cooperation in federal and non-federal settings*, edited by A. Schrauwen. Amsterdam: Europe Law Publishing, 47–57.

Martin, P. and G. Ottaviano. 1995. The Geography of Multi-Speed Europe. *CEPR Discussion Paper Nr. 1292*. London: CEPR.

Philippart, E. and M. Sie Dhian Ho. 2003. *Flexibility and the new constitutional treaty of the European Union*. The Hague: WRR.

Su, H. 2005. The Dynamics of Widening on the Deepening of the European Union – The Constitutionalization of Enhanced Cooperation. *EURAMERICA*, 35, 501–45.

Su, H. 2007. Politics of differentiation: enhanced cooperation in the EU and the pathfinder in APEC. *Asia Europe Journal*, 5(1), 51–66.

Wallace, H. and W. Wallace. 1995. *Flying together in a larger and more diverse European Union*. Working Document 87. The Hague: WRR.

Chapter 8

Designing Democratic Institutions: Legitimacy and the Reform of the Council of the European Union in the Lisbon Treaty[1]

Andreas Warntjen

Introduction

The widely perceived 'democratic deficit' of the European Union has spawned a major debate among scholars and politicians which featured prominently in the discussions leading to the Lisbon Treaty. Even though at first glance the European Union's (EU) institutional set-up is in line with democratic practice at the national level, its policies do not seem to enjoy the same level of legitimacy as those in national political systems. Because the EU has a growing influence on the lives of European citizens, increasing the legitimacy of its policies has assumed high priority on the agenda of European political elites. One of the explicit goals of the treaty reform process leading to the Lisbon Treaty was to address this shortcoming of the Union. The envisaged reform was meant to take up the 'democratic challenge' and bring Europe closer to its citizens according to the Laeken Declaration, which set the agenda for a Convention on the Future of Europe. The Convention was charged with preparing a new treaty and set out to write a constitution for the EU. In the event, a somewhat less ambitious new treaty, the Lisbon Treaty, was adopted. One of the main topics raised by the debate was the reform of legislative decision-making in the Council. The Council is a key body in the legislative process, as all legislative proposals need the consent of the Council to become law.

The scholarly debate on the democratic deficit focused on two issues. First, whether or not there is a democratic deficit. Second, what changes – if any – are necessary to successfully address this issue. With regard to the existence of a democratic deficit, Majone (1998) argues that the EU is (only) setting regulatory policies. To ensure welfare gains it is desirable to limit the direct accountability of its elites. Others have pointed out that the institutional structure of the EU fulfils all

1 Earlier versions of this chapter were presented at the workshop 'Designing Democratic Institutions', London School of Economics and Political Science, May 2008, and at the workshop 'Europe after Lisbon', Aalborg University, March 2011. I am grateful for comments by the participants.

criteria of a democratic polity (Zweifel 2002; Crombez 2003). Moravcsik (2002) argues that the impression of a democratic deficit is misguided for two reasons. First, it overlooks the relationship between the national and European level. Like Majone, he argues that many decisions taken at the European level are in areas which are often *de facto* made by a 'technocracy' because they do not involve redistribution and are of little importance to citizens. Second, the diagnosis of a democratic deficit is in his view often based on a comparison with an unrealistic ideal of democracy. The limited competences of the Union, the regulatory nature of its policies, the increased powers of the European Parliament, and the involvement of national governments via the Council ensure that EU policy-making is nearly always 'clean, transparent, effective and politically responsive' (Moravcsik 2002: 605). In other words, there is no democratic deficit. Even if that is the case objectively, the fact remains that public support for the EU has decreased since the 1980s and continues to be at relatively low levels (Hix 2008: Ch. 4). Furthermore, European citizens currently *de facto* do not have an opportunity to decide on the EU policy agenda or hold their representatives accountable for their actions in the EU (Follesdal and Hix 2006: 552). One proposed remedy for this situation is to increase the level of political contest in the European Union (Follesdal and Hix 2006). Party political competition can link the wishes of the people and the actions of their representatives via elections. However, at the moment, the electoral connection in the European Union is weak. Parties do not compete on European issues. Voters do not vote with EU policies in mind. And political parties do not form a government at the level of the European Union (Thomassen 2009: 9-14). Party political competition could be strengthened if a majority in the directly elected European Parliament would have stronger control over legislative decision-making in this chamber and the legislative process overall, if political camps would openly compete for the office of the Commission President and if debates in the Council would be more transparent (Hix 2008: Ch. 8). However, Bartolini (2006) points out that this politicization of EU policies via a more majoritarian competition among political parties also contains several risks. Indeed, the European Union might provide more favourable conditions for the consociational model of democracy (Gabel 1998: 466–7). It is a culturally – along national lines – segmented polity with no cross-cutting (transnational) political allegiances. Furthermore, there is no European demos which would justify majority decisions, particularly if they involve re-distribution. In this perspective, the legitimacy of the European Union hinges on the involvement of member states. They remain the bearer of both sovereignty and legitimacy; the legitimacy of the European Union is only derived ('borrowed') from their consensual interaction (Scharpf 1999: 25; for a critical discussion see Beetham and Lord 1998: 69–75). The Lisbon Treaty refers to both, the role of member state governments, 'themselves democratically accountable either to their national Parliaments, or their citizens', in the Council and the direct elections of the European Parliament. It also points to the role of political parties at the European level to 'contribute to forming European political awareness and to expressing the will of citizens of the Union'.

This chapter discusses the reform options for the Council that have been considered in the process leading to the Lisbon Treaty in the light of the debate on the EU's democratic credentials. The most prominent topics of discussion on the reform of the Council have been the voting rule, the Council Presidency and whether or not legislative debates should be public. I compare the provisions of the Lisbon Treaty to the ideal-typical prescriptions of democratic theory. Democracies can follow two ideal-types: the majoritarian and the consensual model of democracy. In the majoritarian version, political camps compete with each other for office. The winner enjoys wide-ranging powers to implement the policy agenda of the majority. In contrast, the consensual model comprises broad coalitions, compromise and a minority veto. The next section summarizes these two different ideal-types of democracy. Subsequently, the overall changes in the institutional set-up enacted by the Lisbon Treaty are discussed. Finally, a detailed discussion of the provisions regarding legislative decision-making in the Council is provided. The pre-Lisbon practice of legislative decision-making in the Council resembled the consensual model of democracy. The Lisbon Treaty is unlikely to change this. Whether or not decision-making in the EU should follow the consensual or majoritarian model depends on one's view on the necessity and existence of a common identity for legitimate rule by a majority.

Two paths to legitimacy: majoritarianism and consociationalism

The modern democratic ideal has been famously summarized by Abraham Lincoln in the Gettysburg address as requiring 'government of the people, by the people and for the people'. This notion is closely related to the idea of self-government. 'The role of citizens in a democratic society is to choose the overall aims of the society' (Christano 1996: 207). A political system is democratic if the people are sovereign and hence – directly or through a representative chamber – rule themselves. Democratic systems are, in turn, held to be legitimate forms of government. In general, policies can enjoy input or output legitimacy (Scharpf 1999; Bellamy 2010). Input legitimacy (government by the people) is derived from the consent of those who have to comply with a policy. Output legitimacy (government for the people) is based on policy outcomes: 'policies can claim legitimacy if they serve the common good and conform to criteria of distributive justice' (Scharpf 1997: 153). Thus, policies in a representative democracy advance the interests of the people or have to reflect the will of the people to be considered legitimate. We can distinguish two aspects in this regard. First, a political system has to address the concerns of its citizens. A political system in which representatives ignore issues of concern to the citizens or in which the rule of the people excludes some issues would not be considered legitimate (cf. Dahl 1989: 112–14). Second, decisions by the representatives have to be taken in accordance with the preferences of the citizens. In other words, democratic government has to be responsive (Dahl 1971: 2). Input legitimacy focuses on how political institutions connect the 'wish of the people' to public policy. Output legitimacy asks if public policy is in line with the interests of citizens. The latter form of legitimacy has been criticized as not conforming to democratic ideals (Thomassen 2009: 4–6). In any case, as citizens' preferences are rarely identical, this raises the question of whose concerns and preferences have to be included and in which manner.

According to the majoritarian model of democracy, the answer is the preferences of the majority (or even plurality) of citizens via electoral competition. Power is shared through the alternation of (two) political camps in government. Once in government, the winning side has sweeping powers to implement its will. One mechanism to ensure the effective rule of the majority is agenda control. By limiting the scope of issues to be decided to the ones favourable to the majority, a clear overall shift in policies according to the aims of the majority can be achieved (Cox and McCubbins 2005: 2–5). Because majoritarian democracy concentrates power, '[r]esponsibility for policy is obvious' (Powell 2000: 5). Consequently, citizens (or at least a majority) can directly hold their representatives accountable (e.g., in elections). Majority rule can be based on the notion of input legitimacy if the individuals concerned share a collective identity (cf. Dahl 1989: 146–9; Scharpf 1997: 7–8). Majority rule is acceptable to its subjects the more homogenous they are, the less a structural majority exists which prevents alternation in power, and the less fundamental issues are affected (Dahl 1989: 161).

In contrast to majoritarianism, the consensus model of democracy tries to maximize the number of views included in decision-making and gives veto power to minorities in areas they deem vital (Lord 2004: 26). Power is widely shared and dispersed. A broad coalition is needed to enact public policy (Lijphart 1999: Ch. 1). Whereas the majoritarian version relies on competition for office, consociational theory builds on accommodation. Rather than presenting competing alternative policy packages to the citizens and letting them choose one of them, the political elites in a consociational system would deliberate in private to find a compromise solution that is accepted in a consensual manner. This implies that a minority can prevent a majority from making a decision if it deems that it would unduly reduce its autonomy or violate its minority rights (Lijphart 1996: 261–2). Hence, 'the majoritarian model of democracy is exclusive, competitive, and adversarial, whereas the consensus model is characterized by inclusiveness, bargaining and compromise' (Lijphart 1999: 2). Because of the inclusive nature of decision-making in the consensus model and the possibility of a minority veto, the interests of minorities are protected. Thus, a common identity is not needed to derive legitimate decisions as a (structural) majority cannot overrule the minority (Scharpf 1997: 188). The diffusion of power in the consensus view of democracy, however, also implies that responsibility for political decisions is harder to discern (Powell 2000: 5). Indeed, to reach consensus among the different groups represented in a political system it might be necessary to give their representatives some leeway in negotiations on common policies. 'Negotiated democracy can only succeed in achieving welfare efficiency and distributive fairness [i.e., output legitimacy] *among* units by weakening democratic accountability *within* units' (Scharpf 1997:

189, original emphasis). In general, there is a trade-off between inclusiveness and accountability. The more inclusive a government, the smaller are the chances of alternation and hence accountability (Kaiser et al. 2002).

In the next section I discuss how the reform options for the Council can be associated with the majoritarian and consociational model of democracy.

The changes of the Lisbon Treaty

The Lisbon Treaty has made a number of changes to the institutional set-up and functioning of the EU. It has increased the role of the European Parliament (EP) and national parliamentarians and introduced elements of direct democracy. The co-decision procedure under which the EP and the Council are co-equal legislators (Tsebelis and Garrett 2000) is now the default procedure when adopting EU legislation. The reach of this procedure has been extended to a number of policy fields, where the EP previously had less influence, including politically sensitive areas like asylum and immigration (Craig 2010: 37). Some commentators applaud these changes as likely to increase the legitimacy of the EU (Lenaerts and Cambien 2009). Others remain sceptical regarding the impact of these changes on the widely perceived democratic deficit of the European Union. After all, the changes in the institutional set-up enacted by the Lisbon treaty have not affected the fundamental nature of the EU (Sieberson 2008; Gervan 2009: 173–6). The *de jure* formal monopoly on making legislative proposals still resides with the Commission, but both the Council and the EP can make suggestions (Craig 2010: 33–4). Both the Commission and the Council, in particular the new President of the European Council, should develop a longer-term agenda. Although the office of the President is a new feature due to the Lisbon Treaty, the European Council as a whole already did formulate longer-term objectives of the EU which also potentially affected its legislative capacity prior to Lisbon (Nugent 2006: Ch. 11). The member states have also retained control of the selection of the Commission. Although the Commission President is now 'elected' rather than 'approved' by the EP, the member states are still firmly in the driver's seat because the EP is restricted to electing a candidate put forward by the European Council. Thus, before and after Lisbon, a qualified majority of member states puts forward a candidate for the office of the Commission Presidency which then needs the approval of the EP (Nugent 2006: 150 55; Craig 2010: 89 92). The other members of the Commission are (and have been) appointed by a qualified majority of the European Council subject to the consent of the EP. Thus, the elections to the European Parliament still do not directly determine the composition of the body that (primarily) sets the legislative agenda (Craig 2010: 91–2). Similarly, there have been some changes to the institutional set-up and decision-making rules of the Council. In particular, there is the new office of an elected President of the European Council, the voting rules in the Council have been changed and deliberation on legislative matters are now supposed to be held in public. However, as will be explained in more detail below, they are unlikely to lead to *fundamental* changes in the way the Council takes part in the legislative procedures. Similarly, the provisions on the enhanced role of national parliaments in the Lisbon Treaty and the attached protocols are relatively weak. National parliaments are now supposed to receive more (and more timely) information about what is going on in Brussels, which gives them an opportunity to address issues. But this is only a necessary but by no means sufficient condition to influence EU legislation. In addition, national parliaments have an enhanced role regarding the subsidiarity principle. If one third of the national parliaments considers a legislative proposal to be in violation of the principle of subsidiarity then the Commission must review its proposal. However, the Commission can still press ahead with its proposal despite the objections of national parliaments (Craig 2010: 45–58). Finally, the Lisbon Treaty added a provision regarding direct participation of citizens in the legislative process. In particular, an initiative of at least one million citizens can 'invite' the Commission to consider the adoption of a proposal on a certain topic. Whether this will affect EU legislative decision-making in the future remains to be seen. Thus, the changes in the institutional set-up do not necessarily fundamentally change the nature of the European Union. Some of the suggestions discussed in the lead-up to the Lisbon Treaty, like the direct election of the Commission President (Norman 2005: 120–21), would have implied a drastic change to the institutional status quo; they were, however, not adopted. In addition, it cannot be always taken for granted that institutional changes will lead to higher (perceived) legitimacy. For example, increases in the EP's power in the past have failed to increase participation in EP elections or satisfaction with the EU. Furthermore, whether the involvement of national parliaments leads to a narrowing of the gap between citizens and EU decision-making or only to more bureaucratic delay and gridlock remains to be seen (Emmanouilidis and Stratulat 2010).

The reform of the Council

The reform of the Council was one of the most contested issues in the Convention on the Future of Europe (König, Warntjen and Burkhart 2006) and the subsequent debate on institutional reform. The Laeken Declaration, which mandated the Convention to work out a proposal on institutional reform, raised three issues in particular with regard to the Council:

- The voting system
- The six-monthly rotating Council Presidency
- Public deliberation of legislation

The first two topics had been on the reform agenda before. Since the Single European Act introduced qualified majority voting, discussions on treaty reform have always included the question of a re-weighting of votes and a change of the voting threshold (Nugent 2006: Ch. 5). Extending the term of office of the Presidency has also been repeatedly suggested by expert panels considering institutional reform in the Union (Tallberg 2006: Ch. 3). The Lisbon Treaty grew out of the discussion on a Constitutional Treaty in the Convention on the Future of Europe. In the constitutional convention, which started its work in 2002, the issue of the institutional set-up of the EU was initially not included in the discussion of the working groups because it was deemed to be too contentious. After the Convention Praesidium made a proposal regarding the EU institutions, including the suggestion of a longer-term Council Presidency, several groups of member states put forward their own suggestions regarding the future structure of the Council in 2003. Besides the Council Presidency, the voting weights were a particularly contested issue. The Convention also discussed the possibility of opening up Council deliberations to the public, a proposal that found support from several member states (Craig 2010: Ch. 2; Norman 2005). In the subsequent discussions of the proposed constitutional treaty the member states again took up the issues of the voting system in the Council (Hix 2006: 86). Following the rejection of the constitutional treaty in France and the Netherlands, a reform treaty was drafted that removed all the elements that directly referred to a constitution. The main points of the constitutional treaty were, however, included in the reform treaty as well. The reform treaty was signed in Lisbon in 2007. After weathering two Irish referenda, the first one being unsuccessful, the Lisbon Treaty finally entered into force on 1 December 2009 (Craig 2010: Ch. 2). In the following, the provisions of Lisbon regarding legislative decision-making in the Council are discussed in more detail and are subsequently compared to the majoritarian and consensual ideal-type of democracy.

The choice of a voting rule

In international negotiations, agreements usually require unanimity. Decisions in national legislatures, on the other hand, often only need a simple majority. In the Council of the European Union, unanimity has been giving way to a lower threshold in a large number of policy fields since the Single European Act (Hix 2006: Appendix; Nugent 2006: Ch. 5). This used to be a system of weighted votes, giving more votes to member states with a larger population, and an overall threshold (around 71 per cent) that was close to a three-quarter majority (Hayes-Renshaw and Wallace 2006: Table 10.1). At the same time, however, according to the Luxembourg compromise, agreed upon in 1966, the Council would strive to reach a consensus decision even in areas formally subject to majority voting if one or several member states felt that an issue was particularly important (Hayes-Renshaw and Wallace 2006: 266–7). Similarly, the Ioannina compromise of 1994 effectively increased the voting threshold (Hayes-Renshaw and Wallace 2006: 274–5). The new system adopted in the Nice treaty featured a triple majority requirement: a qualified majority of votes (around 72 per cent) and a majority of member states which had to include at least 62 per cent of the EU population. The distribution of votes was not strictly proportional to population size (Hix 2006: 84-7). In practice, the Council rarely puts a proposal to a formal vote and both at the preparatory and the ministerial level members of the Council generally strive to reach a broad consensus (Bostock 2002; Heisenberg 2005; Hayes-Renshaw and Wallace 2006: Chs 10 and 11; Lewis 2010).

The Laeken Declaration put the issue of extending qualified majority on the agenda again. In general, there was a widespread feeling after Nice that subsequent changes of the institutions would be necessary, not least due to the upcoming enlargement of the Union, which nearly doubled its membership. In the words of British prime minister Tony Blair: '... we cannot do business like this in the future' (cited in Norman 2005: 16). The working group on simplification in the Convention on the Future of Europe proposed linking the use of a qualified majority as a voting rule in the Council to the use of the codecision procedure and even discussed discarding unanimity altogether (Norman 2005: 83). Similarly, the working groups on external policy and the working group on freedom, security and justice proposed to extend the use of qualified majority voting in these often politically sensitive issue areas (Norman 2005: 92–3 and 100–101). The President of the Convention, Giscard d'Estaing, former President of the French Republic, proposed a double majority, consisting of a majority of member states representing a qualified majority of the EU population, to replace the triple majority requirement of the Nice Treaty (Norman 2005: 191). This was criticized by Spain and Poland, two countries who benefited from the Nice Treaty agreement (Norman 2005: 196–7; Hix 2006: 86). The new voting system that was finally adopted in the Lisbon Treaty consists of three criteria (Article 16 (4) Treaty on the European Union): a percentage of member states (55 per cent), a minimum number of member states (at least 15) and a percentage of the population represented by the states (65 per cent). Furthermore, a blocking minority has to consist of at least four member states. The requirement regarding the minimum number of member states is redundant in an EU of 27 member states. Overall, the changes would shift power to the big member states (Baldwin and Widgren 2004). If the Council does not act on a proposal from the Commission or the High Representative of the European Union or when not all member states vote in the Council, different thresholds apply (Article 238 Treaty on the Functioning of the European Union). The Lisbon Treaty increased the areas in which qualified majority applies. However, unanimity still prevails in over 70 policy areas (Craig 2011: 43). By unanimous decision in the Council, further policy fields or topics (except for military or defence issues) can become subject to qualified majority voting (Article 48 (7) Treaty on the European Union). The voting threshold has an effect on inclusiveness, responsiveness and accountability.

In terms of inclusiveness, there is a qualitative difference between unanimity and majority voting, regardless of the required size of the latter. The voting rule of unanimity stands out as it is the only voting rule which grants all members veto power. Having veto power allows a member to prevent any change of the status quo that runs contrary to its interests (Tsebelis 2002). In particular, under unanimity no collective decision can be reached that implies costs for a member without its consent or compensation (Buchanan and Tullock 1965: 81). Thus, unanimity is in line with a consensual version of democracy as it includes all interests and makes broadly supported compromises necessary. All voting thresholds that require less than unanimity allow a member to be outvoted.

Justifications of majority rule build on the argument that the status quo should not be privileged. Any voting threshold requiring more than a simple majority implies that a minority can prevent a majority from adopting its preferred policy. Using the analogy of the case of a minority adopting a policy, proponents of majoritarianism would argue that only simple majority yields legitimate outcomes. In the words of Dahl's advocacy for majoritarianism: 'If it's wrong to allow a minority to prevail over a majority, then isn't it also wrong to allow a minority to block a majority?' (Dahl 1989: 137). Further arguments for the legitimate use of majority rule are that it maximizes the average utility and allows the greatest number of citizens to rule themselves. These arguments are related. While majority rule allows members to be outvoted, under certain conditions the average utility of a group is maximized by majority rule because the losses of the minority are outweighed by the benefits of the majority. Consider a decision to change an existing policy and three voters. Two voters would prefer a change in policy, one prefers the status quo. If they all value their most preferred outcome equally, then majority rule would give the greatest number of voters their most preferred outcome and maximize the utility of the group as a whole. A higher voting threshold would give a minority (in this case a minority of one) the opportunity to frustrate the wishes of the majority, which would lead to lower utility overall.

However, many authors argue that the legitimate use of majority rule presumes the existence of a common identity similar to the one in a nation-state (Dahl 1989: 147; Scharpf 1999: 8; for a critical perspective see Thomassen and Bäck 2009: 185–7 and Beetham and Lord 1998: Ch. 2). 'The authority and legitimacy of a majority to compel a minority exists only within political boundaries defined by a *demos*' (Weiler 1995: 222). In the absence of a common identity, unanimity or a consensual style of decision-making are more likely to lend (input) legitimacy to a decision. This is particularly true in the case of a 'structural majority', which precludes an alternation in power and leaves one group of citizens constantly aggrieved.

In contrast to inclusiveness, responsiveness is inversely related to the voting threshold. Both the average proximity of an outcome to the desired policy and the chances of a new issue being addressed are negatively affected by an increase in the voting threshold. A higher voting threshold can also thwart accountability. Increasing the voting threshold tends to increase the number of interests that have to be taken into account. This leads to an overall compromise that does not directly reflect a position of any of the groups involved in the agreement. Subsequently, it becomes harder for citizens to identify the group responsible for the decision and hold them accountable. Furthermore, a broad coalition makes it harder for citizens to 'throw the rascals out'.

For example, changing the voting threshold from unanimity to simple majority moves the outcome from the lowest-common denominator to the position of the median voter assuming Euclidean preferences on a single dimension (Shepsle 2010). Consider a committee consisting of seven members (P1 through P7) that has to decide on a one-dimensional issue (figure 8.1). According to the median voter theorem, the outcome using simple majority will be the ideal point of the median voter (P4). In contrast, under unanimity the outcome will be the lowest common denominator (i.e., P1). On average, P4 is closer to the ideal positions of the committee members than P1. Hence, the overall utility of P4 is higher than that of P1. The move is however not Pareto-efficient. While it improves the utility of most members, one player (P1) is worse off.

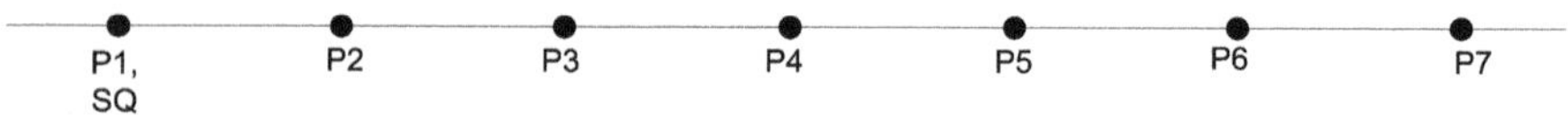

Figure 8.1 The choice of the voting rule

A higher voting threshold, *ceteris paribus*, also decreases responsiveness. A higher voting threshold implies that more actors have to give their consent, effectively turning some of them into veto players (Tsebelis 2002; Warntjen 2011a). This often implies that more policy positions have to be accommodated and might make it impossible to change the status quo. In the example of figure 8.1, any policy that is located between P1 and P7 would be subject to gridlock under a unanimity rule. No unanimous decision could be reached to change a policy in that range. In contrast, under majority rule, P4 through P7 could change any policy to the left of P4. Likewise, any policy to the right of P4 would be changed by a majority consisting of P1 through P4. If the status quo is biased towards a subgroup of citizens, high voting thresholds could lock in decisions that are running against the wishes of a majority of citizens. According to Scharpf (1999) this is the case in the European Union. According to his argument, the high voting threshold in the Council impedes its ability to respond to the wishes of European citizens in (re-)regulating the economy and providing social protection at the European level. In light of enlargement, it was widely expected that the increased preference heterogeneity in the enlarged Council would lead to more policy gridlock (König and Bräuninger 2000). In fact, the Lisbon voting rule might increase the likelihood that a bill passes. The passage probability in an EU of 27 member states with the Lisbon rules is higher than it was in the EU with 12 member states (Baldwin and Widgren 2004). This measure, however, does not take preference heterogeneity into account (Tsebelis and Garrett 1996). In any case, the majority threshold remains relatively high. Furthermore, in practice, informal and consensual decision-making has prevailed in the Council (Heisenberg 2005; Hayes-Renshaw, Wallace et al. 2006). Thus, the voting system in the Council is closer to the consociational idea of decision-making than majoritarianism. The Lisbon Treaty has not significantly changed this.

The Council Presidency

The Presidency is one of the striking features of the institutional set-up of the Council. Originally it was designed as an alternating chairman of the meetings of ministers. Consequently, the Presidency was taken over by a different member state every six months. Since its inception, the office of the Presidency has taken on additional responsibilities. Besides chairing the meetings, it also represented the Council vis-à-vis other EU institutions as well as – in particular in the field of foreign policy –the wider world and offered member states an opportunity to shape the agenda of the EU (Hayes-Renshaw and Wallace 2006: Ch. 5; Tallberg 2006). There is evidence that the member state holding the Presidency can affect the legislative agenda (Tallberg 2006; Warntjen 2007, 2009), pushing forward issues that it deems to be particularly important, and even has a disproportionate influence on legislative outcomes (Schalk et al. 2007; Warntjen 2008b; Tallberg 2006).

How to ensure consistency in the Council's work and whether this required strengthening the role of the Presidency was discussed as early as the 1970s (Hayes-Renshaw and Wallace 2006: 157–61; Tallberg 2006: 47–9). The Laeken Declaration also questions the value of the six-monthly rotation in the context of efficiency. Several proposals regarding the Presidency of the Council were discussed in the context of the Convention on the Future of Europe. The British and Spanish prime ministers together with the French president put forward the idea of a full-time President for the European Council, elected by the European Council by qualified majority for a term in office of up to five years. The Benelux countries and many other smaller states opposed this idea as it violated the idea of the equality of member states in the Council and threatened to upset the institutional balance between the Council and the supranational bodies in the EU. A Franco-German proposal included a variety of different presidencies for the different Council formations. The European Council would be chaired by an elected President. The General Affairs Council, which is charged with coordinating the work of the other Council formations, would be chaired by the General-Secretary of the Council of Ministers. A new foreign minister would be in charge of the meetings on the EU's foreign policy. Several Council formations (on economics and finance as well as justice and home affairs) would elect a chair for a two-year period, whereas the remaining formations would continue using a system of rotation. Most of the speakers at the Convention rejected those plans. In the final proposal by the Convention, two Presidencies were established. The European Council would be chaired by a President who would be elected by the European Council by qualified majority for a term of two and a half years, renewable once. The European Council would not exercise legislative functions. The Presidency at the ministerial level would continue to be based on a system of rotation, but with a minimum term of office of one year. The latter provision was not adopted by the intergovernmental conference following the constitutional convention (Magnette and Nicolaidis 2003; Warntjen 2007b: Ch. 2).

The Lisbon Treaty established an elected President for the European Council, i.e. the meetings of the heads of government (Art. 15 (5) and (6) Treaty on the European Union). The European Council is charged with defining the priorities of the Union, but is not supposed to exercise legislative functions. Sometimes this meeting of the heads of government acted as the final arbiters in legislative disputes which could not be resolved at the ministerial level. The vast majority of decisions are, however, taken by the Council of the European Union, i.e. the meetings of ministers, or *de facto* at the preparatory level by the permanent representatives in COREPER or in the Council working groups (Hayes-Renshaw and Wallace 2006; Häge 2007). At the ministerial and preparatory level where legislative decisions are made, however, Lisbon effectively keeps the current system. Member states hold the Presidency for all council configurations (except for foreign affairs) for six months on a basis of equal rotation 'taking into account their diversity and geographical balance within the Union' (Declaration No. 9 to the Lisbon Treaty). These Presidency terms are organized within team presidencies covering 18 months, similar to the 'troika' system before Lisbon.

In the majoritarian version of democracy, the majority would enjoy wide powers to implement their agenda (Lijphart 1999: Ch. 1). In the legislature, this could be ensured by a partisan leadership office with procedural privileges such as (*de facto*) gate-keeping or agenda-setting powers (Shepsle 2010: Ch. 5; Warntjen 2011a,b). Both powers would allow the majority to skew decisions in line with their preferences, restrict the topics on which a decision is made and prevent divisive votes. The latter is important for the majoritarian model as it allows the political camps competing for office to present clear alternatives (Cox and McCubbins 2005; Tsebelis 2002). Consider a situation where decisions are taken by simple majority (Figure 8.2). If no actor has special powers, the outcome would be the position of the median actor (MC) regardless of the location of the status quo (solid line). Now assume that there is a cohesive fraction that constitutes a majority in line with the majoritarian model of democracy. Let us say that the median of this majority coalition (ML) is located to the left of the overall median (MC). If the majority controls a leadership office with gate-keeping power it could skew the decision agenda in its favour. Whether or not the outcome would differ from the situation where no actor has procedural privileges depends on the location of the status quo. We can distinguish two situations. The status quo can be either closer (II) or further away (I, III) from the ideal position of the majority coalition than the overall median. If the status quo is closer, then the majority will use its gate-keeping power to prevent a change of the status quo to the position of the overall median. Hence, the status quo prevails (dotted line).[2]

2 We should note that some members of the majority coalition would have an incentive to defect from the majority line as represented by its median member. For some members of the majority coalition (e.g., the committee median) the evaluation of the

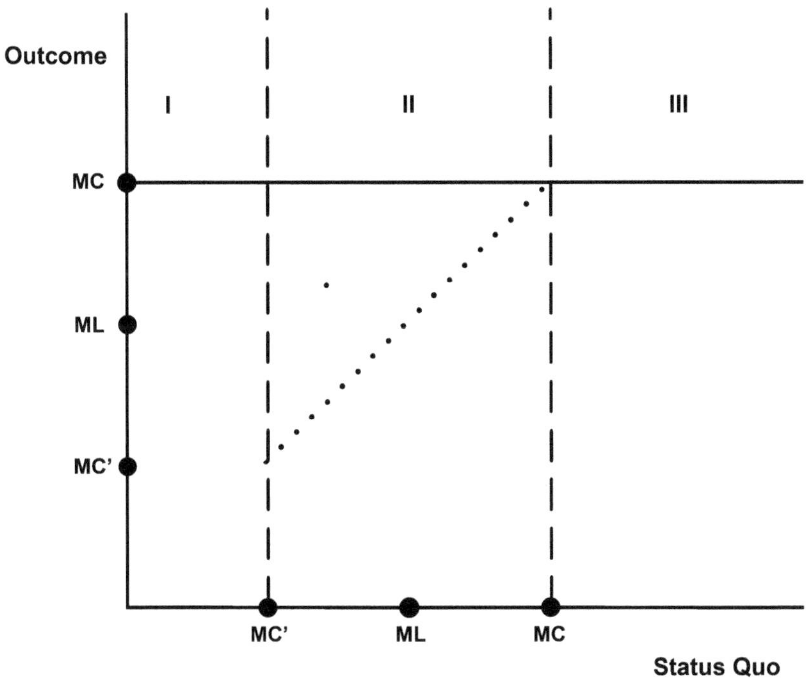

Figure 8.2 The effect of majoritarian gate-keeping

In the majoritarian model of democracy the majority would establish a leadership structure in the legislature as its instrument to control the legislative agenda and legislative outcomes. The leadership office would be elected by the majority and enjoy procedural powers to further the majority's causes. In contrast, the consensus version of democracy would disperse power. A leadership office in the legislature would be reduced to being a mere legislative clerk and/or its use would be shared. The Lisbon Treaty has established an elected Presidency for the European Council. At the ministerial level, however, the system of rotation was kept. Whether the elected President of the European Council will have an effect on legislative decision-making remains to be seen. Furthermore, the procedural powers of the Presidency remain unchanged. The monopoly for making legislative proposals lies with the Commission, which is nominated by the Council members (Hug 2003; Wonka 2007). Despite this link, the preferences of the Commission

relative merits of the majority and committee median differ from those of the majority median. The cohesiveness of the majority faction would have to be ensured by exogenous measures. Furthermore, this version of majoritarianism would not lead to the majority of the citizens' preferences being implemented – even if their representatives have similar or identical preferences – but rather to the rule of a majority of the majority.

might not reflect the majority view in the Council at any given moment as the composition of the Council is subject to change due to national elections (Manow and Döring 2008). A majority in the Council cannot keep items completely off the agenda even if it had complete procedural control over the Council. However, it could in principle delay legislation (in first reading), restrict amendments by the Council to the Commission's proposal, and bias the Council's bargaining position in the conciliation committee. In its current form, however, the Presidency does not enjoy strong procedural powers comparable to the majoritarian office of, say, the Speaker of the US House of Representatives. Nevertheless, establishing an effective leadership structure implies some delegation of authority (Warntjen 2008b). By limiting the Presidency's term in office and by using a system of rotation, however, its power is widely dispersed. In sum, the office of the Presidency in the pre-Lisbon EU conformed to the consensual model of democracy. The changes contained in the Lisbon Treaty are unlikely to change that.

Deliberation in the Council: Public or Private?

One frequent criticism of EU politics is its seemingly untransparent nature. Public access to the Council and its deliberation has increased, starting in the 1990s (Hix 2008: 149–50). Nevertheless, critics of the pre-Lisbon situation argued that the Council was the only legislative body, except for those in North Korea and Cuba, which adopted law behind closed doors (Norman 2005: 116). Others maintained that legislative decision-making in the Council is at least as transparent as it is in national politics (Gabel 1998: 471; Moravcsik 2002: 612–13). In any case, the member states raised the issue of transparent decisions in the Council explicitly in the Laeken Declaration and highlighted the importance of transparency to raise the legitimacy of EU policies:

> The European Union derives its legitimacy from the democratic values it projects, the aims it pursues and the powers and instruments it possesses. However, the European project also derives its legitimacy from democratic, transparent and efficient institutions .... The first question is thus how we can increase the democratic legitimacy and transparency of the present institutions, a question which is valid for the three institutions.... Should the Council act in the same manner in its legislative and its executive capacities? With a view to greater transparency, should the meetings of the Council, at least in its legislative capacity, be public?' (Laeken Declaration on the Future of Europe).

Subsequently, the Convention on the Future of Europe discussed the possibility of having a separate Council formation that would decide on all legislative proposals and would by default act in public (Norman 2005: 111, 150). This suggestion is in line with a majoritarian model of democracy because public debate in the legislature allows for fiercer competition among the political camps vying for office. If citizens can follow the decision-making process, they can hold their representatives directly accountable for their actions (cf. Hix 2008: 101, 103, 150–52). In contrast, in the 'negotiated democracy' of consociationalism, deliberations out of the public eye allow representatives to make the necessary concessions to reach fair agreements that increase welfare overall: 'negotiations could not succeed if all communications at the bargaining table were publicized' (Scharpf 1999: 189). Negotiators might not reach possible mutually beneficial agreements if the public gaze induces them to take on overly uncompromising positions (Stasavage 2004). Thus, transparency involves a trade-off between accountability and efficiency. Whereas the majoritarian model of democracy would emphasize accountability, the consensual model of democracy would lean towards efficiency.

The Lisbon Treaty has further increased public access to its deliberations. Nevertheless, most of the decisions are still *de facto* reached behind closed doors (Lewis 2010: 156). There is still no Westminster style public debate[3] in the Council, facilitating political competition between elected officials from different political parties to galvanize public opinion that a majoritarian view would view as essential (Hix 2008: 98–107). Despite increases in transparency, legislative practice remains be closer to consensual rather than majoritarian decision-making.

In sum, before and after the Lisbon Treaty legislative decision-making in the Council follows the consociational model of democracy (Table 8.1). In institutional terms, a (simple) majority controls neither the agenda-setting process nor the voting outcomes. Furthermore, the most relevant parts of the deliberations are conducted in private, and public Council debates do not aim at political competition between rival political camps.

Table 8.1 Majoritarianism, consociationalism and decision-making in the Council

	Majoritarianism	Consociationalism	Council of EU
Voting rule	Simple Majority	Consensus Minority veto	Unanimity or qualified majority voting 'Culture of consensus'
Legislative organization	Majority control of agenda	Power-sharing	Rotating Presidency with limited procedural powers
Transparency	Full	Limited	De facto limited

3 The Westminster model is based on competition rather than consensus and cooperation; there is a clear majority and the opposition's main task is to criticize the sitting government and to offer an alternative to the electorate.

Conclusion

Democratic theory suggests two paths to legitimacy. The majoritarian model of democracy builds on the competition of political camps, which alternate in power. The consensus model of democracy relies on inclusiveness and power sharing. Applying these models to legislative decision-making in the Council would yield two different institutional settings. The majoritarian version would call for simple majority voting, a strong partisan leadership office and public debates that would clearly set out the different views of the clashing political camps. In contrast, the consensus model would consist of unanimity or consensual decision-making, a rotating and/or weak chairmanship and would lean towards private discussions to find compromises. The agreement reached in Lisbon leads to a change away from unanimity. In practice, however, decision-making will probably remain consensual anyway. In any case, majoritarian voting along clearly demarcated political lines is unlikely as long as the voting threshold remains relatively high. Furthermore, policy positions are often idiosyncratic and depend on the policy field rather than being aligned on one political cleavage. Thus, it is difficult to form competing political camps across several issues. The meetings of the ministers in the Council where legislative decisions are made continue to be chaired by a rotating Presidency. The office of the Presidency also did not gain any procedural powers through the Lisbon Treaty. Although the 2004 enlargement might have *de facto* strengthened the hand of the Presidency, this implies that in effect the power over the decision agenda remains widely dispersed in the Council. Finally, debates continue to be held primarily behind closed doors, with no public clashes of rival political views and legislative agendas to galvanize public opinion.

A normative assessment of this state of affairs depends on one's view on the necessity of a collective identity to reach legitimate decisions via majoritarian means. Furthermore, the choice between the majoritarian and the consensual model involves a number of trade-offs between accountability, responsiveness and inclusiveness.

References

Baldwin, R. and M. Widgren. 2004. *Council voting in the Constitutional Treaty: Devil in the details*. Brussels: CEPS Policy Brief.

Bartolini, S. 2006. Should the Union be 'Politicized'? Prospects and Risks. *Policy Paper No. 19*. Brussels: Notre Europe.

Beetham, D. and C. Lord. 1998. *Legitimacy and the European Union*. London: Longman.

Bellamy, R. 2010. Democracy without democracy? Can the EU's democratic 'outputs' be separated from the democratic 'inputs' provided by competitive parties and majority rule? *Journal of European Public Policy*, 17(1), 2–19.

Bostock, D. 2005. COREPER revisited. *Journal of Common Market Studies*, 40(2), 215–34.
Buchanan, J. and G. Tullock. 1965. *The Calculus of Consent*. Ann Arbor: University of Michigan Press.
Christiano, T. 1996. *The Rule of the Many*. Boulder, Westview Press.
Cox, G. and M. McCubbins. 2005. *Setting the Agenda*. Cambridge: Cambridge University Press.
Craig, P. 2011. *The Lisbon Treaty. Law, Politics and Treaty Reform*. Oxford: Oxford University Press.
Crombez, C. 2003. The Democratic Deficit in the European Union: Much ado about nothing. *European Union Politics*, 4(1), 101–20.
Dahl, R. 1989. *Democracy and its Critics*. New Haven: Yale University Press.
Emmanouilidis, J.A. and C. Stratulat. 2010. *Implementing Lisbon: narrowing the EU's 'democratic deficit'?* Brussels: European Policy Centre.
Follesdal, A. and S. Hix. 2006. Why there is a democratic deficit in the EU. A response to Majone and Moravcsik. *Journal of Common Market Studies*, 44(3), 553–62.
Gabel, M. 1998. The Endurance of Supranational Governance. A Consociational Interpretation of the European Union. *Comparative Politics*, 30(4), 463–75.
Gervan, W. v. 2009. *Wanted: More democratic legitimacy for the European Union*, in European Constitutionalism beyond Lisbon, J. Wouters, L. Verhey and P. Kiiver (eds). Antwerp: Intersentia.
Häge, F. 2007. Committee Decision-Making in the Council of the European Union. *European Union Politics*, 8(3), 299–328.
Hayes-Renshaw, F. and H. Wallace. 2006. *The Council of Ministers*. Basingstoke: Palgrave.
Hayes-Renshaw, F., H. Wallace et al. 2006. When and why the Council of the EU votes explicitly. *Journal of Common Market Studies*, 44(1), 161–94.
Heisenberg, D. 2005. The institution of 'consensus' in the European Union. Formal versus informal decision-making in the Council. *European Journal of Political Research*, 44, 65–90.
Hix, S. 2006. *The Political System of the European Union*. Basingstoke: Palgrave.
Hix, S. 2008. *What's wrong with the European Union & How to Fix it*. Cambridge: Polity Press.
Hug, S. 2003. Endogenous Preferences and Delegation in the European Union. *Comparative Political Studies*, 36(1), 41 74.
Kaiser, A. 2002. Alternation, Inclusion and the European Union. *European Union Politics*, 3(4), 445–58.
König, T. and T. Bräuninger. 2000. Governing the Enlarged European Union: Accession Scenarios and Institutional Reform. *Central European Political Science Review*, 1(1), 42–62.
König, T., A. Warntjen and S. Burkhart. 2006. *The Laeken Convention: Consensus without Unity, in* Preference Formation and European Constitution-Building –

A Comparative Study in Member States and Accession Countries. T. Koenig and S. Hug (eds). London/New York: Routledge,.
Lenaerts, K. and N. Cambien. 2009. *The Democratic Legitimacy of the EU after the Treaty of Lisbon*, in European Constitutionalism beyond Lisbon. J. Wouters, L. Verhey and P. Kiiver (eds). Antwerp: Intersentia.
Lewis, J. 2010. *The Council of the European Union*, in European Union Politics. M. Cini and N. Perez-Solorzano Borragan (eds). Oxford: Oxford University Press.
Lijphart, A. 1996. The Puzzle of Indian Democracy: A Consociational Interpretation. *American Political Science Review*, 90(2), 258–68.
Lord, C. 2004. *A democratic audit of the European Union*. Basingstoke: Palgrave Macmillan.
Magnette, P. and K. Nicolaidis. 2003. *Large and Small Member States in the European Union: Reinventing the Balance*. Brussels: Notre Dame.
Majone, G. 1998. Europe's 'Democratic Deficit': The Question of Standards. *European Law Journa*l, 4(1), 5–28.
Manow, P. and H. Döring. 2008. Electoral and mechanical causes of divided government in the European Union. *Comparative Political Studies*, 41(10), 1349–70.
Moravcsik, A. 2002. In Defence of the 'Democratic Deficit': Reassessing Legitimacy in the European Union. *Journal of Common Market Studies*, 40(4), 603–24.
Norman, P. 2005. *The Accidental Constitution*. Brussels: Eurocomment.
Nugent, N. 2006. *The Government and Politics of the European Union*. Basingstoke: Palgrave.
Scharpf, F. 1997. *Games Real Actors Play*. Boulder: Westview Press.
Scharpf, F. 1999. *Governing in Europe. Effective and Democratic?* Oxford: Oxford University Press.
Shepsle, K.A. 2010. *Analyzing Politics*. New York: Norton.
Sieberson, S. 2008. The Treaty of Lisbon and its impact on the European Union's Democratic Deficit. *Columbia Journal of European Law*, 14(3), 445–65.
Stasavage, D. 2004. Open-Door or Closed-Door? Transparency in Domestic and International Bargaining. *International Organization*, 58, 667–703.
Tallberg, J. 2006. *Leadership and Negotiation in the European Union*. Cambridge: Cambridge University Press.
Thomassen, J. 2009. The Legitimacy of the European Union after Enlargement, in *The Legitimacy of the European Union after Enlargement*. J. Thomassen (ed.). Oxford: Oxford University Press.
Thomassen, J. and H. Bäck. 2009. European Citizenship and Identity after Enlargement, in *The Legitimacy of the European Union after Enlargement*. J. Thomassen (ed.). Oxford: Oxford University Press.
Thomson, R. 2008. The Council Presidency in the European Union: Responsibility with Power. *Journal of Common Market Studies*, 46(3), 593–617.
Tsebelis, G. 2002. *Veto Players. How Political Institutions work*. Princeton: Princeton University Press.

Tsebelis, G. and G. Garrett. 1996. Agenda Setting Power, Power Indices, and Decision Making in the European Union. *International Review of Law and Economics*, 16(3), 345–62.
Tsebelis, G. and G. Garrett. 2000. Legislative Politics in the European Union. *European Union Politics*, 1(1), 9-36.
Warntjen, A. 2007a. Steering the Union. The Impact of the EU Presidency on Legislative Activity in the Council. *Journal of Common Market Studies*, 45(5), 1137–55.
Warntjen, A. 2007b. Through the Needle's Eye. The Council Presidency and Legislative Decision-Making in the European Union. *PhD dissertation*. London: London School of Economics and Political Science.
Warntjen, A. 2008a. The Council Presidency: Power Broker or Burden? An Empirical Analysis. *European Union Politics*, 9(3).
Warntjen, A. 2008b. *Steering, but not dominating: The Impact of the Council Presidency on EU Legislation*, in Games Governments Play in Brussels: Opening up the Council of the European Union. H. Wallace and D. Naurin (eds). Basingstoke: Palgrave.
Warntjen, A. 2009. The Council Presidency and Legislative Leadership: The Case of Occupational Health and Safety. *Paper, ECPR General Conference*, Potsdam, September.
Warntjen, A. 2011a. *Veto player*, in Encyclopedia of Power, K. Dowding (ed.). London: Sage.
Warntjen, A. 2011b. *Veto power*, in Encyclopedia of Power. K. Dowding (ed.). London: Sage.
Weiler, J. 1995. Does Europe need a constitution? Demos, Telos and the German Maastricht Decision. *European Law Journal*, 1(3), 219–58.
Wonka, A. 2007. Technocratic and independent? The appointment of European Commissioners and its policy implications. *Journal of European Public Policy*, 14(2), 169–89.
Zweifel, T. 2002. ... Who is without sin cast the first stone: The EU's democratic deficit in comparison. *Journal of European Public Policy*, 9(5), 812–40.

Chapter 9
The Spanish Presidency – the First Presidency under Lisbon Treaty Trio (relevant institutional 'acquis' and balance)

Blanca Vilà

An open introduction: from the transparency and simplification mandate to the texts of TEU and TFEU

Two years elapsed between the signing in December 2007 of the Lisbon Treaty – consisting of two conventions, the Treaty on European Union (TEU) and the Treaty on the Functioning of the European Union (TFEU), along with 37 final protocols and 65 declarations by Member States and other assorted institutions – and its entry into force on 1 December 2009. This was due to several factors: First there were the (not so trifling) details that needed to be ironed out as a result of the different ratification processes and the rather singular exercise in some cases of the presidential powers provided for to this end in the constitutions of certain Member States. Secondly, there were significant economic developments/crises in both the global and European contexts between the two dates, which led to a certain *neglect* in the preparation of the priority agendas for the implementation of the new institutional and jurisdictional mechanisms to which everyone had subscribed, and gave rise to the need to 'rediscover' the steps to be taken in the immediate future (Martín Pérez de Nanclares 2008).

The initial mandate, linked to the efforts enshrined in the Convention and carried out by earlier intergovernmental conferences (IGCs), required the reform to adapt or, more accurately, to make structural *adjustments* to a 27-member Union that had not yet closed the doors with regard to its capacity to absorb new members. This was to be carried out in the name of *simplifying* decision-making procedures and the delimitation of powers, as well as increasing inward and outward *transparency*, and achieving both greater *proximity* to European civil and political societies and a more clearly articulated democratic *legitimacy* by engaging national parliaments in the debate over how to control well-exercised subsidiarity.

The institutional, jurisdictional and procedural provisions are being implemented within the time-frame of the Spanish Presidency and the Spanish-Belgian-Hungarian Trio Presidency, which is to span the 18-month period in which the aforementioned new institutional developments will be launched, amidst a series of major uncertainties at three different levels as outlined by Blanca Vilà (Vilà, *Mediterranean Yearbook* 2010: 155).

1. the Western financial crisis, with its more or less global repercussions, which specifically affects not only Western economies but also the developing economies and societies of the most fragile countries;
2. the economic and financial construction and social cohesion of the European Union, bound to Western financial architecture and global economic developments, wherein tasks are submitted to 'groups of experts' for reflection, such as the group that, in February 2009, presented the 33 proposals contained in the *Larosière Report* regarding Europe and the transnational financial system to the Commission, or the report commissioned in 2008 from the 'reflection group' headed up by Felipe Gonzalez, which has just now published its proposals for meeting Europe's global structural challenges in the coming years; and
3. the more specific level of the inherent hazards of the eurozone and, in particular, the future of the euro, following the rash attacks by the international market against a Member State, Greece (due to its high levels of debt and implacable deficit), which dragged down the economy of the entire 16-member-strong Eurogroup and, in so doing, revealed the dysfunctions and gaps in the system, as well as the importance of the myriad interests (both domestic and purely speculative).

In short, the three levels of added uncertainty regarding the implementation of the Lisbon Treaty's provisions make fulfilment of the simplification and transparency mandate much more complicated than was originally foreseen (e.g., with regard to the adjustment of methods or the urgency of decision-making). Not only must the efficiency, legitimacy and visibility of the practical solutions to be implemented be addressed, but the additional mission clearly needs to be upgraded.

A detailed reflection on the institutional changes implemented by the Lisbon Treaty: increased institutionalization

The negotiations for the institutional adjustment over the course of the 2007 IGC were ambitious. Renouncing terms that were excessively pompous or that made transfers of national sovereignty too visible, eschewing the common European signs and symbols of the Draft Constitutional Treaty, the Lisbon Treaty– throughout its complex wording – marches firmly and steadily onward towards an institutional change of considerable scope, steering a clear course of both greater institutionalization and greater flexibility and differentiation of its different areas. A quick glance shows that the former institutional balance between the European Council, the Commission and the strengthened European Parliament has been clearly modified, placing greater emphasis on national parliaments and giving a 'boost' to the redoubled presence of the Committee of the Regions and local authorities, as will be seen below. Additionally, the circles have multiplied and the drive towards more comprehensive methods of *differentiated integration* has been made possible through the (most likely less exceptional) use of enhanced cooperation, largely aimed at ensuring efficient action by the Union.[1] In any event, and by way of a brief initial assessment of the scope of its institutional impact, the Treaty places the Union in a new transitional phase characterized by a *lack of formal definition* of the scope of some of its modifications and new *inter-institutional dialectics* as it awaits implementation and empirical readjustment. Let us now examine this situation.

First, the European Council is now a genuine institution rather than merely an institutional formation.[2] This is a visible qualitative change indicative of the increased density at the top of the pyramid, of a top down view or a 'club of senior officials' – in the words of its first President – with a stable presidency vested with decision-making powers (both internal and organizational and, in some regards, external) subject to control by and, in any event, required to report to the European Parliament at the end of its sessions. Pursuant to Article 15.1 of the TEU, 'The European Council shall provide the Union with the necessary impetus for its development and shall define the general political directions and priorities thereof. It shall not exercise legislative functions'. Moreover, pursuant to Articles 235 and 236 of the TFEU, it shall reach its decisions by consensus, but may also vote on issues by simple or qualified majority. These articles also establish something of enormous practical importance in that they separate the General Affairs Council and the Foreign Affairs Council to the benefit of the former, which will collaborate more closely as an actual infrastructure of the European Council. In fact, Foreign Ministers will only attend those General Affairs Councils of utmost importance, such as those addressing economic or energy matters. Again, there is greater institutionalization of 'fundamental' policies.

The Rules of Procedure of the European Council were adopted by the European Council Decision of 1 December 2009 (OJ L 315, 2.12.2009: 51). At its head, the President of the European Council, elected by the Council itself, shall, pursuant to Art. 15.6 of the TEU, chair and drive forward its work, in cooperation with the Commission, endeavouring to facilitate consensus and, as a result of the stability resulting from the term of office of two and a half years for which he or she is elected, essentially guarantee the *cohesion* and *continuity* of the Community's work. Of course, as the first President, Herman Van Rompuy, himself could not help noting, the President of the European Council 'is neither a spectator nor a dictator' vis-à-vis the Council itself. He thus left himself considerable leeway for spontaneity in his actions, including informal meetings and contacts with Heads of State and Government, who avoid him at all costs except in emergencies.

1 See also Chapter 7, Groenendijk, in this volume.

2 See also Chapter 3, Dosenrode, in this volume.

Indeed, he seems determined to fill the gaps in the treaties by means of such impromptu practices, which might be described as calculated 'extemporaneous organization'. The second visible institutional innovation, in which great hope had been placed, is the creation of the office of High Representative of the Union for Foreign Affairs and Security, not to be confused with a Foreign Affairs Minister[3], which basically has two main facets. First, the Representative is double-hatted in that she is both the Union's most senior representative for foreign affairs, second only to the President of the European Council, and as such presides over the Foreign Affairs Councils, and a Vice-President of the Commission, who remains physically ensconced, along with much of her former cabinet, in her old office as Commissioner for Trade.

Second, she has been tasked with setting up the European External Action Service, the new European diplomatic corps, to which end Lady Ashton reached the beginnings of a political agreement with the Union's Foreign Ministers on 26 April 2010. The Service is configured as an autonomous body and began operations in 2011. It seems likely the recent agreement will serve as the basis for immediate consultations with the European Parliament, prior to its adoption by the Council, with the approval of the Commission. The applicable provisions (adaptation of the Financial Rules and Staff Statute, which have budgetary consequences) have been adopted by co-decision with the European Parliament.

In addition to the inherent difficulties of creating any new instrument, much less one that is to be set up as a genuine EU Service, and of consolidating the Commission's many Delegations, which to date have engaged in little more than representation and external management functions, a far cry from classic diplomatic and consular functions, this change gives rise to several questions concerning the specific and genuine spirit of many of the national diplomatic corps in the performance of their functions, characterized by a strictly exclusive view that is both hard to share and hard to force to be shared. This *view*, whereby in many of the minor border conflicts with third countries – e.g., between Spain and Morocco, or between Italy or Greece and Albania – the 'enemy' is most likely the Community neighbour, that is, it is the Community itself that is 'stepping on toes' in Member States' performance of domestic diplomacy, must be corrected. Additionally, the make-up of the quotas for each of the 27 Member States in the institutional Service (RELEX staff at the Commission and Council), a delicate practical task, is already generating tensions. However, the key question may be this: once the 'toy' to be used to *channel* a genuine Foreign Affairs and Security policy has been established, an immensely important and difficult step, and once the Union is able to speak with a single voice in its spheres of competence, will it be able to agree to common, visible positions and content and thus successfully establish its external position? The road will not be easy, but the EU must formulate common positions and build the external dimensions of its different policies with *a single voice*, one that is audible and sufficiently consistent both in a cross-cutting

3 See Chapter 11, Dosenrode, in this volume, for an opposing opinion

sense (diluting state specificities and rendering them invisible) and in terms of inward and outward coherence, like the exterior facet of any domestic policy.[4]

Another extraordinarily important question concerns the *nature* of the European External Action Service under the direction of the High Representative. There are two possible models. One model would be an independent External Service with a legal nature more similar to that of a European Council and the Foreign Affairs Council, which would thus not be directly accountable to the other institutions as an intergovernmental emanation. The other model would be a Service subject to the control of both the European Parliament, with its new powers in the sphere of external action, and, above all, the Commission. The latter body would exercise this control in two ways: institutionally, for not in vain has the High Representative also been a Vice-President of the Commission from the start; and *ratione materiae*, at least in matters, such as trade policy or development aid, that clearly depend on its action.

Will the final model – and the nature thereof – ultimately be found to be strictly attached to the institution that heads it up, that is, the High Representative? For, pursuant to Art. 18 of the TEU, the latter's double-hatting is, to a certain extent, relative: in other words, and with the sole exception of the fact that, like the other members of the Commission, the High Representative must be approved by the European Parliament, it could be argued that the post is more closely linked to *the hierarchy entailed in the exercise of a Vice-Presidency* of the Commission than to membership in it, that is, than to the different Commissioners in their capacities as institutional members. For the post's true 'hat', *ratione materiae*, is the one it wears in relation to the Foreign Affairs Council, which it heads up and whose mission it carries out under the authority of the Union's true external representative, the President of the European Council, to which end the second-to-last paragraph of Article 15 of the TEU provides that the President shall *at his level and in that capacity, ensure the external representation of the Union on issues concerning its common foreign and security policy, without prejudice to the powers of the High Representative of the Union for Foreign Affairs and Security Policy.* In my view, the phrase 'without prejudice', with all the risks it entails, definitively places the body in the European Council's sphere of competence. That is the proper enclave to better understand the nature of the office of High Representative.

Needless to say, the system of rotating Presidencies continues: Spain took over on 1 January 2010. However, with a view to achieving greater institutionalization and to ensuring continuity and coherence, the 'troika' formations are now called rotating *Trio Presidencies*, and they have a common programme, debated and adopted for the entire 18-month period of their duration, although it is also, understandably and perceptibly, subject to the countless hazards of the moment. The question is: have the exercising presidents understood the adjustment made to this point by the new system governing the distribution of this facet of the Community's 'institutional space'? Have they understood that greater

4 See also Chapter 4, Zank, in this volume.

institutionalization of the European Council and the emergence of its President has displaced the 'intergovernmental' quality in its classic sense and ushered back in the 'genuinely European' one, heretofore deposited, albeit perhaps unbeknownst to them, in the Council, precisely due to its role as the potential embryo of a European 'government'?

Yes, a European government that, some years from now, may no longer need an outward dialectic with another institution (the Commission), but rather will undertake this mission itself, in an apparently intra-institutional dialectic. I fear they have not wished to understand anything of the sort. Moreover, continuing in the vein of this brief reflection on the institutional adjustments implemented by the Lisbon Treaty, the European Commission is, for several reasons, the institution to undergo fewest changes, at least at first glance. As is well known, in an unacceptably self-serving act, Ireland imposed, as a condition for its ratification of the Lisbon Treaty, the maintenance *sine die* of an Irish Commissioner; thus, the institution's excessive 27-member composition was not altered. However, from an overall inter-institutional perspective, new hybridizations and interinstitutional contamination cast doubt on the Commission's future in the medium term. First, in the political sphere, the Commission is no longer a true college, but rather seems more like a club of *political representatives* of different national interests, languages and cultures. Thus, Commissioners are proposed who are too tempted to hold domestic political offices, that is, who are contaminated by electoral considerations that are far removed from the spirit of unity that marked the first 40 years of the existence of 'European issues' as a working material and once characterized the Commission. Secondly, the Presidency (tasked with giving voice to the institution's *essential concerns*) has been lacking in charisma of late, and inter-institutional relations have been rather subservient to the dictates, if not of the Council itself, then certainly of the most powerful or demanding Member States, both present and future. Finally, there are the hybridizations and poorly understood double-hattings, which make one think that the *institution as a whole* is in a state of – pardon the oxymoron – 'stable' transition.

A balance of the Spanish Presidency 2010 in the context of Lisbon Treaty implementation: lost in translation?

The programme and the context

As indicated earlier, the Spanish Presidency started on 1 January 2010 under very different conditions about *how to implement* this mandate, and this after an efficient Swedish presidency still under pre-Lisbon conditions. It has been the fourth Spanish Presidency, the previous being in 1989, 1995 and 2002. First of all, the former 'troika' has now become a 'Trio' of presidencies, and Spain started the 18-month first Trio period, with a common programme fixed on July 2009 to be implemented along all three presidencies. This general programme presupposes a general and coordinated Framework for the specific programmes of each presidency, and the Spanish semester programme was articulated around four dimensions, more than four objectives:

The implementation of the Lisbon Treaty institutional novelties, as we have seen in the first part of this chapter, upholds new developments. It covers not only the mission of finding its own place (for the 'new' semestrial Presidencies), learning to hold a convivial institutional environment at the top, but also the mission of having a sort of 'tutelle' on the basic act for the constitution of the new External Service of the EU, the new role of the EP and the enforced presence of National Parliaments, as well as the basic decisions about the new instrument of the 'Citizens Initiative' to be developed.

The Common Strategy against Crisis and Economic Recovery very quickly became the first contextual, but also structural, objective of the Spanish presidency over this period. The main aim was to confirm and to articulate the ability of a common institutional answer to those economic and financial threats, and to enforce the EU's tools for *financial governance* in the face of such crisis.

The accent was on a Citizen's Europe, developing the social dimension of European Integration and enforcing the links between the EU and its citizens through the implementation of the new 'Citizens' Legal Initiative', whose parameters and legal bases can be found in the Lisbon Treaty but whose development needed a wider debate and decisions. The Spanish Act of 2006 was a legal domestic precedent, and this presidency prioritized this dimension, together with the Gender act initiative. On the other hand, the fundamental aim of innovation and the necessity of performance of the 2020 Agenda for Europe, given the weakness of the results of the Lisbon 2010 Agenda, had a central place on Spanish presidency agenda for this first semester.

Finally, the fourth dimension conceived was to reinforce and to upgrade the EU as a Global Actor in international issues, reinforcing the degree of common action, widening its visibility and its leadership for an enhanced common external policy, experimenting with its recent outward institutional tools. Spain had previously organized a roadmap of several first-ranking international meetings, bilateral and multilateral, in a very ambitious programme playing at very different levels (from enlargement to organized regional cooperation, as to Latin America and Asia). One of the most relevant features from the very original Spanish programme was precisely this intensive agenda on international meetings during its presidency.[5]

But this four-dimension programme was to be implemented along a very particular term trying to face economic and financial global and European events. Trio started its experience coming from a simple coordinated troika. Trio implies day by day contacts and at least a unique gaze to main issues. Inwards too, the 'convivial environment' on the European Council President, the Semester's president and the European Commission President was to be handled under special pressures modelling not only the respective 'share' of the leading functions, but

5 See also Chapter 5, Jansson, and Chapter 4, Zank, in this volume.

the outwards position – in front of problems of economic debt or deficit, financial architecture or global voice – for the EU.

A SWOT analysis for the Spanish presidency: Strengths, Weaknesses, Opportunities and Threats

Six months since the end of the Spanish fourth presidency of the European Union, a *prima facie* evaluation shows an ambiguous outcome (Molina 2010: 1): an institutional chapter's appreciation seems to accept that the Lisbon Treaty provisions started their life without any major problems as expected, having the semestrial ruler a discrete position on agenda and organization but losing visibility before the new figure of the President of the European Council. Time factor was a particularly difficult obstacle to achieving and performing, as we shall see, the terms of the second and the fourth chapters of the Spanish agenda for the semester. The external chapter was probably the weakest and the political-economical one too, taken into consideration the context in the sovereign debt arena. In this case, Spanish presidency has an add value as a Laboratory on *what Presidencies will still mean under Lisbon Treaty*, in the institutional context of a Trio, and before a unipersonal EC Presidency, and their conditions and behaviour when facing a very adverse (contextual and structural) conditions for having a leading function. For all these reasons it seems to me of a particular interest to practise in this particular case a test following a SWOT analysis of Strengths, Weaknesses, Opportunities and Threats which could evaluate next member states' semestrial periods on the balance of institutional pressures and global, external or internal economic or political events.

On Strengths issue, the fact of being the fourth presidency held by a Spanish governmental team and its former experiences placed Spanish services in a better place than, for instance, the Hungarian government ruling on 2011, its first European presidency. Another strong point was supposed to be the fact of being part of a new Trio of presidencies, supported by its colleagues and sharing some part of the presidential burden. A third place can be assigned to the social and citizens agenda, as issued from its leftist political positions held by Spanish socialist party government, whose political will for this aim was clear. In any case, all these strong points must be reconsidered: after 15 September 2008, and in particular after the developments of 2009 crisis agenda, the Spanish experience of previous presidencies and all other performing considerations had to be revisited from a weaker perspective.

On the Weaknesses chapter, the unprecedented Greek *sovereign debt crisis* put the case of Spain's deficit on the table in a very early moment of the six months' Spanish Presidency. Normally, other economic crises seem to be seen as an opportunity for European presidencies, trying to enlarge by this fact their leadership along this rotational function. Spain didn't have enough institutional and *economic credibility* during its mandate to do so. Secondly, under the new Treaty,

Spain had a relatively lower profile with regard to the EU external policy and international functions. During 2009 Spain was alone in preparing and organizing a number of important high level international meetings, under a wrong and too ambitious plan. *Time factor* – in so short a period – to deal with on the one hand the extremely organized agenda of any presidency, and on the other major European events of these days can also be considered here. Another weak factor has been the burden of starting as the *first of the Trio* of presidencies without any experience in this particular Lisbon's Treaty institutional implementation, after a very successful Swedish presidency concluding with the Stockholm programme. Finally, a general weakness has been the *historical moment* for this ruling function, from a financial crisis to an economic (sovereign debt and deficit) and monetary crisis, a Eurozone definition crisis (Molina 2010).

The Spanish presidency programme was, before all considerations, quite ambitious. This appreciation means that these opportunities rely on Spanish ambitions during this period. The EU External Service, at least, was politically agreed from the date of 1 December 2010, a number of effectives resources (6000) distributed over 138 diplomatic delegations all over the world.

But the two major axes of this programme were focused on two major international challenges: to enhance Europe's 2020 Agenda for an *innovative* culture, to be highly developed for the Agenda 2020 establishing an Innovation Union (http://ec.europa.eu/research/innovationunion/pdf/innovation-union.en.pdf) which was agreed at the final European Council in June 2010 under Spanish presidency. The second major opportunity was, linked to the first, to conceive Europe as a *global actor* enhancing a new dimension for the EU external policy, not being aware of the new lower role of rotating presidencies, implementing institutional updates and adjustments. This has been at the same time both best opportunity *to act globally* and the lowest Spanish presidency profile. Only the Asian Conference was fully celebrated, Obama's US- EU Conference in May 2010 was suppressed, and EU Latin-American had to cope with the Cuban incident; the meeting in Granada with Morocco was unsuccessful and the meeting of the Union for the Mediterranean's final Council in Barcelona, June 2010, was also not reached.

Finally, a fourth opportunity clearly seen by the ruling Presidency was to consolidate the European *architecture on Financial Supervision*, after the points agreed in September 2009 (European Systemic Risks Board plus three additional mechanisms). Under Spanish presidency the Council has agreed a pack of complementary mechanisms for controlling Funds and Rating Agencies, whose pressure was clearly perceived all along this semester. (Vilà 2009: 3).

Three major Threats have been present in 2010 first Semester term. First, the deepening of this *unprecedented economic and monetary crisis* on Greek sovereign debt, affecting Spain, the presidency's country. Anonymous market forces early started its comparison with Spanish Debt and Deficit, questioning neutrality and authority in the economic arena, includes its voice on European economic governance. 'Eurocrisis' day and solution on 9 May 2010 confirmed that the situation was unattended. Secondly, all *aleatory factors* on institutional Lisbon Treaty's implementations, added to those mentioned above – the delay of two months (February 2010) in constituting the new European Commission Board of Members, paralyzing its minimal good functioning and delaying its main decisions and proposals. And third, many Member States had political domestic instability: a *difficult and uncertain political and economic context*: German Chancellor's behavior and attitude during Greek crisis days, opposite to traditional pro-european former German attitudes, showed a certain German new attitude, after the Constitutional Court Decision on 30 June 2009. Other member States (UK, Netherlands, Czech Republic, Belgium (in a permanent electoral crisis…) and Hungary) held new elections with unsuccessful non-Europeanist governments. On the other side Greece, Portugal, Ireland, Latvia and Spain developed its first structural domestic decisions in an extremely difficult economic and fiscal context (Molina 2010: 3).

Final balance: and the history goes on …

Just some words to remember that as the second member of the Post-Lisbon Trio of presidencies – Belgium – showed that, even the mere existence of a particular government can be irrelevant for the purposes of a successful presidency of the European Union. Let us nevertheless try to draw a very short balance sheet of the Spanish presidency along the first semester of implementation of the Treaty of Lisbon a year after: institutional uncertainty and general economic and monetary crisis have been the most relevant factors for this balance.

2010 First Semester Presidency fulfilled a double error: too *domestic* (general European interests vs national/domestic interests) and too *ambitious* for a so short period of time (under a misunderstood low level of competences, and holding the new decentralized position towards the European Council's President). Let us say that in this 'Liquid Modernity' context (Bauman 2000), threats have to be managed under new circumstances. The updated EU Presidencies will work in the future under a more institutionalized framework, and will have to deal with a series of challenges never before encountered. It requires all European institutions to be flexible and adaptable – 'to be constantly ready and willing to change tactics at short notice…' – Bauman's concept of liquid modernity offers an innovative approach to analysing the complexities of social changes in the contemporary world, and the Lisbon Treaty's first implementation, in a deep Global and European crisis context, marked a new step ahead, full of unattended and unprecedented events.

References

Bauman, Z. 2000. *Liquid Modernity*. Cambridge: Polity.

Castro Ruano, J.L. 2010. Balance de la Presidencia semestral española del Consejo de la U.E: transición hacia una nueva forma de presidencia comunitaria. *Revista Unión Europea*. Aranzadi, Serie *Estudios*.

Closa, C. and P. Heywood. 2004. *Spain and the European Union*. London: Palgrave.

Fernández Solá, N. and A. Sorroza. 2010. La U.E: en el mundo: actuaciones y limitaciones de la Presidencia española. 2010. ARI *Real Instituto Elcano*, 82.

Hayes-Renshaw, F. and H. Wallace. 2006. *The Council of Ministers*. Basingstoke: Palgrave.

Martín Pérez de Nanclares, J. 2008. *Estudio Preliminar* – Tratado de la Unión Europea, *Real Instituto Elcano* (pdf.)

Molina, I. 2010. '*Innovar Europa*' en tiempos de tribulación: Un primer balance de la presidencia española de la UE 2010. *Política Exterior*, 136, julio/agosto.

Powell, Ch., J.I. Torreblanca and A. Sorroza. 2005. *Construir Europa desde España*. Informe Instituto Elcano, num. 2.

Schout, A. and S. Vanhoonacker. 2006. Evaluating Presidencies of the Council of the EU. *Journal of Common Market Studies*, 44(5), 1051–77.

Vilà, B. 2010. 'Post-Lisbone Treaty Europe: Reflections on the Institutional Impact of certain Innovations', IEMed *Mediterranean Yearbook*, 155.

Vilà, B. 2011. The Legal Add-Value of European membership. Some issues on Spain's case, in *25 Years of Spain's membership of the European Union*, J. Roy and M. Lorca (eds). EUCE University of Miami (in print).

Vilà, B. 2011. *A new Playing field for European Microstates? Some appropriated reflexions on the matter for the Trio of Presidencies*. Paris: TGAE, Notre Europe (in print).

Wallace, H. 1985. The Presidency of the Council of Ministers of the European Community: Tasks and Evolution, in *The Presidency of the European Council of Ministers*, C. O'Nuallain (ed.). London: Croom Helm.

Chapter 10
Contradictions in the Market-creating State in Europe

Lars Niklasson

The market and the state in Europe

The purpose of this chapter is to describe and analyse the new strategy for economic growth in Europe, the so called EU 2020-strategy. I will discuss contradictions in the design of the strategy and place the strategy in relation to previous discussions of the contradictions in EU policies for growth. I will furthermore comment on one implication about the design of the European Union as a political system.

The European Union has always been about the creation of an integrated market in Europe. The EU has gradually begun to look like a state, but it is a state with a dominant purpose, to create an integrated European market.[1] With the treaty of Rome in 1957, the principles of a customs union were laid down, together with principles and ideas for the further integration of the national markets. After a slowdown in the 60s and 70s, the project gained speed in the 80s with the adoption of the single market. Barriers were removed and soon the project continued with an Economic and Monetary Union and a single currency, adopted by most member states. With the crisis of the Euro in 2010, one may think about further steps to consolidate what has been achieved. Such steps would include common fiscal and social policies, which would turn the EU into more of a state than it already is.

This perspective is of course simplified and overlooks the large number of steps that have been taken and the conflicts which have been more or less resolved. The Lisbon Treaty is the latest of about a dozen major and minor revisions of the original Treaty of Rome. It is a package of many minor steps towards integration, the effects of which lie in the future. At the same time, several initiatives are taken to support economic growth in Europe. Most important is the launching of the so-called EU2020-strategy, the replacement of the failed Lisbon strategy. It was announced by the European Council late in 2009 and elaborated at the March and June 2010 meetings of the European Council (European Council 2009, 2010a and b). More policies have been added after that.

I will take these documents as the starting point for an analysis of the ideas and contradictions inherent in the EU project of creating an integrated market in Europe. I will then interpret the strategy with the help of some of what has been

---

1 See also Chapter 3, Dosenrode, in this volume.

said about the concepts and ideas inherent in EU-policies and how they often contradict each other. Lastly, I will discuss where the EU can go from here.

The fundamental dilemma for the EU in its economic policies is to choose between horizontal and vertical industrial policies (Smith 2003). Horizontal means general policies, while vertical policies target certain sectors or even certain firms. These two types of policy often have different time horizons. Horizontal policies focus on long-term structural change, to make sure that only competitive firms survive. Vertical policies are more focused on supporting existing firms to maintain jobs. The EU2020 seems to aim for both types of policy at once, where some policies, such as the proposed innovation policy, could be interpreted both ways; are they mainly support for present high tech firms or mainly a key to the development of future firms?

Contradiction is often a good thing in politics. Complicated bargaining is easier if concepts are vague and not always understood. Contradiction can also be a way of giving several parties a piece of the solution. In the long run, however, chances are that contradictions create tensions which make further reforms necessary. To highlight contradiction is a way to understand where conflicts are and where possible areas for reform can be found.

A new strategy for 2020

The EU2020 has a prominent place on the EU website.[2] It gives the appearance of a well-coordinated general strategy for economic growth in Europe, structured in goals, instruments and measurements. It is complex and elaborated, with ambitions for the EU as a whole as well as for the individual member states, for example in the form of national targets. Overall, it looks like a well-designed machinery which will focus European actors on common goals. On closer inspection, the set-up is not so convincing.

Interestingly, the economy is treated as a means rather than a goal in itself. The stated goals are related to individuals and the environment, which most likely will help build support for these policies. The so-called five targets (which are actually eight targets, grouped in five categories) are the following:

- 75 per cent of the 20–64 year-olds to be employed
- 3 per cent of the EU's GDP (public and private combined) to be invested in R&D/innovation
- Greenhouse gas emissions 20 per cent lower than 1990, 20 per cent of energy from renewables, 20 per cent increase in energy efficiency
- Reducing school drop-out rates below 10 per cent, at least 40 per cent of 30–34 year-olds completing third level education
- At least 20 million fewer people in or at risk of poverty and social exclusion.

2 http://ec.europa.eu/europe2020/index_en.htm.

None of the targets deal with economic growth or competitiveness itself. They rather indicate states of affairs which can be achieved if the economy was stronger, but they can also be the means to achieve growth, which is confusing. The employment rate will be an effect of economic growth rather than a means to achieve growth, while the target for R&D could be either a means to reach economic growth or an effect of economic growth. Such complexity implies that the strategy can be interpreted in different ways and that it will be difficult to control or even lead governments, public agencies, firms and individuals to do what the strategy requires.

The monitoring system designed to be part of the strategy deals more directly with economic issues. It focuses on three variables, the macro economy, growth-enhancing reforms and public finances. These intermediary variables are the true goals of the EU2020. They relate to other frameworks already in place, such as the Stability and Growth Pact (Linsenmann, Meyer and Wessels 2007). Setting up a monitoring system may even be a way to integrate economic policies already in place, under a common set of standards.

Apart from the goals (targets), the EU 2020-strategy has three themes and seven flagship activities. The three themes are smart growth, sustainable growth and inclusive growth. These themes refer to activities by which the EU wants to reach its five targets above. There is furthermore a theme labelled 'exiting the crisis', which relates to the crisis of the Euro and the macroeconomic policies of the member states. Here the stated ambition is to get the banking system working, get the public finances back into shape and to restore economic growth.

These latter goals sound like very reasonable ambitions. However, a problem with the approach chosen by the EU is that the wording of the strategy makes it sound as if the goals will automatically be met if one follows the strategy. This is at best a working hypothesis, due to the uncertainties involved in achieving these goals. Economists fight over what to do and governments may not have the strength to do what it takes. Hence, the EU2020 is a starting point rather than a detailed plan of how to exit the crisis and increase economic growth.

A weak mandate

To find out in more detail what the EU wants to do, one has to look at the themes and the seven flagship initiatives, each of which is an elaborated sub-strategy to the EU2020:

- Digital agenda for Europe
- Innovation Union
- Youth on the move
- Resource efficient Europe
- An industrial policy for the globalisation era
- An agenda for new skills and jobs
- European platform against poverty

These initiatives build on policies that are already pursued by the European Union. The strategy furthermore refers to other instruments already in place in the EU ('existing tools'), such as deepening the single market, developing entrepreneurship, investing in growth and trade with other countries. Under these labels we find some battles which have been going on for a long time, such as creating a single market in services. The sceptic can say that a number of Directorate-Generals have produced fancy texts about what they already do, while some of the big controversies are downplayed. The realist can add that this is what most national governments do too.

One of the problems of the EU, which I will come back to, is that President Barroso and his Commission have no electoral victory behind them to give them a mandate for change. The Commission is designed to work as an independent bureaucracy, slowly pushing reform in the member states. Now, within the EU 2020-strategy, it is asked to take a leading role in European politics. Expectations have built up, but the Commission is not given a role which matches the expectations. It works within the limits given by the member states, with little room to ask for a mandate from the citizens of Europe. The leaders of Europe are behind these policies through their decisions in the European Council, but will it be enough? And more fundamentally, can there be a strong common policy when Europe is so diverse? Is diversity a part of the problem or part of the solution?

The layers of goals and ambitions can be summarized in a framework where activities are meant to lead to economic and societal states of affairs (Figure 10.1).

Activities	→	**Growth and competitiveness**	→	**Societal ends**
Themes		Monitoring issues		Targets
Flagship initiatives				
Existing tools				

Figure 10.1 A summary of the causal relationships in the strategy

Too complex and too simple

A general point is that the strategy runs the risk of simplifying too much. It is ambitious in scale and scope, aiming for substantial change in the member states and involving most policy areas where the EU has a mandate. But on the other hand, the specific courses of action are much more difficult than the strategy indicates. Economic growth is an extremely difficult goal to reach, where many factors have an impact. The strategy only highlights the specific instruments in the hands of the EU, when a much more elaborated map of drivers and barriers is needed.

From a perspective of policy analysis, the strategy is interesting as a project management tool. It looks like the logical framework analysis (programme theory) used to design individual projects in foreign aid and other areas (Cooksy, Gill and Kelly 2001). 'For X to happen, Y and Z have to happen first' etc. In this case: to achieve growth, the EU and the member states have to do the following ....

The EU2020 is not so elaborated, and by not elaborating the causal relationships one of the best uses of such a framework is lost, i.e. the identification of contingencies and assumptions. It is often the case that the designer of a project (or a strategy) has overlooked a number of assumptions. 'For Y and Z to bring about X' one has to make sure that all relevant factors are taken into consideration and that there are few side-effects. This often becomes a fruitful exercise in implementation research, understanding causal relations, the role of street level bureaucracies etc. For regular projects this means placing the project in a larger context.

The EU 2020-strategy runs the risk of simplifying too much by not discussing how other factors may help or hinder the achievement of economic growth. In a worst case, it is used as a tool for commanding action, as if nothing else was important. A strategy is a management tool, but needs to be supported by critical analysis, where causal chains can be questioned and tested.

It would be good to stimulate discussion on the specific courses of action and the choice of instruments within the strategy. As it stands, it is wishful thinking based on the tools available to the EU. It may be a great achievement to coordinate EU-policy but not even all of the instruments available to the EU are in the strategy. Cohesion policy was mentioned at the launch in 2009 but is still missing, which may indicate a conflict of interests (see European Economic and Social Committee 2011). Other tools are in the hands of the member states and not given to the EU. This is very interesting for understanding what goes on and how successful the policies can be. The point of a strategy, however, is to end discussion and focus actions. That may not be a wise thing to do if there are serious flaws in the strategy.

Flagship initiatives

The strategy is very vague and one has to look at all the flagship initiatives to understand how the EU thinks about economic growth. The flagship initiative on industrial policy should perhaps be the most central of all, as it relates directly to the health and challenges of European firms. However, its contents are generally quite vague. It consists of ten key actions, some of which refer to annual reporting and review of future policy proposals as well as existing legislation. The rest is a list of things that will be addressed, ranging from a space policy and a strategy on raw materials, to support for small and medium sized enterprises (SME) and improved industrial standards. Areas mentioned where the EU has a mandate are transport, energy and communication. On the list are also actions for specific sectors, such as manufacturing technologies and bio-fuels.

This flagship initiative can be described as the EU doing what it can with the instruments available. It is not primarily a strategy for all the member states to deal with the development of their (individual) industries. Such a strategy is perhaps politically impossible, but it illustrates how limited the EU2020 is and that its contents are more the Commission's strategy than the member states' strategy, in spite of what has been said above about decisions by the member states.

The flagship initiative on Innovation Union sounds more like the creation of a pan-European policy. It refers to initiatives such as the European Research Area and the European Institute of Innovation and Technology. It talks about pooling resources and focusing EU-funding as well as creating a single innovation market, promoting openness and spreading benefits. Reforming research and innovation systems is also a priority.

Here the situation is almost reversed, compared to industrial policy. Innovation policy is an area where many actors want to see a larger EU involvement. One interpretation is that interest groups are using the EU target of three per cent of GDP for R&D as a means to put pressure on their national governments. Hence, universities and high tech firms are united in pursuing this agenda. There are few opponents, which is a contrast to industrial policy, where common ground is more difficult to find.

This short overview is, of course, not a full evaluation of the policies for competitiveness and economic growth. It suggests, however, that the EU is strongly committed to the art of the possible, using the mandate it has been given by the member states. The industrial policies especially are a limited set of actions, mainly focused on specific sectors ('vertical'), even though some more general ('horizontal') policies are presented under the headline of completing the single market. Needless to say, the strategy is focused on action rather than analysis; the thinking behind the design is not presented here.

The overview furthermore implies that the EU pursues several perspectives at once and that this may turn out to be a problem. Inconsistencies or even contradictions may be good for political reasons, but they often reduce the impact of the policies. The EU2020 offers a general overview of EU policies, but the contents are a mix of very different kinds of actions, as before. The strategy adheres to a tradition of mixed or even contradictory policies. Several people have pointed out various kinds of inconsistencies in the economic policies pursued by the EU. This can help us understand the problems with the EU2020.

Several conceptions of the market

The EU has always wanted to build an integrated market in Europe, but this is a vision which covers a number of conflicting aims, all of which can involve the concept of a market. One of the most fascinating analyses of the market-building project of the EU is Nicolas Jabko's *Playing the market. A political strategy for uniting Europe, 1985–2005* (Jabko 2006), where he shows how the Commission has operated with several different conceptions of the market. According to Jabko, it has meant different things in different areas, thereby giving the false impression that all policies of the EU are moving in the same direction.

Jabko discusses the regulation of financial markets and energy markets, as well as cohesion (regional) policy and the economic and monetary union (EMU). In the first, the market plays the role of a constraint on domestic policy, while in the second, the market is used as a norm to deregulate national monopolies. In cohesion policy, the market is seen as a space (territory). Finally, in the EMU, the market is a talisman, a guiding idea for national policymakers.

The policies discussed by Jabko are four areas which are a relevant selection of EU policies, but don't overlap with the EU2020. Financial markets and energy markets are specific parts of the single market, so the analysis shows that there is a variety or even contradiction in the concept itself. The other parts are of course relevant, but some other important policies are missing, like innovation policy (research and development, R&D) and employment policy. Both are areas where the EU only has a weak mandate in relation to the member states.

Focusing on the use of the market-concept is a very fruitful way of showing inconsistencies in EU policies, but neglects interesting contradictions in the views of the role of the state in these policies. There are equally interesting dividing lines on this dimension across the economic policies of the EU. Here, the differences have to do with a focus on safeguarding competition versus supporting European firms, i.e. horizontal versus vertical policies.

Jabko's analysis is an example of a constructivist or sociological institutionalist argument, where the mix of ideas explains how the EU has moved forward. The concepts and ideas are put at the center of the analysis. This helps us understand some of the problems in creating an overall strategy for the EU; that there may not be a unified thinking to support a general strategy for growth.

Asymmetries in the EU

Another approach to contradictions in the policies of the EU is the line of argument pursued by Fritz Scharpf in a number of publications, originating with the essay *Negative and positive integration in the political economy of European welfare states* (Scharpf 1996). Scharpf shows that there is an asymmetry in the making of decisions within the EU, where it is easier to agree on negative than positive integration. In other words, it is easier to agree on taking away national regulation than to adopt new, common regulation.

This argument focuses on the rules of the game and how they produce unintended consequences. It is an example of historical institutionalism, where rules create a path which restricts the options at a later stage. In this view it is the imbalance or even bias in the decision-making rules which explains outcomes, not the ideas behind them. Here, the EU is unable to produce any other strategy than is consistent with its rules.

To some extent, the explanations by Jabko and Scharpf are compatible, though each claims to explain the peculiar mix of policies pursued by the EU. What I want to add to Scharpf's analysis is that the EU is actually pursuing a number of policies which can be labelled positive integration, i.e. member states giving a mandate to the commission to pursue specific policies rather than just safeguarding competition. The EU2020-strategy has a number of these, especially in the innovation policy area, where expansion is supported by actors like universities and high tech firms.

Institutional competition

While Scharpf discusses problems in the choice of a common regulatory framework, there are others who make a case for not adopting common regulation. Victoria Curzon Price (2009) argues from a public choice perspective, that joint regulation is in the interest of producers, while consumers may prefer a greater range of products available. Firms (or nations) with high quality products have an interest in reducing low-cost, low-standards competition. It can be seen as unfair competition when some firms take advantage of lower standards in the protection of consumers, employees or the environment. However, if those standards are seen as politically created barriers, not always in the general interest, then other implications will follow.

The alternative would be to let national regulatory models compete by allowing different standards across the EU. Rather than 'negative integration' the EU could settle for mutual recognition, which was what the ECJ ruled in the famous *Cassis de Dijon-case*. Another label is 'institutional competition', meaning that nations compete with their institutional frameworks. Firms will move to places where they like the institutions (regulations). According to Victoria Curzon Price (2009), there will be less room for institutional competition with the Lisbon Treaty. Policies will be more uniform across Europe.

Scharpf may still be right about a bias in EU regulation, but there are three options rather than two. Ever since the beginning, there have been examples of positive integration – such as equal pay between women and men. With the Single Market the EU opted for reduced barriers (negative integration). The option of (only) mutual recognition may not be politically attractive. Rather than competing, nations prefer similar regulation (see Hix 2005).

Unintended reduction of varieties

In recent writings, Scharpf has drawn the conclusion that imbalances have a further consequence of giving an advantage to some countries rather than other countries. The argument is in the sub-title of a recent article, 'The asymmetry of European integration, or why the EU cannot be a "social market economy"' (Scharpf 2010).

Here, he relates to literature on the so-called Varieties of Capitalism (Scharpf and Schmidt 2000; Hall and Soskice 2001; Schmidt 2002), which points out how different the countries of Europe are in terms of their institutions, i.e. the regulation of their economies.

In the version of Hall and Soskice (2001), there is a liberal market model, not far from the textbook image of a perfect market, and a coordinated market model, where unions, banks and business organizations play a much greater role in coordinating firms. Both models have their advantages and seem to support different kinds of economic development. The key difference is the level of mobility of resources (ibid.). The liberal model is more open to radical change since labour and capital will move around quicker. The coordinated model is better at incremental change for the opposite reason, that capital and labour are more patient due to their influence as stakeholders in the firms.

Scharpf's point is that the EU isn't neutral or even open for a choice among these two models. Rather, the EU actions favour the first model over the second model. It is the design of the single market which leads in this direction. The problem with this situation is that the traditional German and corporatist model is undermined. It can be successful in manufacturing but the EU undermines the networking role of organizations in the German economy.

Scharpf and others are criticizing the EU for an implicit bias against the coordinated market model. This may be a reason to avoid a common model in Europe, hence a reason for avoiding certain issues in the EU2020. Others have argued that the EU has to find a mix which both types of country can live with. This is the message in a recent report by Mario Monti (Monti 2009; Trouille 2010).

From a Nordic perspective, it seems that countries can mix elements of the two models. Sweden in particular is a country which has moved away from corporatism and even tried to become a financial marketplace of the north. Many firms have been sold out to international owners, while much of labour market regulation has been preserved. Denmark provides an opposite example of strong national ownership and flexible labour markets. This variety indicates that other factors, apart from EU regulation, have an impact on national policy choices.

The Varieties of Capitalism-perspective can help us understand why the member states want different things and why EU regulation is implemented differently and has different effects in the various member states of the EU. Basically, the regulations fit in different ways, but other factors are important too. This literature is criticized for downplaying the role of the state, but implicit are different roles of the state in the economy (Hancké, Rhodes and Thatcher 2008). The difference between the models has much to do with the balance of enforcing competition versus providing a supporting environment for firms; i.e. horizontal versus vertical policies.

Neoliberals and mercantilists

In a more normative analysis of the EU, van Apeldoorn, Drahokoupil and Horn (2008) argue that there are three economic ideologies which clash in the EU. This helps us see the different conceptions of the role of the state inherent in EU polices. The authors identify two market-friendly perspectives and one that's adverse. They make the distinction between neoliberal, mercantilist and a social democratic perspectives, which are basically about deregulation, support for national firms or a more interventionist role for the state. Here it is the conflict between the first two, which adds a nuance to the analysis of the role of the state in the market.

Mercantilism, like its 18th-century predecessor, focuses on the present wealth of the nation. The role of the state is to protect and support national firms to maximize national wealth. The nation is often compared to a firm, where public and private actors are part of the same entity or organism. The whole is greater than the parts. Neoliberalism, on the other hand, focuses on deregulation and taking away barriers for entrepreneurs to challenge incumbent firms. The economy is a machine or a discovery process, where public action tends to become a barrier for an efficient market. There is some truth in both perspectives, so how can they be so different? One clue is the time horizon, where mercantilists focus on the present and neoliberals on the future. The first focuses on what is, while the second focuses on what could become.

Van Apeldoorn Drahokoupil and Horn (2008) put the finger on the state, focusing on the outcomes of the economy rather than the set-up of regulation (deregulation). The state becomes an active guardian of the national economy and the means for doing this is to give subsidies to activities which are important for firms, such as R&D. In other words, a vertical policy.

Supply and demand of regulation

All of these perspectives hint at the interests behind economic policies. There are other models which put these political conflicts at the foreground of regulatory design. Among economists, one perspective is to focus on regulations which either enhance efficiency or redistribute wealth. This shifts the focus to winners and losers of regulation. Regulation is in this perspective the outcome of the forces of demand and supply. Firms want regulation in their own interest, such as subsidies for R&D. Politicians want to supply regulation in their own interest. The conclusion of this analysis is often in terms of the need for professional regulators, i.e. bureaucrats rather than politicians. Among political scientists, Simon Hix has applied this model to the EU (Hix 2005).

In this perspective, one of the basic arguments for the independence of the Commission, the European Central Bank and the national central banks is to avoid a political bias for redistribution. However, independent agencies can be captured too.

This model points to an imbalance, like Scharpf's model above. It may shed some light over the design of the EU2020 as a compromise or equilibrium of supply and demand. It can explain outcomes, but pushes the analysis one step further, where we want to know how actors come to think that certain actions are in their interest. Here, Jabko can show how interests are framed.

Market failure and champions

Economists often base their arguments on the idea of market failure, where the state is seen as an instrument for the improvement of the market. There are many such failures in the debate, such as under-investment in R&D. This is close to the mercantilist ideology above, which sees the state as correcting and improving the market, whereas the neoliberal ideology sees too much of state involvement as a bigger problem.

Grahame Thompson relates these perspectives to a neoclassical and an Austrian perspective on the market (Thompson 2001), where the latter focuses on allocative efficiency, distributed information and creative destruction. The neoclassic perspective identifies deviations from the model of perfect competition, where certain parties have more information or a stronger bargaining position than the model supposes. Their solution is government intervention, while the Austrians see the market as the best way to handle these problems over time, where entrepreneurs (may) come up with new solutions, weaker parties learn by doing, etc. In the latter perspective, the risks of government intervention are at least as big as the risk of market failure.

Much of the debate on industrial policy is based on the neoclassical paradigm. It identifies reasons for intervention, often without a balanced discussion of the problems with intervention. The EU has learned to ask for 'additionality' before it funds projects, but it seldom asks about 'crowding out', the risk that it funds projects which would otherwise be funded by private actors.

This way of thinking led to the establishment of 'national champions' (OECD 2009). France especially had a tradition of supporting its major firms to give them a strong position in the world. This was seen as a big problem in the 1980s. One of the ideas behind the Single Market of the EU was to break up these national champions. By means of competition, Europe would in the end get more competitive firms. Some observers have pointed out that we may now have come to the point where the EU supports European champions (Smith 2003). Vertical industrial policy may in fact be a support for European champions.

Support for champions may not be a bad thing, however. The world is not a perfect economy. In the short run the big firms are very important for growth and employment. In the long run there is the risk that they are not flexible enough for survival. But, the business models are changing. With globalization we are witnessing the break-up of the integrated firm. Instead, production is becoming organized in global networks. This will have consequences and industrial policy is only beginning to see the implications.

One of the challenges for industrial policy is to make sure that the benefits from subsidies like R&D-investments end up with those who pay for it. There is a European debate on how entrepreneurs in high tech businesses such as biotech are drawn to the United States. In the end, everyone may gain if European R&D becomes new products and new firms in the US, where the market is more dynamic. However, it may not be the best possible use of European funding, to be a supplier of R&D for the US.

A strategy is not the place to discuss where the world is going, but good strategies are placed in a context. When the world is changing, a strategy should be open or multi-faceted. If the strategy is too simple, it may do more harm than good. There is a risk that the European Council and the Commission focus on solving their daily problems rather than trying to understand where the US and China are going. Should the Council and Commission listen to existing European firms while laying the groundwork for the firms of the future? Can there be a policy for structural change in the EU, speeding up the renewal of European firms or even the transfer of resources from dying industries to expanding ones?

What can the EU do?

The strategy is a summary of what the EU can do. It tells us about the strengths and weaknesses of the instruments given to the Commission. It is a good start to have a focusing device for European debates on the economy, but the holes in the strategy are obvious. One is the near lack of instruments for structural change. Innovative Union is the best hope in this respect. Another hole is the lack of a strong political mandate, mentioned above. These two holes are related; a good principle is to have bodies with power which match the task at hand. As it is now, there is no political body in Europe with the power to upgrade European business for the future. The macroeconomic framework upheld by the European Central Bank may be the best instrument for driving structural change of the economy. If businesses will develop and diversify on their own, the weaknesses of the strategy are not a big problem. If businesses rather exploit weaknesses in EU policies to seek short-term benefits, the design of the strategy may turn out to be a problem.

The two holes of the strategy point to important issues for the future. More work has to be done – or put to use – on where the economy is leading and how to respond. There can be many ways to respond to globalization. Protecting champions is a risky strategy. Protecting national models of organized capitalism makes some more sense. Neoliberal deregulation seems to be the most unpopular option, perhaps because of a lack of popular support for entrepreneurs and 'creative destruction'.

We must not forget that there is an ongoing debate outside of the EU, where think-tanks and the OECD are giving advice on what to do next. The EU used to be much of a think-tank before but has become more of a traditional bureaucracy, with programmes and agencies for many parts of the economy. There is a risk that what was formerly a bureaucracy of reform becomes a bureaucracy defending the status quo. There may therefore be a need to rethink the political underpinnings of the EU.

The Lisbon Treaty makes it easier to make incremental change. In a sense the EU becomes stronger. At the same time, the EU2020 indicates that the lack of a direct political mandate from the citizens can become a problem. Economic policies may become more of support for the status quo than a driver for reform in the member states. If so, it may be time to rethink the fundamental construction of the EU. A lack of politics may have made sense in the beginning, but may now have become part of the problem. A case may be building up for parliamentarianism in the European Union, basing the Commission on a majority in the European Parliament, to balance the heads of state in the European Council.

References

Cooksy, L.J., P. Gill and P.A. Kelly. 2001. The program logic model as an integrative framework for a multimethod evaluation. *Evaluation and Program Planning*, 24, 119-28.

Curzon Price, V. 2009. Institutional competition in the European Union. Causes and consequences of the drive to harmonize, *unpublished paper*.

European Council. 2009. *Conclusions, 10/11 December 2009,* http://www.consilium.europa.eu/uedocs/cms_data/docs/pressdata/en/ec/111877.pdf

European Council. 2010a. *Conclusions, 25/26 March 2010,* http://www.consilium.europa.eu/ueDocs/cms_Data/docs/pressData/en/ec/113591.pdf

European Council. 2010b. *Conclusions, 17 June 2010,* http://www.consilium.europa.eu/ueDocs/cms_Data/docs/pressData/en/ec/115346.pdf

European Economic and Social Committee. 2011. *Working document of the Section for Economic and Monetary Union and Economic and Social Cohesion on The role and priorities of cohesion policy within the EU 2020 strategy (Exploratory opinion requested by the Hungarian presidency),* ECO/291, 28 January.

Hall, P. and. D. Soskice (eds). 2001. *Varieties of Capitalism. The institutional foundations of comparative advantage*. Oxford: Oxford University Press.

Hancké, B., M. Rhodes and M. Thatcher (eds). 2008. *Beyond varieties of capitalism, Conflict, contradictions and complementarities in the European economy*. Oxford: Oxford University Press.

Hix, S. 2005. *The political system of the European Union*. 2nd edn. Basingstoke: Palgrave Macmillan.

Jabko, N. 2006. *Playing the market. A political strategy for uniting Europe, 1985–2005*. Ithaca: Cornell University Press.

Linsenmann, I., C.O. Meyer and W. Wessels (eds). 2007. *Economic government of the EU. A balance sheet of new modes of policy coordination*. Basingstoke: Palgrave Macmillan.

Monti, M. 2009. *A strategy for the single market at the service of Europe's economy and society*. Report to the President of the European Commission José Manuel Barroso, 9 May 2010.

OECD. 2009. *Industrial policy, competition policy and national champions*. Background note, Global forum on competition. Paris: OECD.

Scharpf, F. 1996. *Negative and positive integration in the political economy of European welfare states*. The Robert Schuman Centre at the European University Institute.

Scharpf, F. 2010. The asymmetry of European integration, or why the EU cannot be a 'social market economy'. *Socio-Economic Review*, 8(2), 211–50.

Scharpf, F. and V. Schmidt (eds). 2000. *Welfare and work in the open economy: diverse responses to common challenges*. Oxford: Oxford University Press.

Schmidt, V. 2002. *The futures of European capitalism*. Oxford: Oxford University Press.

Smith, M.P. 2003. From competition to competitiveness: a new EU industrial policy? Paper, Eight biennial international conference of the European Union Studies Association.

Thompson, G. (ed.). 2001. *Governing the European economy*. London: SAGE.

Trouille, J.-M. 2010. The European Union after the Treaty of Lisbon. *Unpublished paper*.

Van Apeldoorn, B., J. Drahokoupil and L. Horn (eds). 2008. *Contradictions and limits of neoliberal governance in the European union. From Lisbon to Lisbon*. Basingstoke: Palgrave Macmillan.

Chapter 11
The Lisbon Treaty – A Treaty of Polity and Politics

Søren Dosenrode

In this chapter we will try to answer our original puzzle: did the Lisbon Treaty really live up to its own preamble? To do so, we will synthesize findings of the previous chapters, and add new analysis when necessary. To systematize we will stick to the concept mentioned in the introduction, that of approaching the Lisbon Treaty through the lenses of polity, politics and policy.[1]

Polity

If one looks at 'polity-ness' at regular intervals beginning with the 1950s, the 1960s, 1970s, 1990s and the 2000s, it has developed from spatial supranationality in 1951 to statehood in the 2000s (cf. Chapter 3 in this volume). Achieving statehood has been a process, and it is open for discussion when it was reached, but since the Maastricht Treaty the fundament was there.[2] In this volume aspects of polity-enhancing and polity-building are discussed in Chapters 3, 4, 5 and 6. But a number of relevant developments are only touched upon briefly, and should be looked at to make a coherent conclusion. Thus the structure of this section will be as follows: first the Union's foreign and security policy developments will be looked at, as the basis of Chapters 4 and 5. This is followed by a discussion of the Charter on Fundamental Rights (Chapter 6). Then comes an overview of the development of the European Council (the Joint Presidency of the European Union), and its precedency, This leads to a discussion on development in the Union's statehood based on Chapter 3.

1 It goes without saying, that the conclusions of this chapter are the responsibility of the editor alone.

2 Jansson opposes the idea of the EU possessing a statehood, cf. Chapter 5 in this volume.

Developments in the European Unions Foreign and Security Policy

Foreign and security policy are vital areas for a polity to be considered a state, and feature prominentely in the new treaty. In chapters 4 and 5 Zank and Jansson respectively look at the EU in the world.

Zank analyses the basics of the EU's foreign policy in Chapter 4. In doing so, he looks at it both from an actorness perspective, and from a structural power perspective.

According to Zank the Union's actorness was strengthened by the creation of the European External Action Service and a High Representative who is a part of both the Commission and the Council of Ministers.[3] One can expect a strengthened cohesion of the Union's foreign policy. But this is countered by the principle of unanimity in foreign policy matters. This, one may expect, will limit the number of concrete actions, although there is accordance on the broad outlines of the Union's foreign policy.

The structural power of the Union has been working since the construction of the Common Market with supranational structures, and has increased each time the internal market has developed. Its strength is the attractiveness of access to the internal market. Zank writes that:

> The EU could use its power of attraction in order to stabilize its surroundings through the perspective of giving membership, based on conditions. In particular under the eastern enlargement the EU acquired an unprecedented power of shaping the societies in neighbouring countries. Without a membership perspective a neighbourhood policy is much weaker. But the attractiveness of the EU market, in combination with assistance, has given the EU influence.

Zank also draws attention to two global processes which, if they continue, are likely to strengthen the EU's possibilities: a) the transition to market economy, and b) the trend towards democracy.

The EU is rightly referred to by Jansson as a project of peace and security (Chapter 5 in this volume). And a substantial part of the Lisbon Treaty deals with the external relations of the EU. According to Jansson, almost half of the amendments made to the Treaty were within the field of security, defence and foreign policy. But he is hesitant in accrediting these new initiatives with a clear 'here and now' effect and Jansson adds that it may be too early to try to evaluate the results yet.

Let us return to the creation of the European External Action Service and the post of a High Representative and Commission Vice-President. It has been seen as a major step forward towards coordination and effectiveness in the EU's

---

3 But one has to be aware that the High Representative seems to be a Vice-President of the Commission more by name than in practice, as she, e.g., never steps in when the President of the Commission is absent, as the other Vice-Presidents do.

foreign policy (cf. Dinan 2011: 104 and Zank, Chapter 4 in this volume). And Michael E. Smith describes the European External Action Service, including the High Representative, as 'one of the most far-reaching attempts to reform EU foreign policy institutions in the long history of European integration' (2011: 1), but he also points to a number of potential problems and weaknesses, among others (2011: 4–7): The High Representative's powers are limited in relation to the Commission, which runs the foreign economic policies (including humanitarian aid, development aid etc.), and the 'representation part' which is shared with the President of the European Council, both have a right to call for 'crisis meetings'. Additionally, the President of the European Commission and the President of the European Council both have a higher diplomatic status than the High Representative.[4] Smith (2011) and Dinan (2011) both agree that the fights between the member states and between and within the institutions have given the European External Action Service a very rough start. But the often-heard criticism of the performance of the High Representative may be too hasty, as Allen and Smith remark (2011: 210), as a) her first duties included negotiating: the basic structure of the European External Action service, various staff regulations, and a budget for the Service, and b) she had 'been given an impossible job that can only be made workable in the long term by providing her with a variety of deputies for her many roles, [...]'. In spite of the odds Lady Ashton is up against, it seems safe to conclude that the Lisbon Treaty did strengthen both the Union's actorness and its structural power.

The Charter of Fundamental Rights

The problems of polity-building were highlighted by the Charter of Fundamental Rights, as Blasi points out in Chapter 6. Having been on the political agenda since the European Council in Cologne in 1999, the Charter was disputed, not least because a Charter on Fundamental Rights, stating rights to the individual citizens is normally found in constitutions. This upset 'the intergovernmental league' of the Union (Denmark, United Kingdom etc.), so in Nice in 2000 the Charter was given a 'political status' only. But as Blasi mentions, this did not prevent the European Court of Justice from referring to it in their decisions from 2003 onwards. The Charter was thus already at that time a sign of the growing constitutionalization of the Union. During the negotiations leading up to the Lisbon Treaty, the question of the Charter on Fundamental Rights' status was solved by a typical EU-compromise. On the one hand the Charter was given legally binding status (Art. 6 TEU), but on the other hand, to comfort the intergovernmentalists, it was placed in an appendix and not in the Treaty proper (only referred to), and a number of states (Poland, the Czech Republic and the United Kingdom) were allowed to limit its use towards

4 And the relationship of the High Representative to the Commission was not helped by President Barroso, when he appointed the Union's first ambassador to the US without first consulting Ashton (Allen and Smith 2011: 210).

their own citizens. So the Charter on Fundamental Rights clearly contributed to polity-building, but did it in a half-hearted way.

The European Council after Lisbon – or the Joint European Union Presidency

An important development in the Lisbon Treaty is the upgrading of the European Council – the joint or collective EU-presidency – and the new permanent presidency.

It was a very important decision to inscribe the European Council as an institution in the Lisbon Treaty, putting it de jure on the same level as the Commission, the Parliament, the Council and the European Court of Justice. De facto its sheer power had not let anyone doubt its supremacy for years. Itself a bastion of intergovernmentalism, the European Council began as an informal affair in the beginning of the 1960s, only to disappear for some years until it surfaced again with The Hague summit of 1969, which inter alia had enlargement and a possible foreign political cooperation as topics. The European Council remained informal and was first 'formalized' at the Paris summit of 1974, and existed in a kind of limbo until the Single European Act, 1986, codified it, and it received a tiny secretariat. The Single European Act, Article 2, merely stated that:

> The European Council shall bring together the Heads of State or of Government of the Member States and the President of the Commission of the European Communities. They shall be assisted by the Ministers for Foreign Affairs and by a Member of the Commission. The European Council shall meet at least twice a year.

As years went by, the European Council developed to become the 'powerhouse' of the European Community, discussing joint approaches to external events, searching for possibilities for internal development, and solutions to upcoming problems. During those years, the European Council also began to become a 'court of arbitration'. When the Council of Ministers could not agree, they happily sent their problem 'up in the system', making the European Council de facto 'co-legislator'.

In the Maastricht Treaty the European Council's importance as a strategic motor was acknowledged, but its tasks were still formulated very generally:

> Article D
> The European Council shall provide the Union with the necessary impetus for its development and shall define the general political guidelines thereof.
> The European Council shall bring together the Heads of State or of Government of the Member States and the President of the Commission. They shall be assisted by the Ministers for Foreign Affairs of the Member States and by a Member of the Commission. The European Council shall meet at least twice a year, under the chairmanship of the Head of State or of Government of the Member State which holds the Presidency of the Council.

> The European Council shall submit to the European Parliament a report after each of its meetings and a yearly written report on the progress achieved by the Union.

To counter the tendency to be used – or abused – by the Council of Ministers in case of disagreement, the *usus* was to meet twice a year only. In that way there was no time for solving conflicts at the Council of Ministers level.

Through the 1990s and continuing in 2000s it became clear that the European Council suffered from both overload and lack of clear procedures (cf. Joint Study 2010: 8). The European Council was not able to live up to its own intentions, not to act as troubleshooter for the Council of Ministers. Often disagreement in the Council of Ministers resulted in the European Council making the decisions. As a result the European Council had an overloaded agenda, and too little time for strategic discussions and decisions. Additionally, the lack of clear procedures led to improvising and non-implementation. One might add to this, that the short time of a presidency (six months) made it extremely hard for the president in office to prepare the meetings thoroughly, get to know all the national positions, and secure and control implementation. Basically, not enough time was available for conducting an efficient presidency. Altogether the European Council performed sub-optimally.

Today the European Council is the supreme executive (a collective presidency) of the EU. In this role the European Council has an extremely potent and important strategic role, setting the aims and defining the direction of the Union's policies, although the phrasing of it in the treaty is grosso modo still formulated in the same way as before.

A sentence was added in the Lisbon Treaty (Art. 15.1 TEU): 'It [the European Council] shall not exercise legislative functions'. This indicates its presidential functions; the European Council is not supposed to be a second chamber de luxe, although the danger is there.

Today the European Council meets at least four times a year, often more – it met six times in 2009 and 2010 and seven times in 2011.

The first permanent president of the European Council, Van Rompuy, described the Council's tasks as (2011: 5):

> Together we establish political priorities, we set the Union's strategic course and we take responsibility in crisis situations.

This interpretation is extending the tasks a little by taking them from a strategic level to include a more action-oriented approach as well as to stress the very important function of crisis-management. By doing so, Van Rompuy adequately describes the de facto role of the European Council today.

An important part of the upgrading of the European Council was the creation of a permanent presidency. In Art 15 (TEU) the tasks of the President of the European Council are listed as follows:

> The President of the European Council:
> (a) shall chair it and drive forward its work;
> (b) shall ensure the preparation and continuity of the work of the European Council in cooperation with the President of the Commission, and on the basis of the work of the General Affairs Council;
> (c) shall endeavour to facilitate cohesion and consensus within the European Council;
> (d) shall present a report to the European Parliament after each of the meetings of the European Council. The President of the European Council shall, at his or her level and in that capacity, ensure the external representation of the Union on issues concerning its common foreign and security policy, without prejudice to the powers of the High Representative of the Union for Foreign Affairs and Security Policy. The President of the European Council shall not hold a national office.

Thus the President of the European Council (a) is entrusted with strategic leadership, (b) with the task of coordinating with the Commission and the General Affairs Council (now the most important Council constellation for the trio-presidency), (c) he must be a broker, finding acceptable compromises when in council, and (d) he is the face of the EU to the outside world (together with the High Representative) and of the European Council towards the other institutions. An additional task not part of the list is to ensure continuity, a necessity for strategic leadership. To facilitate the presidency in the new construction, the President now has what the rotating presidencies did not have: time. Altogether this is an impressive list, which must be countered by the competencies the president does not have: he cannot vote in the Council (but basically decisions are taken by unanimity anyway), he cannot dismiss members of the government (the Commission), he is elected by the heads of state and government, who can also dismiss him, he is not a member of the General Affairs Council which prepares the agenda of the European Council, and his role towards the High Representative is unclear.

The first incumbent, Herman Van Rompuy (cf. Villa in Chapter 9 in this volume), describes his role as 'neither a spectator nor a dictator'. We will try to look into the first experiences from Van Rompuy's presidency, using the list of tasks described above as guidelines. Van Rompuy has taken leadership as well as acted as broker on a number of occasions especially related to the financial crisis (e.g. the 'crisis summit' in July 2011), and his handling of the financial crisis has been appreciated by important players to the extent that he was asked to head the 'Van Rompuy Task Force', set up by the Eurozone leaders in March 2010 to present measures needed to counter the Eurozone crisis. Later Angela Merkel and Nicolas Sarkozy suggested him as chair of a possible 'Economic Government' (EU Observer 18 August 2011). Here continuity comes in as an advantage. Instead of a Spanish presidency having six months to deal with the economic crisis while struggling with economic problems of their own, or Belgium having the EU-presidency while the country was led by a caretaker government, or a Hungarian presidency primarily aiming at promoting Hungarian interests, the EU had the same president throughout the crisis.

Concerning the role of the 'face of the EU', the Spanish and Belgian presidencies demonstrated that the trio-presidencies stepped back to let the President of the European Council and the High Representative enact this role (cf. EU Observer 30 June 2010). Concerning the EU-internal coordination and negotiation, there are regular meetings between the President of the Commission, Barroso, and Van Rompuy once a week. In spite of Van Rompuy's achievements, Dinan clearly sees what the President of the European Council is facing (2011: 107):

> With the possible exception of Juncker, none of the national leaders want the European Council Presidency to be a driving force. At most they are hoping for a good conductor: someone capable of bringing out the best in a large and unwieldy orchestra.

Thus a tentative conclusion is that Van Rompuy indeed fills the job-description well (in spite of his quiet appearance), and that he has managed to establish an important, although not 'absolutistic' position for the role of the president quite in accordance with the quote referred to above.

One consequence of having a permanent President of the European Council is that the rotating presidency lost power and attraction during the first trio-presidency (Spain, Belgium, Hungary) (cf. Dinan 2011: 104). This may have the long-term effect of decoupling the EU from the national political agendas (there used to be a positive exposure of the EU when a country had the 'old' rotating presidency both nationally, in the EU and externally with all the prestige involved). Additionally, the 'intergovernmental' aspect of decision-making will be put under pressure due to the 'sneaking' possibility of majority voting in the European Council.

Summing up, the Lisbon Treaty strengthened the European Council in its role as a collective presidency of the Union, *inter alia* by creating the post of a permanent President of the European Council.

Polity-building measures in the Lisbon Treaty

In Chapter 3 Dosenrode argues that the EU today is in fact a state. He does so by setting up a number of indicators for statehood and analyses them in regard to the EU. For a polity to be a state, he sets up the following characteristics:

1. The state must have recognizable, separate institutions.
2. The state is the supreme power and ultimate authority of all law.
3. The State's sovereignty extends to all individuals within a given territory.
4. The modern state's personnel is recruited and trained in a bureaucratic manner.
5. The state has the right of taxation.
6. The state has the official monopoly to conduct foreign affairs.
7. There is a common core culture.
8. The state is the focal point of the population's loyalty.

In the following, we will look at the indicators specifically with regard to what the Lisbon Treaty added, not what was already there before it.

(1) Was the characeteristic 'the state has recognizable separate institutions' strengthened by the Lisbon Treaty? The EU already fulfilled this characteristic before the Lisbon Treaty, but the Treaty made this even more clear by *inter alia* giving the EU juridical personality, changing the citizenship from complementary into additional[5], giving the European Council the status of institution and creating a president for it (see above), by creating the *de facto* post of a Union foreign minister and by making the Charter of Human Rights legally binding.

(2) Concerning the question of the states as supreme power and ultimate authority of all law, the Lisbon Treaty enhanced this, too, by abolishing the pillar-system of the Maastricht Treaty and including most of the policy-fields from the former intergovernmental pillar 3, Justice and Home Affairs, under the community method of legislating.

(3) The question of the state's sovereignty extending to the people living on its territory was touched upon by the decision to upgrade the Union's citizenship, from a complementary to an additional, or dual one (see above), thus developing the EU's sovereignty over the people slightly.

(4) The question of how the EU recruits and trains its civil service was not touched upon in the Treaty.

(5) The question of the EU's right of taxation is central, and the Lisbon Treaty did include the possibility of it, but not as a 'must' demand. And although the Commission's president and the European Parliament have tried to press for it to come into effect, it is unlikely that it will happen in the near future, because the right to control the Union's budget is an extreamly important instrument in controlling the EU

(6) The ability and right to conduct foreign policy was strengthened (see above), but the European External Action Service (EEAS), the foreign minister, the rotating trio-presidency and the presidency of the European Council are still, at the time of writing, in a process of defining their respective roles (read: turf wars). According to 'rumours' in diplomatic circles in Brussels in summer and autumn 2011 this is by no means an easy task, and it is not being facilitated by an alleged lack of trust between the High Representative on the one side and her staff in

5 An often neglected development is that the Lisbon Treaty changed citizenship from a 'complementary' into an 'additional' or dual citizenship (Art. 20.2 TFEU). It is worth remembering, that it is still only state-like entities which confer citizenship upon people. The idea of several citizenships is not unusual in federations like Germany or Switzerland; e.g. if one would like to obtain a Swiss citizenship, one first has to obtain it from a municipality, then the canton and the federation will add theirs 'automatically'. Buzek sums it up like this (2011: 13–14): Europeans are members of a transnational community which has legal personality, within which they enjoy a number of freedoms that are granted – not curtailed – by virtue of their being a national of a member State of the union. […] Citizenship in the EU has a political, as well as legal, connotation.

the European External Action Service on the other (cf. Dinan 2011; Smith 2011). Adding to this, the major Member States have not been helpful when it comes to the financing of the EEAS, *inter alia* due to their own financial problems (Allen and Smith: 212).[6]

(7) The question of a common core culture was addressed by including the catalogue of values upon which the Union builds. Article 2 of the Nice Treaty had contained the objectives of the EU. In the new Article 2 of the Lisbon Treaty, both the values and the objectives of the Union were listed. The new Treaty confirms the rights to human dignity, freedom, democracy, equality, and the rule of law.

(8) The question of the state, as focal point of loyalty, refers to the coherence and stability of a state. This question was also addressed in Chapter 3, and the problem is that empirical data is lacking at the time of writing.[7]

The conclusion of this section, using these eight characteristics as well as the other elements looked into above, is that the Lisbon Treaty strengthened the 'polity dimension' notably; not as much as if the Constitutional Treaty had been ratified and entered into force, but nonetheless substantially both internally and externally. The Union's statehood has developed progressively.

If this conclusion is accepted, it is logical to ask what form the European state then takes. Seen from the point of view of this author, a federal type has been emerging since the Maastricht Treaty (see Dosenrode 2007). The Lisbon Treaty enhanced this picture, e.g. by structuring the executive level of the EU by adding the collective presidency called 'the European Council', creating the *de facto* foreign minister, strengthening the role of the first Chamber (European Parliament), and by drafting a catalogue of competencies preventing what has been described as a 'one way motorway of competencies' from the member states to the Union. This is obviously a federal model where the member states are very strong, and where the federal level is less powerful if compared to, e.g., the United States of America or Canada. And I see no signs that this balance of power is about to change as long as there is no need to change.

Politics

The journey towards the Lisbon Treaty was, as already mentioned, long; from 2000 to 2009. In Nice (in 2000) the Heads of State and Government had expressed their wish to bring the Union closer to the citizens, strengthen the democratic elements and enhance efficiency. In their Laeken Declaration from December 2001 they stated that the Union had to be brought closer to its citizens, that the citizens

6 If I should dare a quiet guess, the CFSP with the EEAS might be one of the new paths of European integration, the other being some kind of financial 'government'.

7 I refer to Eurobarometer no. 75, Spring (2011) according to which 40 per cent of the Europeans have a positive attitude to the EU; 38 per cent are neutral, and 20 per cent are negative and 2 per cent do not know.

wanted the Union to be more open, effective and democratic (cf. Chapter 2).Thus, the question of how legislation is made was central and was dealt with both during the European Convention, during the Reflection Pause and during the negotiations leading to the Lisbon Treaty. This section will analyse the changes in the Lisbon Treaty in relation to the legislative process as well as a legitimacy aspect, before concluding by comparing the EU-policy process with that of a federation.

Decision-making rules in the Lisbon Treaty

The Lisbon Treaty changed the procedure for legislation seriously. By introducing the 'Ordinary Legislative Procedure' as *the* standard way of doing legislation (Art. 294 TFEU), the balance of power between the Council of Ministers and the European Parliament was altered dramatically. In approximately 75 per cent of the cases where legislation is passed, this procedure is followed, leaving 'only' 25 per cent to one of the old procedures, where it is enough for the Council to 'hear' or 'consult' the European Parliament. In the Ordinary Legislative Procedure the European Parliament is a co-equal legislator to the Council, implying that it may suggest amendments and alterations to Commission proposals, and it has a veto-right, too. The parliament's budgetary competencies were extended to include the whole of the EU-budget, adding to its powers.

In addition, the principle of 'equal treatment' to the European Parliament in legislative and budgetary matters was introduced (Buzek 2011: 11). This implies that the Commission now has to include the Parliament in the legislative preparation in the same manner as the Council is. Altogether, powers of the first chamber, the directly elected European Parliament, have been strengthened (cf. Nedergaard 2010: 63; Buzek 2011: 11). Dinan (2011: 104) sums it up like this:

> As was the case with previous Treaty reforms, the Lisbon Treaty greatly enhanced the EP's [European Parliament's] legislative, budgetary and oversight authority. Also following past practices, the EP lost little time instrumentalizing its new authority. In some cases the EP leveraged provisions in the Lisbon Treaty to influence the outcome of institutional matters in which, according to the Treaty, it should have had only a marginal role.

The procedures in the Council of Ministers were changed in two ways, first the use of Qualified Majority Voting was extended so that unanimity is 'only' needed in approximately 25 per cent of its decisions, whereas some kind of majority voting applies in 75 per cent; in other words the possibility of one state blocking the whole legislative process has been reduced in line with federal principles. The second change was the principle of the double majority. Decisions in the Council of Ministers will need the support of 55 per cent of Member States representing a minimum of 65 per cent of the EU's population. This change has decreased, but not removed, the 'over-representation' of the small member states when voting in the Council.

In conclusion the number of occasions where one member state in the Council of Ministers can veto an initiative has been reduced significantly, and the role of the European Parliament has been strengthened. The first instance, diminishing the legal right to veto proposals, clearly strengthens the effectiveness in the legal procedure, whereas the latter change, to an enhanced involvement of the European Parliament does not necessarily speed up the legislative process.

An important aspect of the politics of the EU, and additionally an aspect of polity-building, is the use of 'enhanced cooperation'. This aspect is analysed by Nico Groenendijk in Chapter 7. After a very long period of non-use, it has now been applied twice, in March 2010 on divorce law and in December 2010 on patents. Groenendijk reminds us that to be called 'enhanced cooperation' the process must follow the rules laid down by the treaties (e.g. it must be proposed by the Commission, it must be heard by the European Parliament, must be used as a 'last resort', etc.). Enhanced cooperation has to do with the working and the deepening of EU-integration. In this sense it very much resembles the activities undertaken in (other) federal states like for example, Switzerland, where cantonal executives meet in sub-groups to discuss and promote cooperation and joint legislation, within fields of common interest but not to be applied in the whole federation.

It is interesting to note that, although enhanced cooperation has existed as an option since the Amsterdam Treaty which entered into force in May 1999, it was under the Lisbon Treaty that it was first applied. This may be interpreted as a new dynamism to deepen integration (deepen, as enhanced cooperation should lay within a policy field allocated to the Union). Groenendijk warns of too hasty conclusions, but he also himself finds it interesting that Germany and France were both among the states deciding to launch the two cases of enhanced cooperation, indicating a willingness to deepen EU integration even when all are not ready to join. Due to the disadvantages of being outside – as in the case of the patents – it is obvious that having the opportunity of enhanced cooperation has given the more integration active states a genuine bargaining chip: 'if you do not join now we will go on; you may join us later, but then you will join a set-up we have made on which you have no influence'. Enhanced cooperation may turn out to be an efficient 'polity enhancing mechanism'; the genie is out of the bottle.

If we turn to the rotating presidency, we see that the Lisbon Treaty seems to have weakened it's ability to set the policy agenda. Vilà, in Chapter 9, notes that the change from the 'troika-presidency' to the 'trio-presidency' limits the possibilities of the presidency in office to set the agenda as they like, as they have to agree on a program with the two other co-presidencies in the 'trio'. Although it is still early to say something definite, the experiences from the first 'trio' (Spain, Belgium and Hungary) points in this direction. This is hardly surprising, given the creation of a permanent president of the European Council as well as the position of a permanent chair of the Foreign Affairs Council. Taking these important roles away from the rotating presidency inevitably weakens it.

Altogether, the efficiency of the EU as a whole has been strengthened, mainly due to the increased use of the Ordinary Legislative Procedure and the reduction of cases where unanimity is a must in the Council of Ministers. Also the opening up of the use of enhanced cooperation points in the same direction. The same goes for the moving of the policy areas which were before in the 'pillar 3' (area of freedom, security and justice) to the group of policy areas where the policy-making process is supranational.

But efficiency and democratic legitimacy do not necessarily walk 'hand in hand'.

Legitimacy[8]

Had the European Union been a 'normal' intergovernmental, international organization the question of legitimacy would be close to irrelevant. But as this chapter claims that the Union possesses statehood and as the majority of the member states legislation originates in the EU this question becomes central, as it was rightly noted down in the Laeken Declaration from December 2001 (cf. above). First this part will look into the enhanced power of the directly elected European Parliament, before it proceeds to the newly introduced citizens' initiative. Then we look into the enhanced protection of personal data, before we look at the formal legitimacy of the institutions. Ending this part we will tentatively discuss and sum up on the question of the EU's legitimacy.

Warntjen reminds us that the Lisbon treaty has made a number of changes to the institutional set-up and functioning of the EU. The Treaty has increased the role of the European Parliament and national parliamentarians and introduced elements of direct democracy. The co-decision procedure under which the Parliament and the Council are co-equal legislators is now the default procedure when adopting EU legislation. The scope of this procedure has been extended to a number of policy fields where the Parliament previously had less influence, including politically sensitive areas like asylum and immigration. The democratic legitimacy has been enhanced relating to the decision-making process.

As noted above, the directly elected Parliament is now a very strong player. This was very visible when the European External Action Service was set up. The Parliament was able to impose its wishes to a large extent, although this had not been the intention (Dinan 2011: 113).

The Treaty also introduced the citizens' initiative, whereby a million citizens from at least one quarter of the member states may invite the Commission to present an initiative on a specific issue – within the power of the Commission. This right was implemented in February 2011 (cf. Official Journal of the European Union). The Commission is not obliged to follow the citizens' request but must

8 Legitimacy is here understood broadly as citizens' acceptance of the governmental system, and that the popular perception is, that the government's power derives from established law and custom, in other words from a political constitution which does not necessarily have to be written down.

react to it. In a situation where the EU wants citizens' participation it is hard to believe that a request will not be taken very seriously.

The role of the national parliaments should be mentioned here, too. Their role has changed over the years. Christine Neuhold (2011: 1) phrases it like this:

> From political players that have largely been side-lined by way of Treaty reform, the Treaty of Lisbon now upgrades the role of national Parliaments in the European Union by foreseeing a number of mechanisms through which national Parliaments are to 'contribute actively to the good functioning of the Union.

The Lisbon Treaty strengthened the right of information of the member states (Art. 12 TEU), as well as the right to delay proposals from the Commission ('yellow' and 'orange' card, Art. 69 TFEU). In this way, the national parliaments get the right to argue that an appropriate initiative is better taken at their, national, level than at the supranational level. Neuhold (2011: 17) ends her analysis on an optimistic note, as she sees the beginning of a new inter-institutional balance and new avenues of inter-parliamentary cooperation. But she admits that it might be hard in practice to reach the quora needed to stop an ongoing legislative process and make the Commission reconsider its initiative.

Blasi, in Chapter 6, analyses *inter alia* the new legal basis for personal data protection as a result of the Charter on Fundamental Rights, the new Art. 47 (TEU), which states that: 'The Union shall have legal personality'. And Art 6.2 (TEU) which allows the EU to join the Convention for the Protection of Human Rights and Fundamental Freedoms (normally called the European Convention on Human Rights). Blasi concludes that the new basis secures the citizens rights better than the old one *inter alia,* due to extra, external, control by the European Court of Human Rights.

Turning to the democratic legitimacy of the institutions, we see that it is (very) mixed:

- European Parliament: Directly elected by the European citizens (Art. 14.2 TEU)
- European Commission: The president is 'elected by the European Parliament', the rest of the Commission is 'subject as a body to a vote of consent by the European Parliament'. (Art. 17.7 TEU)
- Council of Ministers: Appointed and responsible according to national rules (Art. 16.2 TEU)
- European Council: Appointed and responsible according to national rules (Art. 15.2 TEU)
- Court of Justice of the European Union: Appointed by the governments of the Member-States (Art. 19.2 TEU)

Thus the legislative and executive institutions are directly or via elected bodies (sometimes very indirectly ...) responsible to the electorate whereas the juridicative is less so, as a means to secure it against political pressure. One achievement of the Lisbon Treaty was that the scope of the EP's competencies were enlarged, another, that the president of the Commission is now elected instead of being approved by the European Parliament.

Summing up on 'legitimacy' we see that EU legislation must follow the rules laid down in the Treaty, and decisions taken by the institutions must also lie within the powers of the Treaty.[9] The European Court of Justice has as its task to ensure that the rules of the supranational part of the Treaty is kept. Adding to this, the EU gains legitimacy by its output efficiency and also from the new European Citizen's Initiative (ECI). No decision-making is made within the EU without either directly or indirectly elected institutions being involved. The Lisbon Treaty enhanced this a lot … so, what is the fuss about? The 'fuss' is about the Union's 'acceptance' especially among citizens in a number of northern European states. The 'fuss', according to the Glossary of the European Union (written before the Lisbon Treaty), is:

> The democratic deficit is a concept invoked principally in the argument that the European Union and its various bodies suffer from a lack of democracy and seem inaccessible to the ordinary citizen because their method of operating is so complex.

Three factors are mentioned: a) the EU has a lack of democracy, b) the EU seems inaccessible to ordinary citizens, and c) the EU operates according to complex methods.

It was indicated above a) that the power of directly elected institutions had risen, b) that the citizens could now give input directly to the legislative process etc., and c) that formal legitimacy was indeed very much in place within a number of policy areas, but also that there is 25 per cent of legislation which is only made by indirectly elected organs (Council of Ministers at the proposal of the Commission). In other words the degree of democracy is the point of discussion. The next element was that the EU *seems* inaccessible to the citizens. This is a more tricky question because it has little to do with objectivity but with feelings, 'seems': how accessible are national governments? The French? The British? The Spanish? How many Europeans know about the Ombudsman, the European Citizens Initiative etc? This is also the question when one discusses the complexity of the EU system. And yes, the EU decision-making system is messy, but how many national citizens know of the procedure ending in the annual budget of their country? Or the number of readings a law has to have in their national parliament before it is passed by the parliament? These questions are not meant to ridicule those feeling 'left out', as a lack of acceptance or legitimacy is very bad for any political institution, but the questions are meant to illustrate the nature

9 The European Council does not always follow this '*Rechtsstaatsprinzip*', as one has witnessed during the financial crisis.

of the problem. Hoffmann might have the answer to the 'why is it so' question. He introduces the concept of 'constitutional expectation', which he borrows from Richard Primus, in his 2011 paper. Boiled down – perhaps too crudely – Hoffmann's argument is that for Western citizens to feel comfortable with their governmental system it should resemble Montesquieu's division in a legislative, a juridicative and a governmental branch. And he suggests, that one introduces that in the EU. Although it could make sense from a purely academic point of view, especially if one accepts the argument that the EU is a weak state organized like a messy federation, this change does not seem to lay as *the* number one priority for the next treaty revision – remembering the fate of the Constitutional Treaty.

So, it looks as if the 'feeling of a democratic deficit' is hard to change, and it is not likely that the Lisbon Treaty will change this mental perception in spite of objective improvements concerning enhanced democracy. In that sense Dinan is right when writing of the EU's 'chronic crisis of legitimacy' (2011: 103), and a lack of legitimacy is a serious question for any state. This question is bound to occupy statesmen until the problem has been solved.

Policy-making in federations and in the EU after Lisbon

In an analysis from 2007, Dosenrode analyses the policy process in a number of European and Anglo-Saxon federations as well as in the EU. He drew three conclusions which are relevant in connection to the policy-process post Lisbon. They concerned 1) a resemblance between policy-making in the EU and in federations 2) the classification of the policy-process, and 3) the role of the (member-) states.

First; using the phases of the policy-cycle, Dosenrode (2007) demonstrated the resemblance of EU policy-making to that of policy-making in federations, when analysing supranational policy-making. The Lisbon Treaty has strengthened the federal character already present in the Nice-EU, both by adding new policy-areas to the area already covered by the Ordinary Legislative Procedure (e.g. parts of pillar 3, Justice and Home Affairs) and by adding a catalogue of competencies (Arts 3 and 4 TEU; see below). The Ordinary Legislative Procedure grants the European Parliament a number of possibilities to influence EU-legislation by either rejecting it, by a majority of its members, and thus stop it, or by proposing amendments. The latter opens a series of possibilities for the European Parliament to amend and change the original proposal, which it does frequently.[10]

Secondly, the policy-process in the European Union does resemble that of the European-style federations, especially in the later policy-phases where the member-states to a very high degree are included in the process.[11] One finds

10 The Constitutional Treaty, which formed the basis for the Lisbon Treaty, was itself drafted over the federal last, as one could read in the earlier draft versions from the European Convent. But this reference was removed from the final text.

11 See also Burgess' (2000) excellent analysis.

distinctly different styles of the federal policy-processes in European federations vs. the Anglo-Saxon ones; not so much in the problem-definition phase, as in the following phases, where the number of actors, as well as the inclusion of the state level, varies considerably. The number of actors is considerably smaller in the Anglo-Saxon federations than in the European ones, which are more inclusive. This hardly surprises, as the EU (ECSC) was envisaged by its founding fathers as a federation in being on the one hand, and as the Union of member-states who share a common core-culture but have each their own history which tells against a unitary 'construction' on the other hand. The European style is characterized as being cooperative and consensus oriented, contrary to the Anglo-Saxon style, which is majoritarian of nature. A consequence of the European style is that it is not as fast in reaching a decision as the Anglo-Saxon one.

Thirdly; The states are important actors in all the European-style federations (with Austria as a possible exception), but not as important as the member-states in the EU, where, e.g., one member-state is able to block changes in the 'constitution', as one saw with Denmark and the Maastricht-treaty in 1992, with France and the Netherlands with the Constitutional Treaty in 2005, and nearly with the Czech Republic in 2009. The EU member-states play a central role especially in the decision-making phase compared to 'traditional' European states in federations. The compatibility of the policy-making style of the EU and the European-style federation must be assumed to give the EU sustainability as it does not constitute an alien element to the member-states' governmental culture.

The important conclusions here are that there are significant differences between the Anglo-Saxon style federations on the one hand, and the European style on the other, and that the EU in its Lisbon Treaty form constitutes a variation of the European-style, which *inter alia* is inclusive. These findings suit the comments of Warntjen (cf. above) well, making it possible to characterize the policy-process post-Lisbon as consensus-oriented and inclusive.

The conclusion of this section is that the Lisbon Treaty did partly enhance efficiency (reducing the number of cases where unanimity in the Council of Ministers is needed) and it did enhance democracy within the EU, but the question of legitimacy has not been solved in spite of giving the directly elected European Parliament more competencies, and although the member states' parliaments are included more than before, and in spite of the introduction of the citizens initiative.

Policy

This part on 'policy' is the smallest both in this anthology as such and in this chapter. The reason for this is that the Lisbon Treaty was not a 'policy' treaty, adding many new policy areas to the union as such. But it did move the policy areas which before were in the 'pillar 3' (area of freedom, security and justice) to the group of policy areas where the policy-making process is supranational, not intergovernmental.

According to Sbragia (2003: 112) one can categorize the Union's policies in three groups:[12] The first group includes policies which fall under the jurisdiction of the EU. These are often policies seeking to build markets and encourage economic liberalization. They are made to support and strengthen economic growth and prosperity. Secondly, another group of policies which try to soften the consequences of the occasionally rough market forces. These policies are often shared between the EU and the Member States. The last group of policies is not related to the market, but has a polity-building perspective. They can be either supranational (area of freedom, security and justice) or inter-governmental, like the European Foreign Policy. The Lisbon Treaty saw an increase in polity-building policies which were either supranational or had shared competencies due to the already-mentioned shift of the policies in the area of freedom, security and justice from inter-governmental to supranational.

When it comes to policies, Arts 3 and 4 (TFEU) are important, as Art. 3 lists the Union's exclusive policy areas and Art. 4 those where the Union and the Member States share the competence. Such a catalogue of competencies is a novelty in the EU but is known as one of the main characteristics of a federation. The list of exclusive competencies is especially important as it prevents the Union from 'taking over' policy competencies from the member states without a change of the treaties.

The areas listed in Art. 3 (TFEU) are:

1. The Union shall have exclusive competence in the following areas:
   (a) customs union;
   (b) the establishing of the competition rules necessary for the functioning of the internal market;
   (c) monetary policy for the Member States whose currency is the euro;
   (d) the conservation of marine biological resources under the common fisheries policy;
   (e) common commercial policy.
2. The Union shall also have exclusive competence for the conclusion of an international agreement when its conclusion is provided for in a legislative act of the Union or is necessary to enable the Union to exercise its internal competence, or insofar as its conclusion may affect common rules or alter their scope.

The shared competencies work in the way that both the EU and the Member States may legislate within a given 'shared' area, but Member States may only legislate to the extent the Union has not. In that way one has implemented the old

12 Hix and Høyland (2011: 3) operates with five types: regulatory policies, expenditure policies, macroeconomic policies, interior policies and foreign policies.

federal principle, that 'federal law takes precedence over state law' or *Bundesrecht bricht Landesrecht*.[13]

The 'shared' areas are listed in Art. 4 (TFEU):

1. The Union shall share competence with the Member States where the Treaties confer on it a competence which does not relate to the areas referred to in Articles 3 and 6.
2. Shared competence between the Union and the Member States applies in the following principal areas:
   (a) internal market;
   (b) social policy, for the aspects defined in this Treaty;
   (c) economic, social and territorial cohesion;
   (d) agriculture and fisheries, excluding the conservation of marine biological resources;
   (e) environment;
   (f) consumer protection;
   (g) transport;
   (h) trans-European networks;
   (i) energy;
   (j) area of freedom, security and justice;
   (k) common safety concerns in public health matters, for the aspects defined in this Treaty.
3. In the areas of research, technological development and space, the Union shall have competence to carry out activities, in particular to define and implement programmes; however, the exercise of that competence shall not result in Member States being prevented from exercising theirs.
4. In the areas of development cooperation and humanitarian aid, the Union shall have competence to carry out activities and conduct a common policy; however, the exercise of that competence shall not result in Member States being prevented from exercising theirs.

In the following section we will take a look at the EU 2020-strategy.

When discussing the EU 2020-strategy Niklasson, Chapter 8, reminds us of the lack of legitimacy haunting the Commission. President Barroso and the Commission lack a mandate to genuine reform. The Commission is designed to create change slowly, step by step. With the EU 2020-strategy there has been created an expectation for the Commission to take a lead, but the Commission cannot live up to the expectations.

Analysing the EU 2020-strategy, Niklasson writes that the EU is doing what it can, with the instruments it has at its disposal, but also that it is not enough. Looking at the individual member states, Niklasson refers to 'institutional competition'.

---

13 The Joint Study (2010: 190) is critical of this development, which they call 'joint management', and consider a threat to the classical supranational decision-making model.

This implies that the member states are competing through their institutional set-up, and that firms will move to the country suiting them best. Lisbon has made this harder, as policies will be more uniform across the Union now.

Niklasson sums his analysis up like this:

> The Lisbon Treaty makes it easier to make incremental change. In a sense the EU becomes stronger. At the same time, the EU2020 indicates that the lack of a direct political mandate from the citizens can become a problem. Economic policies may become more of support for the status quo than a driver for reform in the member states. If so, it may be time to rethink the fundamental construction of the EU. A lack of politics may have made sense in the beginning, but may now have become part of the problem. A case is building up for parliamentarianism in the European Union, basing the Commission on a majority in the European Parliament, to balance the heads of state in the European Council.

In sum, the 'policy part' of the Lisbon Treaty's main novelties were the catalogue of competencies, setting a limit as to the expansion of the European Union at the cost of the Member States' parliaments, and the transfer of policies from the area of freedom, security and justice to the supranational decision-making procedure. This leads us to the conclusion.

The Lisbon Treaty: a polity and politics Treaty

As quoted in the preface to this anthology, some authors describe the Lisbon Treaty, compared to the previous treaties, as relatively insignificant in terms of institutional and policy reform (Hix and Høyland 2011: 11). As it has hopefully been highlighted in this chapter this is *not* the case.

With regard to *polity*, the Lisbon Treaty continued the process of polity-building begun with the Maastricht Treaty, and it enhanced the statehood of the Union – not dramatically, but still significantly, and much more than one could have expected after the collapse of the Constitutional Treaty.

The Treaty changed the institutional balance significantly.[14] The European Parliament has been strengthened, clearly especially in relation to its status as co-legislator in approximately 75 per cent of all EU legislation and its enhanced budget competencies. The European Council was strengthened, too. Both through its new status as 'institution' (merely recognizing what was *de facto* the case), but also due to the new presidency, which gives continuity and has proved itself effective. The same thing cannot be said about the newly established High Representative/Vice President of the Commission. At the time of writing this, beginning of 2012, the European External Action Service and its head have not really been able to 'take off' yet, but still this new service has a large potential. The Council of Ministers

14 See also Joint Study (2010: 189) for a discussion of the institutional balance.

has been made more efficient through new voting procedures, and potentially the permanent presidency of the High Representative over the Foreign Affairs Council may strengthen it. The Commission has not formally lost – or gained – much power. But in every-day business it is being squeezed by the European Council (e.g. one did not made a Barroso Taskforce but a Van Rumpoy Taskforce), one has had to give 'equal status' to the European Parliament, and the national parliaments now have a right to pull the brake if they feel that the supranational level is not the right place to solve a problem (subsidiarity). On the other hand, the Commission's portfolio was extended to the area of freedom, security and justice. In fact, the joint study (2010: 22) reminds us that the European Council and the Commission are complementary and that:

> Political decisions at the highest level frequently require legislative proposals, which the Commission alone can initiate, or executive measures to be implemented by Commission services.

If one may speak of a loser in the intricate institutional balance, it is the trio-presidency. It has lost much of its attraction due to the high-profile tasks now resting with the President of the European Council and the High Representative. The Lisbon Treaty has definitely created a new institutional balance.

Politics was one of the main concerns of the 'European elite' after the Laeken Declaration in 2001. The priority was to make the Union more efficient, with the Eastern enlargements pending, and to bring the Union closer to the (mainly northern) European citizens, who were skeptical about the project.

Did the Lisbon Treaty manage the 'efficiency task' and strengthen the EU's policy-making procedures? Yes, it did introduce qualified majority voting in a number of cases in the Council of Ministers thus removing individual member states' possibility to block decision making alone. And by abolishing the pillar structure, moving most pillar 3 issues to the supranational pillar, thus reducing veto points in the decision-making procedure. The Lisbon treaty also introduced the Ordinary Legislative Procedure (OLP) as the normal way of making decisions, which may imply more legitimacy (cf. below), but is more dubious when it comes to efficiency defined as 'speed', as a democratic process with hearings, committee work, negotiations etc. take time. Still, using the OLP implies that a single member state or two are no longer able to block an initiative in the Council of Ministers, thus enhancing efficiency,

The question of legitimacy was, and is, hard to solve. In spite of an institutional strengthening of the democratic decision-making, e.g. the introduction of the Ordinary Legislative Procedure as the normal procedure, European Citizens Initiative etc., EU-scepticism is large in northern Europe and now in some southern European countries, too. And it looks as if this will continue.

The aim of the treaty revision process was not an expansion of the *policy areas* and it only did so modestly, by moving the area of freedom, security and justice from the inter-governmental decision-making procedure to the supranational one.

In itself a significant development, as exactly these policy areas are considered 'very sensitive' and symbolic for 'state sovereignty'.

One of the motives for writing this book was our curiosity as to whether the solemn words of the Lisbon Treaty's preamble were in fact just words, or whether there was substance behind them. The words were these:

> DESIRING to complete the process started by the Treaty of Amsterdam and by the Treaty of Nice with a view to enhancing the efficiency and democratic legitimacy of the Union and to improving the coherence of its action, [...].

A conclusion is that the Lisbon Treaty wasn't a quantum leap, but still a solid step forward. The Treaty has a 'score' of 2 out of 3 when it comes to fulfilling its own preamble – efficiency and possible coherence, but with legitimacy still leaving something to be desired. The Treaty was, as mentioned, a polity and politics treaty aiming at deepening the integration, not a policy treaty widening it. So, on paper, Barroso was not quit wrong, when he summed up the situation that day in Warsaw when Poland ratified the Lisbon Treaty on 10 October 2009:[15]

> Now, with the strong foundations of enlargement and the Lisbon Treaty, Europe is ready to move ahead. We have the weight and momentum provided by a truly continental scale, the ability to use our rich diversity to pursue our common goals. And we will have the tools needed to deliver a Europe fully grounded in a firm democratic basis, a Europe with the right mix of institutions to realise change, and a Europe able to play its full role on the global stage.'
> So the next phase for Europe is one of delivery, not a Europe of procedures but a Europe of substance, one where we are not debating structures, but defining and implementing the action we need to take to meet the objectives of our peoples. How we ensure that we emerge from the economic crisis ready to show a Europe of growth, employment and solidarity. [...]. How we ensure that Europe's interests and Europe's values carry their full weight on the global stage.

Hardly the end of the process

And for the future of the EU? In spite of the Preamble's words on 'DESIRING to complete the process started by the Treaty of Amsterdam [...] and Barroso's confident words quoted above, Vilà, in Chapter 9, wrote that the Lisbon Treaty placed the EU in a new transitional phase; and looking at the Lisbon Treaty as a whole it still reflects the tensions between the supranationalists and the intergovernmentalists, and seen from an 'efficiency-point of view' this is still not optimal. This author does not possess the gift of looking into the future, but looking

15 But the jury is still out as to how much the EU delivers with regard to the financial crisis.

at the challenges both to legitimacy and effectiveness, not to mention the financial crisis, this does not indicate 'a completed process'. It is worth remembering, that with the exception of de Gaulle' introduction of the veto right in the 1966, the process of integration never rolled backwards, but forwards – sometimes hardly noticeably at other times fast. So, the Lisbon Treaty is not likely to be the end of the process [16]... although some politicians might wish it was the case....

References

Allen, D. and M. Smith. 2011. Relations with the Rest of the World. *Journal of Common Market Studies*, 49, Annual Review.

Barroso, J.M.D. *EU Commission President Barroso's Speech at Signature Ceremony in Warsaw*. http://www.europa-eu-un.org/articles/en/article_9081_en.htm

Burgess, M. 2000. *Federalism and European Union: the Building of Europe, 1950–2000*. London: Routledge

Buzek, J. 2011. State of the Union: Three Cheers for the Lisbon Treaty and Two Warnings for Political Parties. *Journal of Common Market Studies*, 49, Issue Supplement.

Council of Ministers. 2011. Go-ahead given to the European citizens' initiative. 14 February. http://www.consilium.europa.eu/uedocs/cms_data/docs/pressdata/EN/genaff/119272.pdf

Dinan, D. 2011. Governance and Institutions: Implementing the Lisbon Treaty in the Shadow of the Euro Crisis. *Journal of Common Market Studies*, 49, 103–21.

Dosenrode, S. 2007. Policy-making in Federations and in the EU, in *Approaching the European Federation?*, S. Dosenrode (ed.). Aldershot: Ashgate.

Eurobarometer, Spring 2011. http://ec.europa.eu/public_opinion/archives/eb/eb75/eb75_publ_en.pdf accessed September 2011.

EU Observer. 2010. June 30, 2010: Spain ends invisible EU presidency. 30 June. http://euobserver.com/18/30385

EU Observer. 2011. Integrated EU foreign policy is 'decades away', says EEAS official. 21 June. http://euobserver.com/884/32524

EU Observer. 2011. Van Rompuy tipped to chair new 'economic government'. 18 August. http://euobserver.com/19/113336

EUROPA. http://europa.eu/lisbon_treaty/glance/democracy/index_en.htm. Accessed July 2011.

Fondation Robert Schuman.2010. Question d'Europe, nos167 et 168, http://www.robert-schuman.eu/doc/questions_europe/qe-167-8-fr.pdf

16 At the annual Munich Security Conference the Polish minister of foreign affairs, Radoslaw Sikorski, stated that "The EU must develop into an even stronger, integrated federation" (Jyllands-Posten, Feb. 4th, 2012) indicating a feeling, that the process must go on.

Glossary: http://europa.eu/legislation_summaries/glossary/democratic_deficit_en.htm
Haas, E.B. and P. Schmitter. 1964. Economics and Differential Patterns of Political Integration. *International Organization*, 18(4).
Hix, S. and B. Høyland. 2011. *The Political System of the European Union*, 3rd edn. Houndmills: Palgrave.
Hoffmann, L. 2011. Constitutional Expectations and the European Union: The issue of executive opacity in the Union's continuous constitutionalisation process. *Paper*, UACES Conference: The Lisbon Treaty Evaluated, London, 31 January–1 February.
Joint Study. 2010. The Treaty of Lisbon – A Second Look at the Institutional Innovations, Joint CEPS, EGMONT and ECP Study. http://www.epc.eu/pub_details.php?cat_id=1&pub_id=1150. Accessed August 2011.
Nedergaard, P. 2010. *Lissabon Traktaten – En Politologisk Analyse*. Copenhagen: Jurist- og Økonomforbundets Forlag.
Neuhold, C. 2011. Late wake-up call or early warning? – Parliamentary participation and cooperation in the light of the Lisbon Treaty. *Paper*, UACES Conference: The Lisbon Treaty Evaluated, London, 31 January–1 February.
Official Journal of the European Union, REGULATION (EU) No 211/2011 OF THE EUROPEAN PARLIAMENT AND OF THE COUNCIL, of 16 February 2011, on the citizens' initiative.
RFI. 2011. Paris et Berlin proposent un gouvernement économique de la zone euro (mardi 16 août).
Sbragia, A. 2033. Key Policies, in *The European Union – How does it work?*, E. Bomberg and A. Stubb (eds). Oxford: Oxford University Press.
Smith, M.E. 2011. Building the European External Action Service: Institutional Learning versus Intergovernmental and Bureaucratic Politics. Paper, UACES Conference: The Lisbon Treaty Evaluated, London, 31 January–1 February.

Treaties

Lisbon Treaty; Consolidated Reader-Friendly Edition *of the* Treaty on European Union (TEU) *and the* Treaty on the Functioning of the European Union (TFEU) *as amended by the* Treaty of Lisbon (2007) 2008. http://www.eudemocrats.org/fileadmin/user_upload/Documents/Reader_friendly_til_nettet.pdf
Maastricht Treaty (Treaty on the European Union). http://eur-lex.europa.eu/en/treaties/dat/11992M/htm/11992M.html#0001000001
Single European Act. http://ec.europa.eu/economy_finance/emu_history/documents/treaties/singleeuropeanact.pdf
Treaty of Nice. http://www.proyectos.cchs.csic.es/euroconstitution/library/historic%20documents/Nice/Treaty%20of%20Nice_consolidated%20versions.pdf

Index

THE INTERNATIONAL POLITICAL ECONOMY OF NEW REGIONALISMS SERIES

Other titles in the series

Roads to Regionalism
Genesis, Design, and Effects of Regional Organizations
Edited by Tanja A. Börzel, Lukas Goltermann, Mathis Lohaus and Kai Striebinger

New Regionalism or No Regionalism?
Emerging Regionalism in the Black Sea Area
Edited by Ruxandra Ivan

Our North America
Social and Political Issues beyond NAFTA
Edited by Julián Castro-Rea

Community of Insecurity
SADC's Struggle for Peace and Security in Southern Africa
Laurie Nathan

Global and Regional Problems
Towards an Interdisciplinary Study
Edited by Pami Aalto, Vilho Harle and Sami Moisio

The Ashgate Research Companion to Regionalisms
Edited by Timothy M. Shaw, J. Andrew Grant and Scarlett Cornelissen

Asymmetric Trade Negotiations
Sanoussi Bilal, Philippe De Lombaerde and Diana Tussie

The Rise of the Networking Region
The Challenges of Regional Collaboration in a Globalized World
Edited by Harald Baldersheim, Are Vegard Haug and Morten Øgård

Shifting Geo-Economic Power of the Gulf
Oil, Finance and Institutions
Edited by Matteo Legrenzi and Bessma Momani

Building Regions
The Regionalization of the World Order
Luk Van Langenhove

National Solutions to Trans-Border Problems?
The Governance of Security and Risk in a Post-NAFTA North America
Edited by Isidro Morales

The Euro in the 21st Century
Economic Crisis and Financial Uproar
María Lorca-Susino

Crafting an African Security Architecture
Addressing Regional Peace and Conflict in the 21st Century
Edited by Hany Besada

Comparative Regional Integration
Europe and Beyond
Edited by Finn Laursen

The Rise of China
and the Capitalist World Order
Edited by Li Xing

The EU and World Regionalism
The Makability of Regions in the 21st Century
Edited by Philippe De Lombaerde and Michael Schultz

The Role of the European Union in Asia
China and India as Strategic Partners
Edited by Bart Gaens, Juha Jokela and Eija Limnell

China and the Global Politics of Regionalization
Edited by Emilian Kavalski

Clash or Cooperation of Civilizations?
Overlapping Integration and Identities
Edited by Wolfgang Zank

New Perspectives on Globalization and Antiglobalization: Prospects for a New World Order?
Edited by Henry Veltmeyer

Governing Regional Integration for Development: Monitoring Experiences, Methods and Prospects
Edited by Philippe De Lombaerde, Antoni Estevadeordal and Kati Suominen

Europe-Asia Interregional Relations
A Decade of ASEM
Edited by Bart Gaens

Cruising in the Global Economy
Profits, Pleasure and Work at Sea
Christine B.N. Chin

Beyond Regionalism?
Regional Cooperation, Regionalism and Regionalization in the Middle East
Edited by Cilja Harders and Matteo Legrenzi

The EU-Russian Energy Dialogue
Europe's Future Energy Security
Edited by Pami Aalto

Regionalism, Globalisation and International Order
Europe and Southeast Asia
Jens-Uwe Wunderlich

EU Development Policy and Poverty Reduction
Enhancing Effectiveness
Edited by Wil Hout

An East Asian Model for Latin American Success
The New Path
Anil Hira

European Union and New Regionalism
Regional Actors and Global Governance in a Post-Hegemonic Era.
Second Edition
Edited by Mario Telò

Regional Integration and Poverty
Edited by Dirk Willem te Velde and the Overseas Development Institute

Redefining the Pacific?
Regionalism Past, Present and Future
Edited by Jenny Bryant-Tokalau and Ian Frazer

The Limits of Regionalism
NAFTA's Labour Accord
Robert G. Finbow

Latin America's Quest for Globalization
The Role of Spanish Firms
Edited by Félix E. Martín and Pablo Toral

Exchange Rate Crises in Developing Countries
The Political Role of the Banking Sector
Michael G. Hall

Globalization and Antiglobalization
Dynamics of Change in the New World Order
Edited by Henry Veltmeyer

Twisting Arms and Flexing Muscles
Humanitarian Intervention and Peacebuilding in Perspective
Edited by Natalie Mychajlyszyn and Timothy M. Shaw

Asia Pacific and Human Rights
A Global Political Economy Perspective
Paul Close and David Askew

Demilitarisation and Peace-Building in Southern Africa
Volume II – National and Regional Experiences
Edited by Peter Batchelor and Kees Kingma

Demilitarisation and Peace-Building in Southern Africa
Volume I – Concepts and Processes
Edited by Peter Batchelor and Kees Kingma

Reforging the Weakest Link
Global Political Economy and Post-Soviet Change in Russia, Ukraine and Belarus
Edited by Neil Robinson

Persistent Permeability?
Regionalism, Localism, and Globalization in the Middle East
Edited by Bassel F. Salloukh and Rex Brynen

The New Political Economy of United States-Caribbean Relations
The Apparel Industry and the Politics of NAFTA Parity
Tony Heron

The Nordic Regions and the European Union
Edited by Søren Dosenrode and Henrik Halkier

For Product Safety Concerns and Information please contact our EU representative GPSR@taylorandfrancis.com
Taylor & Francis Verlag GmbH, Kaufingerstraße 24, 80331 München, Germany

www.ingramcontent.com/pod-product-compliance
Ingram Content Group UK Ltd.
Pitfield, Milton Keynes, MK11 3LW, UK
UKHW022126190926
475702UK00013B/1678
9781138256958